KT-195-681

ew   rnali m

From Kelly
To all the great teachers who have graced The Poynter Institute's
classrooms, especially the late Paul Pohlman

From Tom
To Andy Kohut, Amy Mitchell, and all of my colleagues,
forever, at the Pew Research Center

The New Ethics of Journalism
Principles for the 21st Century

Kelly McBride
The Poynter Institute

Tom Rosenstiel
American Press Institute

Los Angeles | London | New Delhi
Singapore | Washington DC

Los Angeles | London | New Delhi
Singapore | Washington DC

FOR INFORMATION:

CQ Press

An Imprint of SAGE Publications, Inc.

2455 Teller Road

Thousand Oaks, California 91320

E-mail: order@sagepub.com

SAGE Publications Ltd.

1 Oliver's Yard

55 City Road

London EC1Y 1SP

United Kingdom

SAGE Publications India Pvt. Ltd.

B 1/I 1 Mohan Cooperative Industrial Area

Mathura Road, New Delhi 110 044

India

SAGE Publications Asia-Pacific Pte. Ltd.

3 Church Street

#10-04 Samsung Hub

Singapore 049483

Printed in the United States of America

Library of Congress Cataloging-in-Publication Data

The new ethics of journalism : principles for the 21st century / Kelly McBride, The Poynter Institute; Tom Rosenstiel [editors].

pages cm
Includes bibliographical references and index.

ISBN 978-1-60426-561-3 (pbk. : alk. paper)
ISBN 978-1-4833-0133-4 (web pdf)

1. Journalistic ethics. 2. Journalism—History 21st century. I. McBride, Kelly, editor of compilation. II. Rosenstiel, Tom, editor of compilation.

PN4756.N49 2013
174'.907—dc23   2013012147

This book is printed on acid-free paper.

Acquisitions Editor: Matthew Byrnie

Editorial Intern: Gabrielle Piccininni

Production Editor: Stephanie Palermini

Copy Editor: Jacqueline Tasch

Typesetter: C&M Digitals (P) Ltd.

Proofreader: Jeff Bryant

Indexer: Rick Hurd

Cover Designer: Rose Storey

Marketing Manager: Liz Thornton

Permissions Editor: Jennifer Barron

SFI® Certified Sourcing
www.sfiprogram.org
SFI-00453

13 14 15 16 17 10 9 8 7 6 5 4 3 2 1

CONTENTS

Journalism Ethics Then And Now

Bob Steele

T his is an essential book about a profoundly important subject published at a critical time. *The New Ethics of Journalism: Principles for the 21st Century* focuses intensely on the role that journalism plays in our society, a role that remains urgent and unique even as so much changes in the profession and in the business of journalism, as well as in our global society.

It remains imperative that those who practice journalism strive for excellence and aspire to high ethical standards, regardless of systemic structural changes in media, increasingly fickle and cynical news consumers, and sharp scrutiny from a wide range of critics.

The essays published here matter because the public must have confidence in the integrity of the journalistic process and the credibility of the product, even more as journalism is being redefined and recreated in real time.

This book represents another chapter in the decades-long effort by The Poynter Institute to address important issues of journalism ethics. It was my great privilege to be part of Poynter for nearly 20 years as we taught, advised and guided thousands of journalists and hundreds of news organizations and wrote extensively about ethics and values. *The New Ethics of Journalism: Principles for the 21st Century* continues that Poynter commitment.

The book's editors, Kelly McBride and Tom Rosenstiel, are two of the sharpest minds I know. With this project, they bring their considerable experience, expertise and intellectual energy together with a group of thoughtful, provocative essayists who explore and expound on what journalism can be and should be in the midst of this extreme transformation. The editors and the essayists in this collection generally write with optimism. That's appropriate, although it would be unwise and unrealistic to minimize the chaos of the recent years and the profound consequences. We should recognize the continuing peril even as we see promise ahead.

The traditional economic models for the business of journalism have been badly battered and often shattered. New models are emerging, but we are still years away from stability. Some approaches are financially promising and respect ethical, excellent journalism. However, other ill-conceived business decisions savage essential ethical and journalistic values and fail to serve the public good.

At the same time, the technology for gathering, processing and delivering news keeps developing at seemingly warp speed, creating dynamic possibilities but too often producing distorted coverage and diminished quality. In this period of intense adaptation, journalists and news executives are employing digital tools and creating innovative content with varying degrees of exuberance and alarm, skill and stupidity.

The information needs, desires and behaviors of the public are also shifting, sometimes dramatically. Those who practice and produce journalism must pay attention to what the marketplace dictates and to what consumers demand as they participate in the creation and distribution of journalism. Yet there is danger, too, as we rely increasingly on social networks and algorithms to deliver important information.

Journalists must continue to cover unpopular topics and tell stories that don't draw the most eyeballs. Despite the vagaries of a "most viewed stories" popularity contest, we must honor the fundamental duty to report accurate, fair, substantive and indispensable information while surviving in the marketplace. Journalism cannot be judged exclusively by the same bottom-line financial criteria as other commercial products. The old adage of reporting the news "without fear or favor" retains value, whether it's vigorous coverage of contentious issues or courageous decisions that insulate against outside pressures that could compromise journalistic independence.

Journalism has a special role in society, serving the public good like no other business or profession. Journalism has an obligation to support the democratic process by informing and educating. Journalism has a responsibility to give citizens meaningful information so they can better understand the issues in their communities and beyond, make good decisions in their daily lives and effectively carry out their civic duty.

This anthology spotlights the ethical challenges that constantly arise for those reporting and sharing the news. Some of these challenges have existed for decades. Some ethical issues are new, or at least have a new shape or different shade to them reflecting all that is changing in this era.

At Poynter, we've written extensively about the core values of accuracy and fairness, often praising sound ethical decision-making and excellent journalism and many times spotlighting flaws and failures. In our seminars, we've used hundreds of case studies to examine ethics concerns with confidential sources, conflicts of interest, invasion of privacy, deception and fabrication. We've helped journalists recognize the ethical potholes and pitfalls that always emerge in covering politics, natural disasters and wars. Believing that guidelines are more meaningful than rigid rules, we've written protocols for covering suicide, school violence, racial tensions and much more.

The emergence of digital technology and the evolution of the role of journalism—including much more active participation by the public—has intensified some of the traditional ethical challenges and created new ones.

Think about the role social networks like Twitter and Facebook now play in the coverage of civil unrest in our communities and in countries around the globe. Recognize the challenges that exist for news organizations when facts, photos and audio of breaking news stories come from citizens rather than staff journalists, raising concerns about sourcing, authenticity and fairness. Consider the looser editing standards that often exist with a "digital first" philosophy that emphasizes speed over verification, with content that goes public and potentially viral without effective front-end checks and balances.

The essays, the case studies and the accompanying questions explore the value and values of journalism and the complex relationship between journalists and those they serve. This book identifies and champions the guiding principles that can inspire and influence those who practice journalism. It offers reasoned reflection for individuals and news organizations to set strategy and to use in making sound ethical decisions built on the values of expertise, knowledge, commitment, courage, independence, transparency, and accountability.

I don't agree with every position or proposal in this book, nor will you. Journalism ethics inevitably creates contention. However, we gain insight from the probing essays even as we challenge some ideas they present. I'm confident you will sharpen your thinking as you work through the dynamic case studies and grapple with the analytical questions that follow each essay.

My hope is that this book will remind you how vital and valuable journalism is in our society, imperfect though it is. I also hope you will be inspired to take action to make journalism even better.

T his book has a thousand authors, and really more. Yes, there are two editors, 14 named authors, a case study writer and the man behind the foreword. You'll find their biographies in the back of this volume. But many more have influenced these pages. All those who have worked to innovate—who have tested new technologies, who have experimented with new ways to tell stories and deliver journalism—have had a hand in shaping the ideas found here. If you've been to a seminar at The Poynter Institute or a Committee of Concerned Journalists workshop, if you've phoned in for advice, or shared your triumphs and failures on Poynter.org, then you too helped write this book. Especially if you were there in New York at our symposium in October 2012, you influenced this book.

We want to specifically acknowledge a handful of people who help us out by keeping us informed, sharing their knowledge and experience with us, and taking our calls when we need advice. They include David Folkenflik of NPR; Brian Stelter, Sewell Chan and David Carr of *The New York Times*; Eric Wemple of *The Washington Post*; Amanda Michel of *The Guardian*; Vivian Schiller of NBC; Drew Curtis of Fark; Alexis Ohanian of Reddit; David Boardman of the *Seattle Times*; and Jennifer 8. Lee of everywhere.

This book is in part the collective work of The Poynter Institute, where almost everyone on staff had some role. Specifically, the support and encouragement of President Karen Dunlap and Dean Stephen Buckley were instrumental. Paul Tash, chairman and CEO of the Times Publishing Company, opened some important doors. Other key players include Jessica Blais, Nafi Sallah, Ann Madsen, Butch Ward, Bobbi Alsina, David Shedden, Maria James, Jennette Smith and the amazing Foster Barnes.

So, too, are we indebted to the staff of the Pew Research Center, whose intelligence and integrity sustained one of the editors of this book for many years and on whose data and insight we, like so many others, rely. In particular, Mark Jurkowitz, Scott Keeter, Michael Dimock, Carroll Doherty and Lee Rainie deserve special thanks. So, too, does our good friend, Paul Taylor. And, of course, two people above all with whom Tom worked most closely and for so long, Andy Kohut and Amy Mitchell.

The ideas here are also influenced by the unerring friendship of Bill Kovach, who has always understood journalism more deeply than most, and by the late James Carey, who explored the idea of communications as culture and journalism as community and conversation decades before those phrases were ever typed by someone imagining the digital age.

We owe a great deal, more than we could ever repay, to Julie Moos, who jumped into the churn to save us from ourselves, organizing the final editing efforts, serving as a our backstop and our unflinching critic. Her name should be on the cover. In turn, Mallary Tenore carried a tremendous load at Poynter Online so Julie could help with the editing of this book.

Kelly would like to personally thank Charisse Kiino at CQ Press, for not letting this book die, the first, second or third time it was on life support. Matthew Byrnie at Sage Publishing inherited this book without complaint, and among those helping out were Gabrielle Piccininni, editorial intern; Stephanie Palermini, production editor; Jacqueline Tasch, copy editor; and Liz Thornton, marketing manager.

Tom also thanks his family, who excused yet again his absences as he disappeared to work on this, and his new colleagues at the American Press Institute and the Newspaper Association of America. Thank you, Caroline.

And Kelly thanks her children, Molly, Clarke and Maggie Jacobson, for stepping up and her boyfriend Kyle Parks for stepping in.

None of this would have been possible without the support of several organizations. In addition to Poynter, Pew and the Committee for Concerned Journalists, we found support from the Ford Foundation, the Knight Foundation and The Paley Center for Media, who gave us an enthusiastic yes when we asked if they would host a symposium with us in October 2012. There we publicly tested the ideas you will find in this book, and videos of that day are online at Paley's website. Specifically, we treasure the involvement of J. Max Robins, Joel Topcik and Marisa Laureni.

Vadim Lavrusik of Facebook, Andrew Heyward formerly of CBS News, Emily Bell of the Columbia Journalism School and John Paton of Digital First Media all played a significant role that day.

Finally, we need to offer up a loud and clear thank you to Craig Newmark of craigconnects.org. Without his generosity, the New York gathering could not have happened. Along with his project director, Jonathan Bernstein of Bernstein Crisis Management, Newmark turned out to be one of the best partners ever. His involvement allowed us to build upon a project that was already in progress, making it stronger and extending our reach. Thanks, Craig!

New Guiding Principles for a New Era of Journalism

Kelly McBride and Tom Rosenstiel

One of the fundamental challenges facing journalism in the 21st century is what ethics should guide the production of news. When people discuss ethics in journalism, the conversation tends to get stuck between two polar impulses: to cling to tradition so tightly we resist progress, on the one hand, and to throw away the most important values in journalism and charge blindly ahead thinking everything has changed on the other.

We consider this a false choice.

The digital age has transformed how journalism is created and delivered. Certainly, we must change the ethical decision-making that supports that. Just as certainly, however, some guiding stars remain. Journalists, for instance, cannot give up dedication to truth and accuracy on behalf of the public, but they must find new ways to fulfill that commitment. This book is not an attempt to predict the future or mourn what's been lost. Nor does it try to deny what has changed or declare all that came before obsolete. Rather, it is an attempt to look at what is happening in journalism in the early part of the 21st century, to define and articulate new tensions that challenge journalism's core principles, and to suggest practices that further truth and community in service of democracy.

To do this, we asked different thinkers about contemporary journalism to draft essays on what we identified as key issues. Then, we gathered in New York and worldwide via the Web a larger group of journalism observers to help contemplate the ideas presented by our essayists. We distilled all of this into organizing principles, and we went back to work along with the writers to refine those ideas. This book of essays, and the organizing principles outlined in this first chapter, is the fruit of that labor.

This is not the first time The Poynter Institute has tried to help distill core principles of journalism into a book on ethics. In the early 1990s, the institute developed Guiding Principles for Journalists. Those principles were simple by design, organized under three concepts: Truthfulness, Independence and Minimize Harm.

That work was led by Bob Steele, the author of the foreword to this book. This book builds on the shoulders of that work. All of those principles remain vital and are resident here.

The new list of ethical principles mainly elevates two concepts that have been expanded by the digital age. Transparency, which was always a part of truth seeking, is now its own principle because it is so essential a part of how modern journalism attains credibility. Community, which may have been taken for granted in an age when the press had a monopoly on the audience, is the new third principle. It was always the final purpose of journalism, even if it seemed somewhat remote when the audience was a more silent partner in the transaction of news. Now journalism is enriched, and made more relevant, by the range of voices and expertise of the community—even if its production has been made more complex.

It may be years before journalism settles into economic stability and we know what shape that will take. Yet as the invention and adoption of new technologies continues to accelerate, it is clear journalism will come from varied sources—from many smaller and a few large for-profit organizations (although maybe not as large as they used to be), small nonprofits, citizen initiatives and the work of lone individuals and passionate advocates. Journalism may come from think tanks, even corporate sources. Journalism in the United States may eventually come to rely more on government subsidy. The concept of journalists as clearly independent of those they cover will be more complex because the opening of the information system to all means those who make the news will also cover it. When anyone can make journalism, it becomes even more important that its production be ethical and that the community be able to recognize and identify when it is and isn't.

In whatever form, we all have a stake in the survival of reliable journalism. Without it, democracy fails. The powerful will be less accountable and more likely to abuse their influence. The public will be more at risk. Social problems will go unspotted and unaddressed. Information that a few want hidden will remain in the shadows longer.

Journalists and those who value journalism are in the midst of a great diaspora. They are packing up the remnants of a belief system and carrying it forward to new places, where those pieces will evolve into a new foundation. This is not an easy or painless journey. At the same time, it is impossible to deny the exciting possibilities presented by the changes that have already occurred.

This book was conceived more than four years ago at the dawn of the worst of the economic upheaval that unmoored so many professional newsrooms. You are finally seeing it now because it was only recently that we in the profession have been able to see a few years into the future and accept that journalism will never return to its past economic state.

We begin this book then by looking ahead, with a new set of Guiding Principles for Journalists, which meld the core values of journalism with the democratic values of the digital era.

1. Seek truth and report it as fully as possible.

   - Be vigorous in your pursuit of accuracy.
   - Be honest, fair and courageous in gathering, reporting and interpreting information.

- Give voice to the voiceless; document the unseen.
- Hold the powerful accountable, especially those who hold power over free speech and expression.
- Be accountable.

2. Be transparent.

- Show how the reporting was done and why people should believe it. Explain your sources, evidence and the choices you made. Reveal what you cannot know. Make intellectual honesty your guide and humility (rather than false omniscience) your asset.
- Clearly articulate your journalistic approach, whether you strive for independence or approach information from a political or philosophical point of view. Describe how your point of view impacts the information you report, including how you select the topics you cover and the sources that inform your work.
- Acknowledge mistakes and errors, correct them quickly and in a way that encourages people who consumed the faulty information to know the truth.

3. Engage community as an end, rather than as a means.

- Make an ongoing effort to understand the needs of the community you seek to serve and create robust mechanisms to allow members of your community to communicate with you and one another.
- Seek out and disseminate competing perspectives without being unduly influenced by those who would use their power or position counter to the public interest.
- Recognize that good ethical decisions require individual responsibility enriched by collaboration.
- Seek publishing alternatives that minimize the harm that results from your actions and be compassionate and empathetic toward those affected by your work.
- Allow and encourage members of the community to self-inform. Make journalism a continuing dialogue in which everyone can responsibly take part and be informed.

If you compare these principles to those that were originally drafted at Poynter in the 1990s and subsequently adopted by numerous newsrooms and professional organizations, including the Society of Professional Journalists, you will notice many similarities and some significant differences. But nothing has vanished.

That original list looked like this:

1. Seek truth and report it as fully as possible

- Inform yourself continuously so you in turn can inform, engage and educate the public in a clear and compelling way on significant issues.

- Be honest, fair and courageous in gathering, reporting and interpreting accurate information.
- Give voice to the voiceless.
- Hold the powerful accountable.

2. Act independently.

- Guard vigorously the essential stewardship role a free press plays in an open society.
- Seek out and disseminate competing perspectives without being unduly influenced by those who would use their power or position counter to the public interest.
- Remain free of associations and activities that may compromise your integrity or damage your credibility.
- Recognize that good ethical decisions require individual responsibility enriched by collaborative efforts.

3. Minimize harm.

- Be compassionate for those affected by your actions.
- Treat sources, subjects and colleagues as human beings deserving of respect, not merely as means to your journalistic ends.
- Recognize that gathering and reporting information may cause harm or discomfort, but balance those negatives by choosing alternatives that maximize your goal of truth telling.

Truth is still the greatest value, the first among equals. Seeking and reporting truth is the primary function of journalism. And yet, so much has changed, including how one would identify truth and disseminate it with authority. The first section of this book focuses on our ability to discern the truth (essays by Clay Shirky and Roy Peter Clark), identify truth in political speech (Steve Myers), and tell the truth in stories (Tom Huang) and images (Kenneth Irby).

Where we once argued for independence, we now advocate transparency. Independence is a part of that principle, and we still believe in its essential value. But we recognize that journalism in the future will take many more forms and will intertwine with the proliferation of opinion in the digital marketplace—the two no longer so easy to distinguish. Journalism with a point of view can be just as powerful as work that starts from a position of neutrality. Both can and do move people to democratic action. Both can seek truth. The test is in how the journalism is produced—not necessarily who produces it.

The transparency that we urge in these guiding principles demands that the public see how the journalism of the future is produced and calls for an openness that encourages constant conversation between journalist and citizen, newsroom and community.

As a principle, transparency will drive journalists to actions and accountability that independence did not. A transparent news organization will approach its work with greater self-awareness, recognizing how its business model impacts the topics and types of stories it considers news. Transparent journalists will strive for intellectual honesty and integrity in every step of their work, acknowledging where they get their ideas and how they sort the relevant from the irrelevant. Transparent journalists and news organizations will embrace the practice of corrections across platforms.

In the second section of the book, we move from the outside in as we look at this issue of transparency. We start with an exploration of the competing values between journalism and the private platforms that increasingly deliver journalism (Dan Gillmor). Sticking with private platforms, we look at the revelatory value of the data that grows out of those platforms (Gilad Lotan). Finally, we move inside newsrooms, looking at evolving funding models (Adam Hochberg), the intellectual habits of reporters (Ann Friedman) and the methods journalists use to correct their mistakes (Craig Silverman).

The principle of transparency informs not just how we judge our conflicts of interest, but how we tell the story of journalism itself. The stories created by journalists rely heavily on systems like social media platforms, outside of our control, yet suddenly crucial to the marketplace of ideas. Journalists must be dedicated enough to the notion of transparency to examine these systems and help communities hold them accountable for their incredible power.

We have enlarged the principle of minimizing harm into a principle of engaging community. Journalists still have a moral obligation to seek alternatives that minimize the harm they cause. But that duty is not an abstract notion. Instead, minimizing harm is part of a greater contract with the members of a community that journalists serve and the sources they tap into to tell stories. It is a promise to act in the interests of informing a community and upholding democracy, acknowledging that the community itself has a substantial ability to contribute to the conversation. By elevating respect for the community, we note that journalistic decisions cannot be made in a vacuum. Instead, these values guide us toward an ethic of diversity (Eric Deggans). They help us resist the temptation to manipulate through fear and sensationalism (Kelly McBride and danah boyd). Together, the values of truth and transparency are interpreted in relation to a specific community and the common good (Steven Waldman and Mónica Guzmán.)

These essays are written by individuals who were invited into the process because of their different perspectives and experiences. Each speaks with a distinct voice and tone. At the end of each chapter is a workshop meant to root the ideas of the essay in a contemporary application. These can be used in a newsroom, classroom, or discussion group to make clear the new trends and ethical challenges, which evolve as quickly as journalism itself.

Poynter's efforts in the 1990s were hardly the first to imagine the ethics or responsibilities of the press or the last. If one were to look at other work from the 1940s on—from the Hutchins Commission or the Society of Professional Journalists or Committee of Concerned Journalists—one would be struck by the similarities of the efforts. Each has informed the other.

Nor do we pretend to have all of today's answers, so when you've completed this short book, we don't expect you will have all the answers either. We hope instead that you will be a more informed, active participant in shaping the critical conversation about how to produce journalism and consume it in the 21st century. For the principles that guide ethical decision-making in the production of news to have meaning, they need to be thought through anew by each generation in its new circumstances. That is the process of renewal and the point of rigorous self-reflection. Only then is journalism a vibrant and a living exercise on behalf of the public.

The Complicated Pursuit of Truth

INTRODUCTION

Kelly McBride and Tom Rosenstiel

Telling the truth has always been the simplest and most complicated function of journalism. That critical but elusive task starts with describing what happened, sometimes based on a reporter's own eyewitness account (the first of the Twin Towers collapsed into a cloud of smoke and debris at 9:59 a.m. on Sept. 11, 2001), more often based on the accounts of others (when the tsunami hit East Asia in 2004, few if any journalists were present), and, in the case of investigative work, after the journalist has assembled enough accounts, documents and other evidence to declare something of significance with authority (the U.S. government deceived the American people about its early involvement in Vietnam and miscalculated and mismanaged the war, according to the Pentagon Papers).

When asked to consider the question philosophically, journalists sometimes struggle to articulate what they do. Are they capable of more than accuracy? We can point to exposés and analyses and answer: yes. Truth emerges not only in a single story but also in the sorting out that occurs over time as different accounts probe an event and its implications. This form of journalistic or practical truth is a living, continuing process, as co-editor Tom Rosenstiel and his colleague, Bill Kovach, have described it.

Journalism also may lend itself to some kinds of truths more easily than others. The media are on firmer footing, for instance, identifying what words the president said or how many people died in a fire than they are in describing the motivations that drive the people in the news.

Nonetheless, while acknowledging that getting the facts right remains journalism's core function—and that includes trying to get at "the truth about the fact," as the Hutchins Commission put it in 1947—much of how we discern and articulate the truth is changing.

This section's first two authors, Clay Shirky and Roy Peter Clark, explore two dimensions of a long-standing debate: the degree to which truth is ascertainable.

They propose somewhat differing answers to the questions of how society knows what the truth is, how we designate truth-tellers and how technology and new forms of communication have impacted our ability to arrive at consensus. Together, they describe the spectrum of truth that journalism covers and how the process of fixing on truth on that spectrum is made both more challenging and richer today. The demands on journalists are higher. So is the need for journalism that goes beyond the stenographic task of simply describing the public argument.

Tom Huang then analyzes the principal means by which journalists have tried to describe truth: the story, which is being transformed by digital technology. Huang's essay offers a disciplined tour through the virtues and challenges of the main new storytelling forms possible today.

In the essays that follow, Steve Myers and Kenny Irby look at two even more precise developments in journalism's pursuit of truth: the growth of the fact-checking movement and the changing role that photographic storytelling plays in our understanding of the world.

These five chapters, arranged from the more abstract (Shirky and Clark) to the more specific (Huang, Myers and Irby), remind us that truth, at least as it relates to journalism, is not the same as meaning. We might, for instance, know who won the election, or even what occurred in a tragic school shooting. What it means to us is something more individual. On some level, journalism commands our attention because it tells us what to think about: what is new, what is changing, even perhaps what is important. But it does not, nor has it ever, tell us what to think.

As you read these essays, you will undoubtedly draw connections of your own to other phenomena occurring in journalism and the wider world of communications. Just as surely, the rapid pace of change will continue to alter the way we seek truths and tell stories.

chapter 1

Truth without Scarcity, Ethics without Force

Clay Shirky

T he first item in the Society for Professional Journalist's Ethics Guide is "Seek truth and report it." This seems simple enough, yet the contemporary media environment has seen a dramatic increase in spurious claims about everything from hydraulic fracturing to the funding of Medicare to the president's birthplace and religious affiliation. With the Internet opening the floodgates to ideological actors of all persuasions, the exhortation to seek truth and report it seems less widely practiced than ever.

The Internet's effect on our respect for the truth has been frequently discussed in the last decade, in books such as *Republic.com* and *True Enough: Learning to Live in a Post-Fact Society* and in any number of essays over the years. As an example, *The Atlantic* ran a piece just before the last elections called "Truth Lies Here," which suggested that the Internet, by allowing us to pick and choose what we listen to, is corroding our shared commitment to facts.[1]

"Truth Lies Here" included the usual high points: the Daniel Patrick Moynihan quote ("Everyone is entitled to his own opinion, but not to his own facts"), the observation that news consumers are replacing professional editors with our friends as arbiters of news, and frustrated wonderment that so many Americans have been willing to make, and so many media outlets willing to report, basic errors of fact, like the notion that President Obama is a Muslim.

This "post-fact" literature is certainly on to something; *the Internet is changing the conditions under which ordinary citizens are willing to regard any given statement as true.* There comes a moment, however, when anyone making this case has to employ what journalist William Safire used to call a "but of course" paragraph, a brief nod to a possible counterargument before setting it aside.

In the Atlantic, the "but of course . . . " was this:

None of this is to argue that we should—or could—return to the old order, wherein *The Times* or Walter Cronkite issued proclamations on the credibility and import of news from around the world.

This yearning for mainstream concurrence without cultural dominance is what gives that lament for lost consensus its poignant feel since these two desires are mutually exclusive. It's not as if, in the mid-20th century, we Americans had a small group of white men who could speak to and for the public without fear of contradiction or amendment, and we also happened to have mainstream consensus about the news of the day. The latter state is impossible without the former; the former is how we got to the latter.

We have never all agreed with each other. What looks like a post-truth journalistic environment is actually a post-professional environment and a post-scarcity environment. Truth isn't a stable "thing," it's a judgment about what persuades us to believe a particular assertion. And for anything outside our direct personal experience, what persuades us is evidence of operative consensus among relevant actors. This journalistic formula for truth is far more difficult to attain in this new environment.

Of course, many truths are knowable, verifiable and undeniable, like the number of children (20) killed in the Newtown, Conn., shooting, or the amount of revenue your local city council collected last year in parking fines. These truths are the bulk of the substance in journalism.

What the Internet changes is how many different opinions are now in circulation when we try to determine the meaning of a truth, a change that in turn alters our idea of whose opinion is relevant and where consensus actually lies. People no longer have to shut up while Walter Cronkite tells them "that's the way it is," no longer have to sit alone, shouting at their televisions, wondering if they are the only ones who think that something has gone wrong with the country they live in.

It's tempting to want to make the shouters admit they are the ones who are wrong, to insist that facts are facts. The history of life in democratic societies, though, suggests our inability to shut the shouters up is fairly essential.

DISTINGUISHING CONSENSUS FROM TRUTH

Homosexuality is a mental illness; that assertion was just as factual as a fact could be, circa 1969. A group of professionals, the American Psychiatric Association, arrived together at a list of the conditions and behaviors that were evidence of mental imbalance. The APA's professional judgment was then published in the canonical psychological work, the *Diagnostic and Statistical Manual.* Homosexuality was in the DSM.

Being gay is no longer an illness. Concern over same-sex attraction was progressively downgraded and finally removed altogether over several successive revisions of the DSM, starting in 1970. How did that happen?

It happened because people attracted to members of the same sex insisted, persistently and publicly, that the DSM diagnosis, almost universally reported as fact, was nothing but prejudice dressed up in clinical language. As the APA argued over the issue, its members came to agree.

This process of removing the sense of homosexuality as pathology is not over, of course; there are still people ready to say that it would be better if gay teens killed themselves than try to make a public place for themselves in society. But in the decades since the first person stood up to the cops at the Stonewall

Inn, the ability of gay-hating members of American society to speak or act as if their views represented an obvious truth has weakened with each passing year. This was in part because our sense of who the relevant actors are has changed, as with psychologists being increasingly willing to listen to the accounts of gay citizens themselves.

People fighting for the inclusion of gays in society have had to fight against many things. Some of the things they had to fight against were the facts, as constituted by society and regularly reported in the press.

We could try to rescue the virtue of mainstream consensus from our historically benighted views about homosexuality by insisting that its existence as an illness was never *really* a fact, that it was merely something people wrongly believed.

Unfortunately, the stray flick of that observation is enough to cause the whole majestic zeppelin of Truth to burst into flame. If some facts are not in fact facts, we need a way of separating these seemingly true but secretly false facts from real actually true facts. But, since we kick beliefs like homosexuality-as-illness out to the curb retroactively, any such mechanism is pretty clearly not going to be universal or fast-acting. Journalism, that famous first draft of history, is especially vulnerable to the damage to mainstream consensus.

The philosopher Richard Rorty described truth as whatever everybody declines to be arguing about at the moment. This is less nihilistic than it sounds, since it describes the progress of both social and scientific beliefs. People used to argue about whether photons had mass and about whether women should vote. Now those are settled questions. We used to have consensus on whether gay couples could marry and how many dimensions the universe has. Now people argue about those things all the time. Scientists and politicians have different rules for fighting, of course, and different standards for what constitutes a worthwhile argument, but in both cases, the process is one of competing claims adjudicated by argument and settled by consensus.

We could thus describe public expression without using the label truth at all by simply locating any given statement on a spectrum of agreement, running from "The sky is blue" through "Inflation is always and everywhere a monetary phenomenon" to "The Earth is flat." The statements we describe as true are the ones that enjoy operative consensus among relevant actors. As a consequence, any statement presented as true can also be described as an assertion; that the people who believe the statement are the people whose opinions on the subject matter, and those who don't, aren't.

The last decade of public conversation on climate change has turned on this axle. Because journalists often aspire to report from a position of dispassionate arbitration, evidence of consensus is taken as evidence of truth, and lack of consensus signals an unsettled issue. This was a workable strategy only when people with views outside mainstream consensus were locked out of the mainstream media and thus had no way to make their opposing view known.

That strategy is now broken. The Internet broadens the range of publicly expressed opinions, to put the matter mildly, making it simple to find people who will vigorously contest any consensus view, no matter how widely held or carefully tested. This has, in turn, allowed climate change deniers to exploit the press's discomfort with adjudicating disputes, a journalistic trope my colleague Jay Rosen calls "we have no idea who's right!"

There is no neutral position from which to stand; every assertion the press publishes is backstopped by the relevance of the community making that assertion, whether that means scientists, politicians, the Chamber of Commerce, or the *vox populi*. Even for something as tied to physical reality as climate change, the press is perforce in the business of refereeing community disputes, not merely ascertaining and then recording facts.

With the Internet's expansion of public speech, journalistic attempts to publish the truth must shift from reporting consensus to telling the public whose opinions are relevant and whose aren't. This shift in focus to describing who is and isn't a relevant actor is a return to an older pattern, more common in the days of the partisan press.

As Walter Lippmann put it nearly a century ago,[2]

> There is no defense, no extenuation, no excuse whatsoever, for stating six times that Lenin is dead when the only information the paper possesses is a report that he is dead from a source repeatedly shown to be unreliable.... If there is one subject on which editors are most responsible it is in their judgment of the reliability of the source.

Yet reporters and editors working on climate change have often been unwilling to say, "These scientists are more credible than those scientists" or "This set of data was more relevant than that set of data." The perception that the press itself is an actor in the public conversation, not just a conduit for that conversation, can still produce discomfort in the nation's newsrooms (even though that perception is obviously correct).

WHEN BELIEFS AND FACTS COLLIDE

We are accustomed to the idea that certain beliefs are contained in particular communities, such as "Jesus is Lord" or "Tennessee barbecue is superior to Texas barbecue," but this is also the case for sentiments like "The world is round" or "Al Qaeda attacked the Cairo Embassy." As it is, of course, for sentiments like "Obama is a Muslim."

There is a story in my family of my father-in-law taking his fiancé (my future mother-in-law) home to Ethiopia to meet his family. His mother was charmed by my mother-in-law, who, even though she was white, seemed perfectly well behaved. She was, exclaimed his mother, "very nice—just like a Christian!"

Now my mother-in-law *was* a Christian by any American standard—a good Scots/German Protestant. But my grandmother-in-law, Ethiopian Orthodox, used "Just like a Christian" to mean "Just like us."

Depending on who's asking and how, up to one-fifth of U.S. citizens have been willing to say that Barack Obama is a Muslim. This despite the fact that

Obama was raised a Christian, calls himself Christian and worships in a Christian church. But as with my mother-in-law, the question isn't so straightforward. When conservatives say things like this, it's often as a form of protest, just as, during the Bush administration, liberals circulated obviously faked images of a gun-toting Sarah Palin in an American flag bikini as if they were real.

Furthermore, liberals generally think of religion as a personal choice—you are the religion you say you are and no other. Many of our fellow citizens, however, think we're wrong, and that religion is tied to family identity. In this view, the fact that Obama's father was Muslim and that he is named after a grandson of the Prophet counts for something. Reckoned this way, Obama is clearly the most Muslim president in history.

When liberals want those conservatives to admit that Obama is not a Muslim, we are not asking them to accept simple facts. We are asking them to replace their conception of religion with ours, a conception that says having a Muslim parent or an Arabic name says nothing whatsoever about religious identity. In presenting our sense of religious identity as factual and the conservative one as obviously false, we are asking them to agree that, in the ways that matter on the issue, Obama is just like them. And they don't agree.

In 2010, *Newsweek* ran an article, based on Pew Research, on the subject of the president's religious identity.[3] A comment on that piece, by someone going by the nickname Bigfoot, highlights the issue: "I do not know what 'religion' he professes to be, but he definitely is NOT christian! I know that he is a 'Wolf' in sheeps clothing and do not buy any of his garbage for one second!" (sic)

Bigfoot doesn't deny the president is a Christian because he thinks Obama says the Shahada every day. He denies the president is Christian because he doesn't buy any of Obama's garbage for one second. As a consequence, he is unwilling to admit to *any* important similarities between the president and himself.

It's easy to characterize our contempt for Bigfoot and his ilk as high-minded concern for their grasp of the facts, but that's fairly obviously not the case. If we really cared that much about people's grasp of the facts, we'd have lain awake for decades fretting about the alien abduction people. We don't, though, because we're perfectly willing to regard them as harmless morons, alongside the flat earthers and that time cube guy.

The alien abduction people don't upset us because we simply refuse to account for their beliefs in our beliefs. The way people talk about their abduction by aliens doesn't strike us as legitimate, so we simply ignore their claims. With people like Bigfoot, however, we can't ignore them as easily because, in an inexplicable turn of events, *Newsweek* has handed Bigfoot a megaphone.

The thing that alarms us about people like Bigfoot isn't their beliefs, it's their right to assert those beliefs in our newly expanded public sphere and their ability to act on those beliefs in ways that affect us. When people disagree with us about things like the president's religion, we say we wish they wouldn't deny the facts, but really, we just wish they were more liberal or that their definition of religion was the same as ours. Failing that, we sometimes wish that public speech was still restricted to the pros.

THE PROFESSIONALIZATION OF NEWS

In a technical sense, journalism is a trade, not a profession. Its core skills are not arcane, and there are no requirements for either formal studies or certification. (Indeed, in the United States, any certification that barred amateurs and novices from competing with incumbents would be not just illegal, but unconstitutional.)

Curiously, much of the 20th century was marked by impulses toward professionalization—from trade associations to journalism schools, and the second half of the century created a situation in the news ecosystem that looked very like professionalization. Federal Communications Commission decisions favoring large broadcast areas and national networks created a television cartel. The death of the evening newspaper at the hands of the evening news strengthened the remaining metro dailies, which achieved something like a monopoly on local display ads. The postwar economic boom turned these scarcities into persistent and sizable income growth.

Newspaper chains standardized hiring and training practices across huge swaths of the country, and their hiring preferences increasingly turned to college-educated members of the middle class. In symbiotic adaptation, the country's journalism schools began training their students in the current professional practices of existing businesses, turning out graduates ready to plug into increasingly complex production processes.

The roots of nonpartisan centrism as a press ideology go back to the 19th century and grew with the spread of advertising as a means of financing journalism in the 20th. But the twin postwar forces of large scale and lack of competition helped push the national press even further away from partisan argumentation. Moderate centrism became the house ideology of *The New York Times, The Washington Post* and CBS News. On the national stage, truth was whatever educated, straight, white men declined to be arguing about at the moment, a consensus view of reality that included the views of Walter Cronkite but excluded those of a large number of his viewers.

In an environment like this, industry self-regulation proved a powerful force for censuring journalists who didn't adhere to shared standards. Reporters couldn't have their licenses revoked, as doctors or lawyers can, but in an industry whose senior leadership could fit in a hotel ballroom, an informal blackballing, as in "Don't hire Janet Cooke," was enough.[4]

The Internet does not alter this model. It destroys it. No matter how many news outlets continue to hew to moderate centrism, there is no longer any way to keep partisans and fabulists out of the public sphere, nor is there any way to revoke access after heinous affronts to truth-telling. Even the challenge presented by the openly partisan Fox News is nothing like the explosion of reporting and opinion from across the political spectrum the Internet is ushering in.

It's tempting to conclude that this stuff doesn't count, precisely because the people publishing it don't abide by the methods or norms favored by mainstream journalists, but the people in the news industry no longer get to decide what the public counts as news. In this environment, the definition of news has much more to do with demand than supply. When the New York Police Department raided Zuccotti Park in November of 2011 to oust the Occupy Wall Street protesters who had been living there to draw attention to their cause, the event was better documented by the occupiers themselves than by the press, since the police went out of their way to block traditional reporters. In contrast to reporting from people with press passes, largely operating behind police barricades, first-hand accounts from people like Tim Pool, who streamed the police activity and the occupier's reactions live from his phone, constituted the news as many observers experienced it.

Similarly, the passionate and knowledgeable cyclists at NYVelocity did more to unmask Lance Armstrong's years-long doping regime, though they were journalistic amateurs, than all the professional sports journalists covering Armstrong combined.

We are now watching the quasi-professionalization of journalism in the 20th century run in reverse. It is certainly possible to tell the difference between Tim Pool and Scott Pelley or NYVelocity and *The New York Times*; it is no longer possible to find a sharp discontinuity at some midpoint between them, where *amateur* stops and *professional* starts.

The old gap separating journalists from the public, producers from consumers, has turned into a gradient. At the same time, public consensus has shrunk dramatically, and the ability of mainstream outlets to limit public voices to mainstream values has collapsed altogether. We are entering a world where the consensus view of truth no longer rests on scarcity of public speech and one where ethical norms can't be backed up by force.

"POST-FACT" JOURNALISM

Here's what the "post-fact" literature has right: The Internet allows us to see what other people actually think. This has turned out to be a huge disappointment. When anyone can say anything, we can't even pretend most of us agree on the truth of most assertions any more.

The post-fact literature is built in part on nostalgia for the world before people like Bigfoot showed up in the public sphere, for the days when *Newsweek* reflected moderately liberal consensus without also providing a platform for orthographically challenged wingnuts to rant about the president. People who want those days back tell themselves (and anyone else who will listen) that they don't want to impose their views on anybody. They just want agreement on the facts.

But what would that look like, an America where there was broad agreement on the facts? It would look like public discussion was limited to the beliefs held by straight, white, Christian men. If the views of the public at large didn't hew to the views of that group, the result wouldn't be agreement. It would be argument.

Argument, of course, is the human condition, but public argument is not. Indeed, in most places for most of history, publicly available statements have been either made or vetted by the ruling class, with the right of reply rendered impractical, illegal or both. Expansion of public speech, for both participants and topics, is generally won only after considerable struggle, and of course, any such victory pollutes the sense of what constitutes truth from the previous era, a story that runs from Martin Luther through Ida Tarbell to Mario Savio, the drag queens outside Stonewall, and Julian Assange.

There's no way to get Cronkite-like consensus without someone like Cronkite, and there's no way to get someone like Cronkite in a world with an Internet; there will be no more men like him because there will be no more jobs like his. To assume that this situation can be reversed, that everyone else will voluntarily sign on to the beliefs of some culturally dominant group, is a fantasy. To assume that they should sign on, or at least that they should hold their tongue when they don't, is Napoleonic in its self-regard. Yet, this is what the people who long for the clarity of the old days are longing for.

Seeing claims that the CIA staged the 9/11 attacks or that oil is an unlimited by-product of volcanism is enough to make the dear dead days of limited public speech seem like a paradise, but there are compensating virtues in our bumptious public sphere.

Consider three acts of mainstream media malfeasance unmasked by outsiders: Philip Elmer-DeWitt's 1995 *Time Magazine* cover story[5] on the prevalence of Internet porn, which relied on faked data; CBS News'[6] 2004 accusations that President George W. Bush dodged military service, which was based on forged National Guard memos; and Jonah Lehrer's[7] recycling and plagiarism in work he did for the *New Yorker* and *Wired,* as well as the fabrication of material in his books. In all three cases, the ethical lapses were committed by mainstream journalists and unmasked by others working on the Internet, but with very different responses by the institutions that initially published the erroneous material.

In Elmer-DeWitt's case, he was given what seemed to be an explosive study that claimed, among other things, that 85 percent of the images on the Internet were pornographic. This was the basis for a *Time* cover story, his first. But the conclusions he drew seemed fishy, and a distributed fact-checking effort formed in response, largely organized on the digital bulletin board system called Usenet. It quickly became apparent that the research was junk; that the researcher who had given the report to Elmer-DeWitt was an undergraduate who faked the data; that the professors listed as sponsors had had little to do with it, and so on. The study was in fact largely faked, and Elmer-DeWitt and the *Time* staff did not vet it carefully.

Elmer-DeWitt apologized forthrightly:

> I don't know how else to say it, so I'll just repeat what I've said before. I screwed up. The cover story was my idea, I pushed for it, and it ran pretty much the way I wrote it. It was my mistake, and my mistake alone. I do hope other reporters will learn from it. I know I have.

Almost no one saw this apology, however, because he said it only online; the correction run by *Time* sought to downplay, rather than apologize for, misleading their readers, even though the core facts reported in the story were faked: "It would be a shame, however, if the damaging flaws in [the] study obscured the larger and more important debate about hard-core porn on the Internet."

In 1995, *Time* could count on very little overlap between its readership and the country's Internet users, so Elmer-DeWitt's ethical lapse and subsequent apology could be waved away with little fear that anyone else could dramatize the seriousness of the article's failings.

Contrast the situation a decade later, in 2004, when CBS News aired a "60 Minutes Wednesday" story about President Bush's time in the National Guard. Like the Elmer-DeWitt story, the CBS story was based on faked documents; as with that story, the forgery was discovered not by CBS itself or another professional media outlet, but by media outsiders working on the Internet; like *Time* in the Elmer-DeWitt case, CBS spent most of its energy trying to minimize its lapse.

Unlike the Elmer-DeWitt story, however, the strategy didn't work. Charles Johnson, blogging at Little Green Footballs, produced an animated graphic[8] demonstrating that the nominally typewritten documents from the early 1970s were actually produced using the default font in Microsoft Word. By 2004, Internet use had become so widespread that the *Time Magazine* tactic of writing off Internet users as a cranky niche was ineffective; Johnson's work was so widely discussed that CBS couldn't ignore it. When the network finally did respond, CBS spokesmen admitted that the documents were questionable, that members of the news staff did not check their authenticity carefully enough, that their defense of the reporters involved compounded the error, and that the lapse was serious enough to constitute a firing offense for the senior people involved, including producer Mary Mapes; Dan Rather resigned after some delay.[9]

A more recent example of this pattern, almost a decade after the National Guard memos, was the science writer Jonah Lehrer's use of recycled, plagiarized and fabricated material, including, most famously, invented quotes from Bob Dylan.[10] Again journalistic ethics were breached in mainstream publications—in Lehrer's case, in writings for *Wired* and the *New Yorker,* and in his book, *Imagine.* His lapses were uncovered not by anyone at publisher Conde Nast, however. His most serious lapse was uncovered by Michael Moynihan, a writer and editor at *Reason and Vice,* who published his discovery of the Dylan fabrication in *Tablet,*[11] an online-only magazine of Jewish life and culture. Moynihan's revelations, the most damning of the criticisms Lehrer was then facing, precipitated his resignation from the *New Yorker.*

The Lehrer example demonstrates the completion of a pattern that we might call "after-the-fact checking," visible public scrutiny of journalistic work after it is published. After-the-fact checking is not just knowledgeable insiders identifying journalistic lapses; that has always happened. Instead, the new pattern involves those insiders being able to identify one another and collaborate on public complaint. Group action, even loosely coordinated, has always been more visible and powerful than disaggregated instances of individual action; the rise of loose, yet collaborative networks of fact-checking creates a concomitant weakening of strategies by traditional media for minimizing the effects of such lapses.

The difference between Elmer-DeWitt and Lehrer isn't that the latter's lapses were worse, it's that the ability to hide the lapses has shrunk. The nominal ethics of journalism remain as they were, but the mechanisms of observation and accountability have been transformed as the public's role in the landscape has moved from passive to active, and the kind of self-scrutiny the press is accustomed to gives way to considerably more persistent and withering after-the-fact checking.

"THE INTERNET IS A TRUTH SERUM"

The truth is not dead. Those who issue such laments have correctly identified the changes in the landscape of public speech but often misdiagnose their causes. We are indeed less willing to agree on what constitutes truth, but not because we have recently become pigheaded, naysaying zealots. We were always like that. It's just that we didn't know how many other people were like that as well. And, as Ben McConnell and Jackie Huba put it long ago, the Internet is a truth serum.

The current loss of consensus is a better reflection of the real beliefs of the American polity than the older centrism. Several names can be applied to what constitutes acceptable argument in a society—the Overton window, the sphere of legitimate controversy—but whatever label you use, the range of things people are willing to argue about has grown.

There seems to be less respect for consensus today because there is indeed less respect for consensus. This change is not good or bad per se; it has simply made agreement a scarcer commodity across all issues of public interest. The erosion of controls on public speech have enabled birthers to make their accusations against the president public; it also allows newly emboldened groups—feminists, atheists, Muslims, Mormons—to press their issues in public, in opposition to traditional public beliefs, a process similar to gay rights post-Stonewall, but now on a faster and more national scale. There's no going back.

One of the common ways journalists identify truth is by looking for operative consensus among relevant actors. For the last two generations of journalism, the emphasis has been on the question of consensus; the question of who constituted a relevant actor was largely solved by scarcity. It was easy to find mainstream voices and hard to find marginal or heterodox ones. With that scarcity undone, all such consensus will be destroyed unless journalists start telling the audience which voices aren't worth listening to.

A world where all utterances are putatively available makes "he said, she said" journalism an increasingly irresponsible form, less a way of balancing reasonable debate and more a way of evading the responsibility for informing the public. "Seeking truth and reporting it" is becoming less about finding consensus, which has become rarer, and more about publicly sorting the relevant actors from the irrelevant ones. The shrinking professional class of journalists can no longer fall back on experts, as if every professor or researcher is equally trustworthy.

Journalists now have to operate in a world where no statement, however trivial, will be completely secured from public gainsaying. At the same time, public production of speech, not just consumption, means that the policing of ethical failures has passed out of the hands of the quasi-professional group of journalists employed in those outlets and has become another form of public argument. This alters the public sphere in important ways.

The old days, where marginal opinions meant marginal availability, have given way to a world where all utterances, true or false, are a click away. Journalists have always had to make a call about what constitutes legitimate consensus and who constitutes relevant actors. They just didn't used to have to work so hard to do so. An environment where public speech was scarce, and where access was generally limited to people with mainstream views, was an environment where the visible actors were the relevant ones and vice versa. It was also an environment where the absence of dissent was a rough and ready metric for measuring consensus.

Now, public speech is accessible to brilliant people and crazy people and cantankerous people and iconoclastic people. No assertion more complex than "the cat is on the mat" generates universal assent. In this environment, journalists have to get practiced at sorting relevant from irrelevant actors and legitimate from illegitimate objections.

In an even more significant rupture with the past, they have to get practiced at explaining to their readers why they are making the choices they are making. Prior to now, when a news outlet didn't publish the opinion of someone whose views it considered irrelevant, there was almost no way that person could reach those readers on his or her own. Also prior to now, only the people creating the weather page had to admit to the readers that there was a specific probability connected to their assertions.

Now, though, both of those traits have broken down. Views not covered in mainstream outlets can nevertheless find large audiences. The public thus operates with increased awareness that some voices are being intentionally ignored by some media outlets. (Indeed, all media outlets ignore at least some voices.) This means not just including some voices and excluding others but explaining why you are doing so.

This is destroying the nominally neutral position of many mainstream outlets. Consider, as an example, Arthur Brisbane's constitutional inability, as public editor of *The New York Times,* to process universal public disdain for his proposed methods of fact-checking politicians.[12] His firm commitment to avoiding accusations of partisanship, even at the expense of rigorous checks on putative facts, helped raise the visibility of the fact-checking movement in the 2012 presidential campaign, as pioneered by PolitiFact and its peers. These fact-checking services have now become a new nexus of media power in the realm of political speech.

Yet Brisbane is onto something, though it may have more to do with self-preservation than with commitment to truth: A world where even mainstream news outlets tell their readers when politicians lie, or publicly assess various speakers' relevance on any given issue, is a world where neither powerful public actors nor advertisers will be automatically willing to trust or even cooperate with the press.

Even as the erosion of consensus makes for an unavoidable increase in oppositional reporting, it also makes the scrutiny journalists face from their audience far greater than the scrutiny they face from their employers or peers. Trust in the press has fallen precipitously[13] in the last generation, even as the press itself increasingly took on the trappings of a profession.

One possible explanation is that what pollsters and respondents characterized as *trust* was really *scarcity*—like the man with one watch, a public that got its news from a politically narrow range might have been more willing to regard those reinforced views as accurate. Since Watergate, however, along with increasingly partisan campaigning and governance, the lack of shared outlook among existing newsmakers, coupled with the spread of new, still more partisan newsmakers, makes this sort of trust impossible.

There's no going back here either. The era when there was something called "the press," and it had a reputation among something called "the public," is over. Each organization will have to try to convince each member of its audience that it is trustworthy. Any commitment to ethics will involve not just being more reactive to outsiders' post-hoc review, but also being more willing to attack other outlets for ethical lapses in public, more ready to publicly defend their own internal policies, rather than simply regarding ethical lapses as a matter for internal policing.

The philosophy of journalism ethics—tell the truth to the degree that you can, 'fess up when you get it wrong—doesn't change in the switch from analog to digital. What does change, enormously, is the individual and organizational adaptations required to tell the truth without relying on scarcity and while hewing to ethical norms without reliance on a small group of similar institutions that can all coordinate around those norms.

This will make for a far more divisive public sphere, a process that is already under way. It's tempting to divide these changes into win-loss columns to see whether this is a change for the better or the worse—birthers bad, new atheists good (relabel to taste)—but this sort of bookkeeping is a dead end. The effects of digital abundance are not trivially separable—the birthers and the new atheists used similar tools and techniques to enter the public sphere, as did the Tea Party and Occupy Wall Street. More important, the effects are not reversible. Even if we conclude that the collapse of moderate centrism is bad for the United States, there's no way to stop or reverse the exploded range of publicly available opinion.

Now, and from now on, journalists are going to be participants in a far more argumentative sphere than anything anyone alive has ever seen. The question for us is not whether we want this increase in argumentation—no one is asking us, and there's no one who could—but rather how we should adapt ourselves to it as it unfolds.

NOTES

1. Michael Hirschorn, "Truth Lies Here," *The Atlantic,* November 2010, http://www.theatlantic.com/magazine/archive/2010/11/truth-lies-here/308246/.

2. Walter Lippmann, "News, Truth, and a Conclusion," in *Public Opinion* (New York: MacMillan Co. 1922), http://xroads.virginia.edu/~hyper/lippman/ch24.html.

3. David A. Graham, "Silly Things We Believe about Witches, Obama and More," *The Daily Beast,* http://www.thedailybeast.com/newsweek/galleries/2010/08/24/dumb-things-americans-believe.html; "Growing Number of Americans Say Obama Is a Muslim," *Pew Research Center for the People and the Press,*" August 19, 2010, http://www.people-press.org/2010/08/19/growing-number-of-americans-say-obama-is-a-muslim/.

4. *Washington Post* reporter Janet Cooke won the Pulitzer Prize for her 1980 story, "Jimmy's World," about an 8-year-old heroin addict. The Pulitzer Board subsequently stripped her of the prize when it was revealed that Jimmy was a fabrication. For more information, see Elaine Dutka, "Janet Cooke's Life: The Picture-Perfect Tale," *Los Angeles Times,* May 28, 1996, http://articles.latimes.com/1996-05-28/entertainment/ca-9096_1_janet-cooke.

5. Philip Elmer-Dewitt, "Online Erotica: On a Screen Near You," *Time Magazine,* July 03, 1995, http://www.time.com/time/magazine/article/0,9171,983116,00.html.

6. Jarrett Murphy, "CBS Ousts 4 for Bush Guard Story," *CBS,* February 11, 2009, http://www.cbsnews.com/2100-201_162-665727.html.

7. Articles about "Jonah Lehrer," *Poynter.org,* last modified March 4, 2013, http://www.poynter.org/tag/jonah-lehrer/.

8. Charles Johnson, "NPR Rewrites Rathergate History to Cover Up Fraud," *Little Green Footballs,* December 23, 2008, http://littlegreenfootballs.com/article/32256_NPR_Rewrites_Rathergate_History_to_Cover_Up_Fraud.

9. Al Tompkins, "Mapes: Decision to Air National Guard Story Was Made by CBS Superiors, Including Heyward," *Poynter.org,* January 10, 2005, http://www.poynter.org/uncategorized/29491/mapes-decision-to-air-national-guard-story-was-made-by-cbs-superiors-including-heyward/.

10. Steve Myers, "Jonah Lehrer Resigns from New Yorker after Fabricating Bob Dylan Quotes in 'Imagine'," *Poynter.org,* July 30, 2012, http://www.poynter.org/latest-news/mediawire/183298/jonah-lehrer-accused-of-fabricating-bob-dylan-quotes-in-imagine/.

11. Michael Moynihan, "Jonah Lehrer's Deceptions: The Celebrated Journalist Fabricated Bob Dylan Quotes in His New Book, *Imagine: How Creativity Works,*" *Tablet,* July 30, 2012, http://www.tabletmag.com/jewish-news-and-politics/107779/jonah-lehrers-deceptions?all=1.

12. Steve Myers, "Brisbane: 'I Ended Up as a Pinata on This One'," *Poynter.org,* January 23, 2012, http://www.poynter.org/latest-news/mediawire/160444/brisbane-i-ended-up-as-a-pinata-on-this-one/.

13. Andrew Beaujon, "Gallup: Americans Mistrust Media More Than Ever," *Poynter.org,* September 21, 2012, http://www.poynter.org/latest-news/mediawire/189225/gallup-americans-mistrust-media-more-than-ever/.

Caitlin Johnston

In his essay, Clay Shirky suggests that it has become more difficult to determine "operative consensus among relevant actors" and, therefore, more difficult to discern the truth. This case study illustrates how professional newsrooms might shift their approach to covering a story in response to that new reality.

Pinellas County (Fla.) Commissioner Norm Roche led an effort in 2011 to eliminate fluoride from the county water supply. The county government had been adding fluoride since 2004, a common practice throughout the United States that had been lauded as one of the greatest public health achievements of the 20th century.

The treatment, which cost the county roughly 30 cents per person per year, was widely reported by dentists and medical professionals to help prevent tooth decay. But critics used research showing that too much fluoride could have side effects on young children, such as causing white spots on their teeth, as a foothold to argue that the government should not force its citizens to consume the supplement. Members of the Tea Party compared the government-backed fluoride treatment to Soviet and Nazi practices.

"Fluoride is a toxic substance," said Tea Party activist Tony Caso in a *Tampa Bay Times* article about the commission's decision. "This is all part of an agenda that's being pushed forth by the so-called globalists in our government and the world government to keep the people stupid so they don't realize what's going on . . . This is the U.S. of A., not the Soviet Socialist Republic."[1]

In a 4-3 vote in October 2011, the county commission passed the law eliminating the treatment from county water. The backlash was immediate.

Commissioner Ken Welch, who voted to keep the fluoride in the water, voiced his outrage over a minority group's ability to override the majority of public opinion.

"We are going to the backwoods of urban counties with this move," Welch said in a *Tampa Bay Times* article.[2]

The four commissioners had ignored the voices of most of the county's dentists, pediatricians, medical groups, health officials and the public in order to pass legislation supporting a minority-held belief. Welch told the *Tampa Bay Times* that professionals supporting the use of fluoride outnumbered critical ones before the commission 20-1. But that didn't faze his fellow commissioners.

In the year that followed, the *Tampa Bay Times* ran more than a dozen editorials and columns about the fluoride battle, excoriating the county commission for failing to protect public health. The news side of the staff covered the debate vigorously throughout the year as residents struggled with how to compensate for the now fluoride-free water. Apart from writing articles before and after commission meetings, they also included the issue in articles surrounding the 2012 re-election campaign of two commissioners who had voted to remove fluoride from the water supply.

In their news stories, *Times* reporters characterized the opinions and studies supporting fluoride supplements in water as solid, well-accepted science. They questioned or ignored the few studies that contradicted the belief that fluoride should be added to public water supplies. In the run-up to the 2012 election, the *Times* editorial staff advocated strongly for citizens to vote out of office two of the commissioners who were up for re-election.

"Two of the Fluoride Four are on the ballot Tuesday seeking re-election to their countywide seats: Nancy Bostock and Neil Brickfield," the editorial board wrote. "Their challengers, Charlie Justice and Janet Long, support restoring fluoride to the county's drinking water. It only takes one new commissioner to reverse the backward decision—and save Pinellas County families time, money and frustration."[3]

Both Bostock and Brickfield were voted out of office, by significant majorities.

Their successors brought the fluoride issue back on the commission agenda. During the subsequent hearing the chamber was once again packed with vocal opponents to fluoride. The law restoring fluoride to the water passed 6-1, with Roche again voting against fluoride.

The paper's strong coverage seemed to influence the election and the fluoride vote. The *Times* would go on to win the 2013 Pulitzer Prize for editorial writing.

QUESTIONS

• How should journalists determine if a group's arguments should be characterized as legitimate or illegitimate? In this case, what evidence would you use to counter the claims that fluoride is potentially harmful?

• Journalists are frequently criticized for quoting opposing sides as if they had equal standing. Assume that you have determined that those who oppose fluoride in public water supplies do not have equal or substantial scientific evidence for their arguments compared with those who support the addition of fluoride. Identify three strategies you could use in your news coverage to ensure that opposition voices are heard by the audience in context. Would you quote them directly? Would you openly challenge the accuracy of their claims on the air or in text? Would you ignore them altogether? What are the advantages and disadvantages to each of your strategies?

• Name another topic on which there is significant opposition to mainstream beliefs. Find an example of a story where the two sides are presented equally. And find an example of a story where the reporter gives more weight to one side or the other. What techniques does each reporter use? Can you identify the audience for each story? Why might news organizations opt for one approach or the other?

Editors' Note: The Tampa Bay Times _is owned by The Poynter Institute, which employs this book's co-editor and several contributors._

CASE NOTES

1. David DeCamp, "Pinellas County Commission Votes to Stop Putting Fluoride in Water Supply," _Tampa Bay Times_, October 5, 2011, http://www.tampabay.com/news/localgovernment/article1195147.ece.
2. David DeCamp, "Pinellas County Commission Stands Firm in Decision to End Fluoridation," _Tampa Bay Times_, October 12, 2011, http://www.tampabay.com/news/environment/water/article1196224.ece.
3. "The Real Cost of the Fluoride Fiasco," _Tampa Bay Times_, November 1, 2012, http://www.tampabay.com/opinion/editorials/the-real-cost-of-the-fluoride-fiasco/1259225.

chapter 2

Kicking the Stone: The Search for Reliable Evidence in Journalism

Roy Peter Clark

Like many English majors, I have been fascinated by the stories of the great British man-of-letters Samuel Johnson, who towered over the 18th century like a lighthouse. One story still makes me laugh. It concerns how Johnson refuted the philosophy of Bishop George Berkeley, who argued, in essence, that all experience was subjective.

In *The Life of Samuel Johnson* (1791), James Boswell, Johnson's friend and biographer, describes how the good doctor came to the rescue:

> After we came out of the church, we stood talking for some time together of Bishop Berkeley's ingenious sophistry to prove the nonexistence of matter, and that every thing in the universe is merely ideal. I observed, that though we are satisfied his doctrine is not true, it is impossible to refute it. I never shall forget the alacrity with which Johnson answered, striking his foot with mighty force against a large stone, till he rebounded from it—"I refute it *thus.*"

Journalists are, by training and disposition, stone kickers. In general, they are skeptics who prefer a world of things to a world of ideas and theories, or at least they act as if they do. At their best, they engage the world as it is, rather than as they wish it would be. They go out. They find things out. They judge those things to be either important or interesting — or both. They report things back to the rest of us. Their purpose is to enrich our experience, individually and collectively. Reading Boswell's *Life*, we benefit from the knowledge that it takes a big kick to move a big stone.

HOW DO WE KNOW WHAT WE KNOW?

But how do journalists come to know things? And how do they know what they know? If we believe that seeking truth is an essential purpose of journalism, even as it expands into the digital age, answering these questions becomes essential.

One man who offered an answer was Melvin Mencher, an influential professor at Columbia University's Graduate School of Journalism and the author of a best-selling journalism textbook. In a curmudgeonly style, Mencher passed along to his students a reliable and responsible method of reporting. By *reporting,* I think he meant a democratic craft of learning, knowing and sharing knowledge.

Mencher understood that journalism was not science, but the process of working a story could still begin with a hypothesis, a preconception of what the reporter might discover. It is important to note here that Mencher's method does not presume that the reporter is a blank slate or an empty vessel. The reporter brings experience and learning to the task, but whatever she thinks she knows, she must in the end be guided by the available evidence.

"Who are the homeless?" an editor may ask. Even before the search begins, the reporter is thinking: "If people sleep and keep their stuff in subway tunnels, does that make them homeless?" Or, "I wonder how many people begging on the streets and claiming to be homeless are really alcoholics or drug addicts?" Or, "If a person has every chance to have a home but chooses to live out on the street, should that person have the same homeless status as someone who is forced out of work and gets a foreclosure notice?"

Based on the early evidence, one or more of these will pan out, leading the reporter to choose a focus for the story, a central governing idea that helps the reporter and editor select the most telling details from everything that has been gathered. Let me repeat Mencher's key to responsible practice: If the evidence points the reporter in a different direction, the story must be reconceived. Many of us who serve as sources have had to deal with reporters who are determined to kick the stone, even after we point out to them that it's the trunk of a tree.

No reporters I know think of themselves as Truthtellers, with a capital T, not because they are humble but because they find themselves so often wallowing in a world of uncertainty, a world, as Clay Shirky points out in his essay in this volume, where a practical consensus on how things work is increasingly difficult to find. Who can hope to make sense of the global economy—or even a school board budget? This may be why accuracy becomes a fetish for journalists. At least we can spell the names right and copy the numbers right. Perhaps a higher or deeper level of understanding may come over time.

Journalists are truth-seekers, with a lower-case *t*, pragmatists who follow their instincts and evolving routines designed to mark their work as trustworthy. Their reports will deliver information in the public interest: for example, that rear-end collisions have increased since the city placed video cameras at dangerous intersections. Now, instead of running red lights, drivers are slamming on the brakes and getting hit from behind. Their stories will transport us to places we cannot go and experiences we could not otherwise have, to the ruins of the Jersey Shore created by Hurricane Sandy or to the Atlanta gravestone of the great golfer Bobby Jones, where visitors leave golf balls as tokens of tribute. Don't believe me? Go to the cemetery and kick the stone.

Our ethic of small-*t* truth-telling follows a set of standards and practices that I've described in essays and articles since 1980, when *Washington Post* reporter Janet Cooke fabricated a story about an eight-year-old heroin addict. A fiction writer might have performed a public service with such a story, but the *Post* wound up returning its Pulitzer Prize.

Until now, the cornerstone principles of responsible reporting have been these: Do not add. Do not deceive. A kind of distortion, argued the author John Hersey, is inevitable in journalism when you gather a hundred facts but only publish ten. It is distortion by subtraction, as can occur when a photograph is badly cropped or a quote is ripped from its larger context. Journalists work to avoid such problems, but even bad journalism by subtraction is recognizable as journalism.

Something essential changes with addition. Responsible journalists do not add to an article facts they know not to be true, they do not add details to a story that didn't exist, and they don't add words in a quote that were never uttered.

The strongest antidote to deceptive practices—such as composite characters, or improper manipulation of time and space, or even bias—is transparency. In a skeptical, some might say cynical, age authors can no longer count on the benefit of a willing suspension of disbelief. At best, we get a grudging suspension of disbelief, which can evolve into something stronger only if we journalists are willing to disclose to audiences—with more humility than we have done in the past—what we know, how we came to know it, what we don't know, what we are still trying to learn and what we may never know.

When I started practicing journalism as an amateur, I was unaware of these norms and in my ignorance violated some of them. In one freelance op-ed piece from the 1970s, I created an argument, in the form of angry dialogue, between two Catholic parishioners to dramatize the rifts between the liberal and conservative factions of the Church. Honest, I didn't know any better. On another occasion, I created a composite Alabama automobile, one festooned with all the kinds of political and cultural bumper stickers that were common in the South in the 1970s. Ten cars became, in my story, one car.

Speed ahead to the 21st century and two forces seem at work at the same time now, headed for a broad cultural collision. I would argue that the ethical norms of journalism have never been tougher—nor tougher to enforce. The more people work and play within the field of public communication, forming what has been called a Fifth Estate, the more difficult it will be to create standards and practices that most will adhere to. Can you practice forms of journalism without identifying yourself as a journalist? Yes, you can—as eyewitnesses to historical events have demonstrated over the centuries.

Forms of journalism are not eternal. They are invented to solve certain sets of social and political problems and take advantage of emerging markets and new technologies. The human interest story, for example, was created for readers of the penny press as an intentional diversion from traditional politics and business news. The idea was to attract new immigrant readers by the hundreds of thousands, especially in the big cities.

Such forms can become exhausted from overuse, only to be reimagined or adapted to match an innovation, the way short forms of the inverted pyramid have been used to convey breaking news on the Internet. But I see nothing new under the sun—or in *The Sun,* for that matter—that would license bloggers or tweeters, or iPhone photographers and videographers to add stuff that never happened or to deceive audiences with tricks of invention.

Wanna be a journalist, kid? Go out there, find stuff out, check it out and deliver it straight. If you prefer taking some fancy steps, be sure to admit what you are doing to the community you want to reach. Adhere to a social contract.

Truth (with a small *t*), transparency and community. These are values and virtues that will continue to define responsible journalism even as technologies, platforms and audiences evolve.

In his useful and provocative essay, Professor Shirky argues that journalists must be ready to serve a world in which consensus is increasingly difficult to find and where truth will become a frustratingly fragmented and relative commodity. As an example, he cites the way that psychiatry decided homosexuality was a disease and then decided it was no longer a disease, another step in a social revolution toward the recognition of sexual orientation. As a journalist, I am already uncomfortable. I'm not sure expressions of human sexuality are stones that I can kick. They seem too big. And maybe they aren't even stones at all. Maybe they are something much less solid. Maybe they are clouds of abstraction. Can you kick a cloud?

NEW IDEAS ABOUT TRUTH—OR "TRUTHINESS"

If I understand correctly, this is Shirky's larger point: In professional environments, new ideas about the nature of truth replace old ones through argument and consensus. While individuals may change their minds on an issue or, in the parlance of waffling politicians, "grow," many amateurs or civilians—abetted by digital technology—define reliable evidence as that body of knowledge that confirms what I already know or think I believe, an ideology derided by comedian Stephen Colbert as "truthiness."

In late 2012, while I was beginning to think through the question of what constitutes reliable evidence in journalism, a young man, Adam Lanza, shot and killed 26 people, including 20 first-graders, at Sandy Hook Elementary School in Newtown, Conn. One of the questions that has emerged from the catastrophe is whether Lanza, who also killed his mother and himself, had Asperger's syndrome and, if he did, whether that created in his mind an unempathetic worldview that could lead him to unthinkable violence.

Theories about truth just slammed into one of the most dramatic domestic news stories of the new millennium. In what sense was the mass murderer mentally ill? Had he been examined and diagnosed with Asperger's? If so, to what extent does that shine any light on his motivations or actions? In the absence of consensus, such questions become more valuable than ever, and no public practitioners are more prepared to ask them than journalists.

At least since the invention of the telegraph and the formation of the wire services, journalists have followed paths of understanding described collectively as the Five Ws and H—who, what, where, when, why and how—questions that govern the gathering, sorting and presentation of evidence. Acts of responsible journalism are designed, by tradition, to lead to public comprehension on issues of importance, knowledge that can turn into action (such as trying to keep guns out of the hands of dangerous people or improving the quality of mental health care).

It's been widely acknowledged, by practitioners and scholars, that the hardest of the Five Ws to solve is the fifth, the "why," a category that the late professor James Carey once described as the "dark continent" of the practice of journalism. You may be able to kick a large stone, even a boulder, but can you kick a mountain?

An epistemology of journalism—a phrase that reporters and editors are likely to piss on because of its academic pretentions—is mocked, more often, by the malpractice of professional journalists themselves. How can we make sense of what constitutes responsible evidence within professional or amateur practice when the day-to-day routines that attend public information so often fail the test of reliability? How can we begin to get to the why of a mass shooting—with all its multiple, complex and interconnected causes—when we find it so hard to render the who, what, where and when?

In the case of the Newtown shootings, The Poynter Institute's Andrew Beaujon described the surprising number of inaccuracies and distortions generated by the earliest reports. Let's stipulate that what is sometimes called "the fog of breaking news" is difficult even for professionals to penetrate. We also recognize that time is the co-author of good judgment and that a news cycle measured by the minute (or less) provides a powerful force against getting things right.

Even with those qualifiers, it is amazing how much of the early reporting out of Newtown was wrong, as Beaujon reported:

> Adam Lanza was not buzzed in to Sandy Hook Elementary School. His mother, Nancy, did not work at the school. He didn't have an altercation with school officials the day before. He used a Bushmaster rifle, not the Glock and SIG Sauer pistols he was carrying, to carry out his massacre. The children he killed were first-graders, not mostly kindergartners.
>
> Adam Lanza's name was not Ryan (which was his brother's name).[1]

These were just the first published inaccuracies. Others followed. To acknowledge such failures is not to suggest that the professional press is wholly responsible for them. In some cases, mistaken information, rumors and theories were delivered to journalists by sources usually considered official, such as someone representing the police. Sources, journalists and audiences were acting under the usual pressures, intensified by social media's distribution of information (some of it right and some of it wrong) coupled with expectations that knowledge should be delivered as quickly and widely as possible. In such an environment, truth becomes a by-product of this social energy, rather than its primary purpose.

"Oh, what a world, what a world," mourns the Wicked Witch of the West as she melts from the water in Dorothy's pail. "O brave new world," says Amanda in Shakespeare's *Tempest*, "that has such people in't." So which is it?

AN ETHIC FOR THE DIGITAL AGE

The purpose of this collection of essays is to find the shape of an ethic of journalism in the digital age, an age in which traditional norms are being challenged by technology, demography, economics and other cultural upheavals and surprises, such as the competition from amateurs. This last point is both a sign of the times and a cause of it. It took most of the 20th century to professionalize those who deliver public information. Joseph Pulitzer created the Columbia University Graduate School of Journalism and his much coveted prizes to cultivate and reward practitioners who were working at the highest levels. Walter Lippmann and John Dewey began scholarly arguments about the definition of news and the means to gather and transmit it. The Hutchins Commission in the 1940s and the Kerner Commission in the 1960s held journalism practice up for close inspection and offered ideas on how it could be improved. Occasional scandals led to codes of conduct, standards and practices espoused by professional organizations that represented various groups of journalists and media leaders.

When Professor Shirky dismisses this movement as somehow antagonistic to First Amendment freedoms—where the licensing of speech would be deemed unconstitutional—he does not recognize that they were most often self-imposed, a process of internal (some might say tribal) direction, correction and self-protection designed to ward off government imposition.

The most powerful of these norms, and the most often mischaracterized, is objectivity. In its original frame, this was not an argument for blank slate reporting. Of course, every person brings an autobiography to the experience of every act, and that includes such players as the reporter, editor or photographer. W. H. Auden argued that a poem was a "contraption" with a person inside of it: a poet. The products of journalism are contraptions, too: stories, articles, columns, photos, radio interviews—and now blog posts, tweets, status updates and slide shows. And the person inside, the governing intelligence, comes with them.

As Bill Kovach and Tom Rosenstiel (a co-editor of this book) emphasize in *The Elements of Journalism,* the routine practices that developed under the rubric of objectivity were built not to suggest reporters could be unbiased, but in recognition that they were indeed biased. The checks and balances that required being assigned by professional editors, acquiring expertise in important beats, avoiding conflicts of interest, getting to the other sides of arguments, the stuff now touted with little credibility as fair and balanced—all of these gave value to words and ideas such as *nonpartisanship, independence, disinterestedness,* not having a dog in the fight.

As these norms evolved during the 20th century, they were never the only ways of knowing that existed for journalists. An ethic of pragmatic detachment that came to dominate beat reporting, say, held little sway in the world of investigative reporting. In their important work "On the Epistemology of Investigative Journalism," Professors James S. Ettema and Theodore L. Glasser reveal a different set of norms developed from the early muckrakers and perfected through the days of Bob Woodward and Carl Bernstein.

"Investigations into crime and corruption usually arise outside of the news net and may cite bureaucratically *in*credible sources. We find, however, that this investigative reporter has worked out for himself an elaborate process which justifies to himself and his colleagues the knowledge claims embodied in his stories," write Ettema and Glasser.[2] The investigators establish their credibility by going through a set of "intellectual exercises," which the authors describe as:

- Screening the tips
- Weighing the evidence
- Fitting the pieces
- Evaluating the story

I remember experiencing the product of such a process while reading a special investigation published by *The Providence Journal*, which began "Jewelry work in Rhode Island is life at the bottom of industrial America."[3] The old factories that manufactured jewelry turned out to be sweatshops that, among other abuses, employed underage children—including my wife. When I first read that lead, I said to myself: That's not news writing, that's an opinion, an editorial. But after reading the story, I saw it as something different: an unmistakable conclusion based on the weight of the evidence, a strong, reliable revelation of the truth.

There have always been amateur reporters, and their best work usually came in the form of eyewitness testimony. Look at the countless times now that the first images of a catastrophe—an earthquake, tsunami, hurricane, airline crash or mass shooting—come not from trained professional photojournalists but from amateurs working with cellphone cameras. The quality of the lighting or the composition may be lacking, but never mind. If the image is delivered quickly, if it captures breaking news, audiences will embrace it. If it arrives just in time, it's good enough.

My Poynter colleague and social media expert Ellyn Angelotti argues that the primary assets of social media involve a level of control over time and distance, so any proposed standards need to account for those strengths—even magnify them—rather than hinder them or pull them back. This makes sense to me. We are not likely to encourage television journalists to tone down the visual elements of their craft or ask reporters from NPR to minimize the use of natural sound.

The tweet is the vehicle of the quick take, a form of knowledge delivery that now exists in journalism, but its knowledge claims stand in distinction from beat reporting or investigations. However new this seems, remember that telegraph dispatches from the Civil War were quick takes. A telephone dictation from a "leg" reporter in the 1940s was often a quick take. These takes could be expanded, improved on, corrected by updated versions in subsequent editions of the paper. At its best, the eyewitness news account reported on Twitter has the feel of being on the scene as news is happening now.

Take, as an example, this tweet of Joanna Smith reporting for the *Toronto Star* on the earthquake in Haiti: "Fugitive from prison caught looting, taken from police, beaten, dragged thru street, died slowly and set on fire in pile of garbage."[4] That is powerful narrative in 140 characters. More important, I believe it. Smith has kicked the stone.

Journalism professor and news media critic Jay Rosen has characterized political writing from a supposedly nonpolitical stance as "the view from nowhere." For every word or phrase devoted to the canons of neutrality, many more describe the evolving manifestations of subjectivity: opinion, point of view, spin, propaganda, take, column, frame, satire, bias, leanings, snark, slant, angle, peg, social construction, post-modern, memoir, paradigm, political, loaded, master and slave narrative, the death of the author and many more.

I once heard a genial publisher describe to an audience of writers what was happening in his world, especially with scholarly studies on academic topics. He said that no one these days would use W. J. Cash's famous title: "The Mind of the South." The honest question these days, said the publisher, is "whose mind" and "which South."

We've reached a kind of impasse—and it has finally squeezed into journalism—where the large truths attached to modernism seem woefully inadequate for understanding the rich diversity of the human experience. And yet the postmodern perspectives that have replaced them leave us feeling alienated, fragmented, small. There may not be Truth with a capital *T*, but that does not mean we have to settle for a lower, lower and lower-case version of reality until we can barely see that first letter at all. Must *truth* become *ruth*?

TRUTH AND THE KNOWLEDGE COMMUNITY

Let me offer a compromise based on an analogy from the study of linguistics. It involves the phrase *discourse community*. This slightly inflated term refers to all the language clubs to which people belong. Every person learns to negotiate and communicate with the world using a rich variety of language levels. The words I use to lodge a business complaint will feel different from those I use to eulogize a grandparent. The words of my family Christmas letter will differ from those I use to text. Different words for different purposes for different audiences at different levels of formality. Some days I wear my tuxedo, on others I wear my Hawaiian shirt.

Somewhere on the spectrum from empirical objectivity to postmodern nihilism stand communities of knowing. Cognitive communities, if you will. This is not a figure of speech or analogy. We already recognize that the constitution of reliable evidence differs as we move from theology to philosophy to science to law. The practical meaning of Asperger's syndrome will differ depending on whether you are writing an article for a psychiatric journal, a police report, a news account, a legal brief or a new piece of legislation. While these may differ significantly, we know from practice that, at the highest level, they need not contradict each other or be framed antagonistically. They can co-exist, the way that breaking news reporting, beat reporting, tweet reporting and investigative journalism can co-exist and complement each other.

Here's the kicker: The quality of the practical truth revealed in a work of journalism will depend on a transparent methodology made operational in one or more knowledge communities. I already know that the account of 9/11 on a Wikipedia page is different from the Pulitzer Prize–winning nonfiction book, *The Looming Tower* by Lawrence Wright. The moderated crowd-sourcing that creates the former makes it both better and worse than the tome that takes the long view. Time, it turns out, *is* the co-author of good judgment, and Wright was able to trace the road to 9/11 from the formative days of Egypt's Muslim Brotherhood in 1948. But what if Wright is sitting in a New York City penthouse when the building starts to shake and the power goes out? What is it? A terrorist attack? An earthquake? He wants to know, and he wants to know right now what is going on. He'll probably turn to Twitter or Wikipedia or Google News or any other technology that provides quick and immediate information. Wouldn't we all?

The seeds for these arguments have been sown for decades—some would say centuries. As far back as the 1730s, the New York attorney Andrew Hamilton defended printer John Peter Zenger, imprisoned for his attacks on the colonial government, by arguing that liberty depended on the ability of "exposing and opposing arbitrary power . . . by speaking and writing truth."

In 1922 in his famous book *Public Opinion*, Walter Lippmann made a strong argument for distinguishing between news and truth. He traced the failure of the press and all democratic institutions to a common source:

> the failure of self-governing people to transcend their casual experience and their prejudices, by inventing, creating, and organizing a machinery of knowledge" [think for a moment of the Internet as a machinery of knowledge]. . . . It is because they are compelled to act without a reliable picture of the world, that governments, schools, newspapers and churches make such small headway against the more obvious failing of democracy, against violent prejudice, apathy, preference for the curious trivial as against the dull important, and the hunger for sideshows and three legged calves.[5] [Think of YouTube or Buzz Feed!]

Perhaps there is embedded in Lippmann's argument a new role for all professionals or amateurs who connect in any sense with the mission of journalism or its practices. For Lippmann, news was like a searchlight that scanned the dark sky looking for this person or that event. Because it was so scattered, journalism could never have claims on the truth, that picture of reality on which people could act. Perhaps the methods and technologies now available to us offer hope for a greater congruence between news and truth, not through a process of consensus building but from an emphasis on reliability. Through our pursuit of truth, our transparent methods and our new ability to work within communities of interest, we may be better prepared to direct citizens not there, not there or over there, but, yes, over there!

When Thomas Jefferson offered his famous defense of newspapers—that he would prefer them without government rather than the other way around—he added a sentiment that is often deleted in the retelling. He wished, most of all, "that every man should receive those papers and be capable of reading them." In a sense, Jefferson argued for a form of critical literacy we now see as an ideal for all audiences confronting all messages. As a rough contemporary of Dr. Johnson, Jefferson was something of a stone kicker himself, someone who believes that the ideals of liberty could be realized only by the actions of an informed citizenry. Their message to us, perhaps, suggests the possibility of a new enlightenment (with a lower-case e), one in which the authorizing powers of the First Amendment inspire both professionals and amateurs alike, where side by side, if not hand in hand, we can travel a road looking for stones worth kicking.

NOTES

1. Andrew Beaujon, "Sandy Hook Coverage: Is 'Good Enough' Good Enough?" *Poynter.org*, December 17, 2012, http://www.poynter.org/latest-news/mediawire/198545/sandy-hook-coverage-is-good-enough-good-enough/.
2. James S. Ettema and Theodore L. Glasser, "On the Epistemology of Investigative Journalism," in *Journalism, the Democratic Craft*, eds. G. Stuart Adam and Roy Peter Clark (New York: Oxford University Press, 2006), 126.
3. Bruce Butterfield, Working in Jewelry Series, *Providence Journal Bulletin*, June 21–27, 1981; "Jewelry Workers Face Health, Safety Problems," *The Free Lance-Star*, June 24, 1981, http://news.google.com/newspapers?nid=1298&dat=19810624&id=ZvZNAAAAIBAJ&sjid=FosDAAAAIBAJ&pg=4712,3603808.
4. Mallary Jean Tenore, "What Twitter Teaches Us about Writing Short and Well," *Poynter.org*, August 30, 2012, http://www.poynter.org/how-tos/newsgathering-storytelling/186371/what-twitter-teaches-us-about-writing-short-well/.
5. Walter Lippmann, *Public Opinion* (New York: Harcourt, Brace and Company, 1922), 365.

Caitlin Johnston

Roy Peter Clark says there is a difference between "truths" and "Truth." WBEZ's This American Life *found itself exploring this distinction after a contributor substituted one for the other.*

In January 2012, the popular public radio show, *This American Life,* aired an hour-long segment that detailed alleged abuses at factories in China where iPads and iPhones are made. "Mr. Daisey and the Apple Factory," a documentary-style story narrated by Mike Daisey, described the monologist's quest to discover what it was like inside the industrial complexes where our most popular technology is manufactured. It quickly became the most downloaded podcast in the history of *This American Life.*

On hearing the show, which was broadcast by hundreds of public radio stations in the United States and Canada, other journalists working in China were immediately suspicious. Among the obvious errors, Daisey had described armed security guards at the factory, when in fact guns are highly regulated in China and carried only by police and military personnel. Daisey said he met workers at Starbucks, which seemed unlikely since a cup of coffee at Starbucks in China would cost 25 percent of a day's wages for an Apple factory worker. Daisey described interviews with workers who had been poisoned by n-hexane. Although the poisoning had been well-documented by other journalists, it happened in factories more than 1,000 miles from those Daisey visited in Shenzhen.

One of the suspicious journalists, Rob Schmitz, is the China correspondent for *Marketplace,* a program produced by American Public Media and broadcast on public radio stations. He tracked down Daisey's translator after Daisey "lost her contact information," making it difficult for *This American Life* to complete a thorough fact-check.

The interpreter debunked most of the narrative, Schmitz reported for *Marketplace.*[1] Daisey had not interviewed underage children. An illegal union gathering he attended included three or four workers, not 25 to 30. He did not interview several hundred workers for his research; instead it was fewer than 50 people. A particularly poignant interview in which Daisey describes a factory worker, whose hand had been mangled in a machine accident, touching a fully assembled iPad for the first time and describing it as "magic" did not happen, according to the interpreter.

Schmitz helped *This American Life* host Ira Glass put together an hour-long show on Daisey's deceptions, called "Retraction."

That show quickly surpassed the original Daisey show as the most downloaded podcast ever. It was a humbling moment for Glass and his staff, as well as a raw examination of the difference between "truths" and "Truth."

Not a single time during the retraction episode did Daisey ever say the words "I lied." Not even after host Ira Glass called him out on the fabrications discovered after interviews with Daisey's translator and other knowledgeable sources.

Daisey had added and removed details as he saw fit. In addition to misrepresenting the number of people he spoke to and the number of factories he visited, he admitted fabricating interviews with sources to better serve his story arc.

He did it all, he said, to help expose a greater truth.

"And everything I have done in making this monologue for the theater was bent toward that end, to make people care. I'm not going to say that I didn't take a few shortcuts in my passion to be heard. But I stand behind the work."[2]

The shortcuts Daisey referenced—the same information Glass and other called lies and fabrications—were acceptable in his mind, he said, because they served the larger "story." Daisey had performed this same material as a theater piece for two years before it was shared on the radio.

The mistake, Daisey said, was in allowing it to be broadcast on *This American Life* as a piece of journalism. But he stood by its veracity as a larger truth, arguing that there were different definitions of truth:

> I don't know that I would say in a theatrical context that it isn't true. I believe that when I perform it in a theatrical context in the theater, that when people hear the story in those terms, that we have different languages for what the truth means.

But that didn't sit well with Glass. Whether it was presented as a piece of journalism or of theater didn't matter, he said:

> I understand that you believe that, but I think you're kidding yourself, in the way that normal people who go to see a person talk—people take it as a literal truth . . . I thought it was true, because you were on stage saying, this happened to me. I took you at your word.

Part of the problem was that Daisey had lied to Glass and other staff members during the fact-checking process before the episode aired. "We have gone through his script and fact checked everything that was checkable," Glass told his audience during the original episode.

That included trying to contact Daisey's interpreter. However, Daisey had changed her name and then told the staff that he no longer knew how to contact her. "I can say now in retrospect that when Mike Daisey wouldn't give us contact information for his interpreter, we should have killed the story rather than run it," Glass said during the retraction episode.

Most of the hour-long retraction episode focused on Daisey's deceit and clarifying what was and was not true about the story in China. Only in a few instances did Glass talk about himself and the staff of *This American Life* sharing some of the responsibility for broadcasting the false story.

I wanted to say before we leave this subject that I and my co-workers at *This American Life* take our mistake in putting Mike's story onto the air very seriously. As I said earlier in the program, when Mike told us that it would be impossible for us to talk to his interpreter for fact-checking purposes, we should have killed the story right there and then. And to do anything else was a screw-up.

The popular, but not entirely truthful, episode of the show was broadcast to a national audience as a work of journalism because (1) Mike Daisey believed there are different definitions of truth and that he was justified in his theatrical presentation of the facts; (2) he lied to staff who attempted to verify the information in his presentation; and (3) the staff trusted him and did not press further in attempts to contact his translator.

QUESTIONS

- What is Mike Daisey's definition of truth? What is Ira Glass' definition of truth? Why is it important, in journalism, to stick with Ira Glass' definition?

- Mike Daisey originally created his monologue as a piece of theater, which he performed on the stage. Is it possible that he could have accurately disclosed his research methods and preserved his credibility in a journalistic setting? What would such a disclosure look like?

- The original podcast, "Mr. Daisey and the Apple Factory" is still available on *This American Life*'s website. What steps has *This American Life* taken to ensure that people who read the transcript or download that podcast, know about the problems? Some people argue that the show should be taken out of circulation. What's an argument for leaving it up?

- Listen to the "Retraction" episode on *This American Life*. What specific responsibility does the staff take for letting Mike Daisey on their program? Do they identify any systemic faults? Is there anything more the staff of the program could do to take responsibility or change their systems?

- Is it possible that the staff at *This American Life* was predisposed to believe the story of human rights abuses? Why or why not?

CASE NOTES

1. Rob Schmitz, "An Acclaimed Apple Critic Made Up the Details," *Marketplace*, March 16, 2012, http://www.marketplace.org/topics/life/apple-economy/acclaimed-apple-critic-made-details.
2. "460: Retraction Transcript," *This American Life*, March 16, 2012, http://www.thisamericanlife .org/radio-archives/episode/460/transcript.

Storytelling in the Digital Age

Tom Huang

O n a flight from Dallas to Chicago, I caught a glimpse of the future of storytelling. A thin, gray-haired man turned from his window to talk to a young mother. She was holding a 2-year-old in her lap. From my aisle seat, I could hear the two strangers make small talk about raising children.

The man took out his iPhone. He tapped on the device's screen and showed the mother a few short video clips that he had shot. In one, his granddaughter, who was probably 4 or 5 years old, searched a wooded area for Easter eggs. In another, the girl was learning a tumbling routine as part of her gymnastics team.

The 2-year-old boy watched the videos, mesmerized. Soon enough, he moved to the grandfather's lap. As the flight began its descent, the two of them peered out the window at the world below.

We witness such quiet moments all the time: strangers telling their stories, sharing something important about themselves, something funny or sad or poignant, through words, images and video on their digital devices. On the surface, there was nothing extraordinary about that moment.

And yet, maybe there was.

As someone who is passionate about telling stories, I've been thinking about how digital innovation is transforming the craft of storytelling. As a veteran journalist, I could present a grim knee-jerk reaction. "The traditional story will soon be dead," I could say.

(For this essay, I will rely on the definition of *story* that narrative journalist Jon Franklin proposed in his classic *Writing for Story*: "A story consists of a sequence of actions that occur when a sympathetic character encounters a complicating situation that he confronts and solves.")[1]

"Young people aren't interested in reading long, linear stories any more," I might say. "Not with their short attention spans, and especially not on their phones." But I suspect that the transformation of storytelling will be more complicated and more surprising than that.

I believe that the traditional story will endure, and even thrive, in the digital realm, as it has in every medium we human beings have created to share information and experience, in books, songs, plays, film, newspapers, radio,

TV and now digital platforms. Digital innovation—and advances in mobile technology, in particular—will reinforce the values of storytelling.

At the same time, digital innovation will bring profound changes and add new pressures to those values. Journalists will have to adapt to these changes and pressures—and take a proactive role in sparking more innovation—if they hope to help their news organizations survive.

So far, though, most news organizations have been slow to embrace that change. As Bill Adair, the creator of the *Tampa Bay Times'* PolitiFact, has argued:

> Editors and reporters haven't stopped to invent new forms of storytelling—or even consider how they might do things differently on the Web and mobile devices. Their automatic response is to do the same basic thing they've always done: "Go write a news story about that."[2]

In this chapter, I will explore how digital innovation is enhancing storytelling in three fundamental ways:

- It is introducing new story forms that break out of the traditional narrative structure—in some cases, allowing readers to guide the storytelling themselves.
- It is expanding the group of people who can be storytellers—and broadening their reach.
- It is increasing the access people have to in-depth stories and creating different access points for different demographic groups.

At the same time, there is an ethical dynamic to all this. These changes are also challenging the traditional values of storytelling, values that support journalism's underlying purpose of creating public understanding. While the iPad and other digital tablets will make it easier for people to consume stories, and social media will make it easier to share them, the advent of new story forms also could:

- Make it harder for readers to find a coherent storyline within a complicated event or issue, even as readers may also benefit from reading stories with more contributors and perspectives
- Make it easier for those who want to manipulate or deceive the public to introduce false information or rumors into the public's understanding
- Break the audience into fragments, making it more difficult for people to find common ground through stories.

THE TRADITIONAL VALUES OF STORYTELLING

Let me start by sharing a story about stories.

I began telling stories when I was 6; I drew primitive comic books. And by primitive, I mean primitive. The comic books were about the Supers, a team of superheroes consisting of some misfit cavemen and cavewomen, some mean teachers I knew, and some stick figures representing other oddballs I had already met in my young life.

If I were to examine these comics now, I'd see their underlying meaning: They were about the struggle of the Supers to fit into society, much like my family's struggle to fit in as immigrants still finding our way in the United States.

You probably have your own story about how you first started telling stories. Your stories might have first appeared in your diary, or in postcards to your parents, or in essays that your teacher encouraged you to write.

Telling stories is how we explain who we are, what we do and why we do it. Sometimes, the very act of storytelling is how we discover something that we didn't initially know about ourselves. As Joan Didion wrote in *The White Album*, "We tell ourselves stories in order to live."[3]

Storytelling is what makes us human. And it's a safe bet that our ability to tell stories and learn from them helped us survive those terrifying early days as apes throwing bones into the air a la *2001: A Space Odyssey.*

Jack Hart, a legendary editor who recently retired from *The Oregonian*, believes that human beings are hard-wired for story. "The myriad ways we use story to cope with the world make it hard to imagine that narrative isn't part of our fundamental nature," he wrote in *Storycraft: The Complete Guide to Writing Narrative Nonfiction.*[4]

For more than three decades, Hart, Franklin and other journalists have made narrative storytelling an important part of newspapers. They have argued that this particular kind of news presentation—in which stories are told with characters; a beginning, middle and end; a complication or conflict; and a resolution—engage and enlighten readers in ways that more common news story formats, such as the inverted pyramid structure, often do not.

In realms outside journalism, success can depend on how well one tells and understands narrative. Lawyers know that they must persuade juries with the stories they tell. The best doctors know they must listen to their patients' stories to truly understand what's ailing them. The most effective political communicators (think of Abraham Lincoln, Ronald Reagan or Bill Clinton) are often noted for how they tell stories—about their own lives and challenges they've had to overcome; about the lives of people who have been affected by policies they support or criticize; and about their visions for the country.

Ted Anthony, an Associated Press national writer, recognized the importance of storytelling at the 2012 political conventions. Speechwriter Curt Smith explained to Anthony: "Storytelling forms the heart of political rhetoric. Ronald Reagan once told me, if you give someone 10 facts and one story and if the story is told well, it's the story that you recall."[5]

The traditional values of storytelling can be distilled to these three.

Clarity: Stories help readers understand and make sense of complex issues and processes.

Nuance: Stories provide readers with enough room for nuance and ambiguity, particularly when it comes to describing people's emotional lives.

Empathy: Stories help readers connect with others, sometimes those who are very different from us, by allowing us to share our experiences.

In his book *Storycraft,* Hart summed it up well:

> Story makes sense out of a confusing universe by showing us how one action leads to another. It teaches us how to live by discovering how our fellow human beings overcome the challenges in their lives. And it helps us discover the universals that bind us to everything around us.[6]

DIGITAL STORY FORMS

How is digital technology affecting these values?

It wasn't that long ago when print journalists considered photo essays, explanatory graphics, chunky text and summary boxes to be alternative story forms. Journalists used these forms as additional ways to engage readers, especially those who preferred to scan newspapers rather than read in-depth.

A few newspapers—most notably, *USA Today* and *The Virginian-Pilot*—placed a top priority on using these story forms prominently and consistently. Even *The New York Times,* long known as the Gray Lady, began to excel in informational graphics. Still, many journalists considered these story forms to be value-added items (some might say afterthoughts), not integral to the storytelling process.

Digital innovation is forcing us to reconsider this mind-set. New story forms (and some not so new) are thriving on digital devices. In this section, I will identify several digital story forms: some that have become stalwarts and others that have only recently emerged. (No doubt, there are even fresher ones that are emerging even as I write this.) I will also discuss what storytelling values these forms reinforce and what values they challenge.

Interactive Graphics

One of the most powerful new story forms is the interactive graphic, which leverages the power of data visualization while giving readers some control over how they digest information. Journalists now have the data visualization tools to tell sophisticated stories through interactive graphics. Many of these "interactives" are strong enough to stand on their own, rather than merely providing supporting data for a traditional story. A number of outlets can boast outstanding examples of interactive graphics.

The New York Times has had several outstanding examples of interactive graphics. Let me highlight one.

In "How Class Works," a 2005 *New York Times* interactive graphic about the factors that go into class differences, we can input data about ourselves, including our job, income, education and wealth.[7] We can use these factors to estimate what socioeconomic percentile we fall into. We can learn about how the population breaks down by education and income, and we can understand the concept of mobility, the movement of families from one income spectrum to another.

The multi-component graphic accompanied an 11-day series, but I found that I could understand the main concepts by interacting with the graphic on its own. While the "Class" graphic doesn't tell a strictly linear story, we as readers can discover our own stories within the data. That made the story less abstract and more personal. Even without reading the entire *New York Times'* series on class, we still discover how important one's education (and obtaining an advanced degree) can be in determining one's class. We also see how class mobility has slowed down; the American rags-to-riches story does not happen all that often these days.

Edward Segel and Jeffrey Heer, two Stanford researchers studying narrative visualization, explained what they saw as the difference between an author-driven approach to storytelling and a reader-driven approach. "Stories in text and film typically present a set of events in a tightly controlled progression," they wrote in a 2010 paper for *IEEE Trans. Visualization & Computer Graphics.* "While tours through visualized data similarly can be organized in a linear sequence, they can also be interactive, inviting verification, new questions, and alternative explanations.

"Visualizations," they wrote, "are increasingly striking a balance between the two approaches [author-driven and reader-driven], providing room for limited interactivity within the context of a more structured narrative. This is a relatively recent development, with most mainstream examples coming from online journalism."[8]

The best interactive graphics are a hybrid of the author-driven and reader-driven approaches. They provide introductory text (or an introductory video) to set up the piece, and then they provide explanatory text to guide the reader along the way. Some also provide a structure in which the reader can interact with the graphics in a meaningful sequence.

These examples differ from traditional storytelling in some significant and subtle ways. Most important, they typically don't have a central character, a line of action, or a beginning, middle and end. Still, they can have the same effect as traditional storytelling. They can provide both clarity and nuance on a complex topic. And, actually, they can often do a better job at this than in a conventional text, especially on topics with large amounts of data.

Interactive graphics are, however, less effective in engendering empathy from the reader. Traditional stories transport readers to other places and help them imagine the experience of the central character. It's possible that someday we will be able to better integrate interactive graphics within a traditional narrative and build empathy and an emotional response through the combination of both.

Video Storytelling

Video is one of the richest multimedia tools that journalists can use for storytelling. From short breaking-news clips captured on smart phones to longer, more complex documentaries, video has the power to take viewers to a place, allow them to witness the action, and let them listen to people tell their stories in their own voices.

These digital video story forms are quite different from traditional broadcast television stories in that they typically have no correspondent or anchor. In general, they don't have the same high production values or elaborate sets. And sometimes they don't even have narration. But they are told in the fashion of documentaries. Video is also a highly accessible form of storytelling: I see more and more people watching videos on their phones and digital tablets, especially as captive audiences on airplanes.

One of the most powerful videos that I have watched was produced as part of "Choosing Thomas,"[9] a narrative series written by Lee Hancock and photographed by Sonya Hebert for *The Dallas Morning News*, where I work.

The 2009 series and video (I edited the series, but not the video) followed a North Texas couple as they learned that their unborn child had Trisomy 13. The rare genetic disorder meant the baby would not live long after birth. The Lauxes decided to give birth to Thomas anyway. For them, his life mattered, even if it would last just a few days. Hebert's combination of photos and video documented the 5 days that the Lauxes took care of Thomas before he died. When I watch the 9-minute video, I am immersed in the Lauxes' journey, and I am still brought to tears. It exemplifies the authenticity and intimacy that the best journalism has—in any form.

Videos like the one on Thomas Laux reinforce the values of traditional storytelling, especially when they are produced as minidocumentaries. The "Choosing Thomas" video brings clarity to what it's like to have a baby with Trisomy 13. It does not gloss over Thomas' birth defects, or the deeply painful moments that his parents experience. The camera's eye is unflinching as Thomas' health fails.

The video is nuanced: We see the Lauxes' joy and sadness, anger and sense of humor. And while some viewers may not agree with the Lauxes' decision, they can at least begin to empathize and understand what it was like to be in the couple's situation.

Data Centers

Data centers are websites or Web pages that compile sets of information focused on a certain theme. These sites are typically organized so that readers can access and analyze the data for themselves. These data centers often use a combination of interactive graphics, maps, stories and photos to tell a larger, ongoing story.

Homicide Watch D.C. is a well-known data center, a website that tracks murder cases in Washington, D.C. Launched in 2010, the site is run by journalists Laura and Chris Amico. The site breaks down each case into pieces of data, which tells the story of murder through "original reporting, court documents, social media, and the help of victims' and suspects' friends, family, neighbors and others [to cover] every homicide from crime to conviction."[10] (See Case Study for more discussion of Homicide Watch D.C.)

The Washington Post's Neighborhoods site provides comprehensive data on D.C., Virginia and Maryland neighborhoods. The reader can find out the average price of homes sold and the average monthly rent in any given neighborhood, plus a profile of that neighborhood by demographic, real estate and transportation data. The reader can also access maps that show the location of schools, recent crimes, homes sold and homes for sale and for rent.

While readers don't get a traditional story about the neighborhood, they get a wide-ranging snapshot of the area in the data. In effect, they are provided with the raw data for themselves that journalists would have used to compose more traditional stories. They can quickly tell how much it would cost and how safe it is to live in a neighborhood, where they might send their kids to school, and how long the typical commute is to downtown.

Whether it's a Washington neighborhood or a murder case, sometimes all readers want are some quick takeaways based on data. They don't always need to read a traditional story. They can gain clarity on a subject with the help of these sites, which organize and highlight important pieces of data and present the results in a structured way. In other words, given what they are looking for—easy-to-find prices or crime rates—readers may not need the pathos, context, linear progression or deeper sense-making that a traditional story can provide.

But for all their virtues, the data centers also cannot provide something that traditional stories can. While you can study the data of a neighborhood, you might not truly get the feel of the neighborhood unless you read about it. Meanwhile, Homicide Watch D.C. draws its nuance and empathy through the reported stories, guest columns and online memorials to the victims—all examples of traditional storytelling.

Story Clusters and Streams

Digital technology also challenges one of the most basic components of traditional daily news presentation—the concept of the daily story. In traditional news formats, each new development is its own story, and the narrative written the day before is disposed of, in the same way that the physical paper is discarded and each day's paper or newscast is new again. In a digital format, what was produced earlier does not need to disappear, and this opens the way for whole new forms—stories that grow and build, in the same way that a Wikipedia entry builds on itself rather than starting over. These new forms can be called story clusters or streams.

One of the best examples of story clusters came from the Living Stories project run by the now-defunct Google Labs from December 2009 to February 2010. In partnership with *The Washington Post* and *The New York Times*, Google built story clusters around significant ongoing stories such as health care reform, global warming and the war in Afghanistan.

Each story cluster included an overview; links to news stories, features and opinion pieces on the topic; a timeline of events (including stories aligned with the chronology) and interactive graphics. The stories could also be sorted by themes, people and multimedia.

According to the Google blog,[11] Living Stories, when compared to traditional news coverage:

> try a different approach that plays to certain unique advantages of online publishing. They unify coverage on a single, dynamic page with a consistent URL. They organize information by developments in the story. They call your attention to changes in the story since you last viewed it so you can easily find the new material. Through a succinct summary of the whole story and regular updates, they offer a different online approach to balancing the overview with depth and context.

Google News has incorporated some of the Living Stories' approach, but as a story stream. On significant news stories, the reader can get a stream of related "real-time" stories and news videos that are updated minute by minute, similar to a news ticker. The reader can also find in-depth stories and opinion pieces related to the news topic.

One high-profile sports website, Vox Media's SB Nation, is making prominent use of the story stream concept (they have even trademarked the term). The site's streams typically consist of blog posts surrounding a specific game or race, as well as ongoing game-day coverage from sports leagues like the National Football League. Dipping in and out of the stream, the reader can get constant updates on the evolving story, as well as perspectives from a variety of bloggers.[12]

I'm intrigued by Google's Living Stories and SB Nation's Story Streams because they promote the idea that a story can act like a living organism: evolving, expanding and splitting into new stories that take divergent paths. Readers can see stories develop over time, and there doesn't have to be just one traditional story at the end of the day.

The first experiment with Living Stories didn't last, but the virtues of the experiment continue to suggest themselves. My guess is this is not the last we have seen of the idea. If a news site embraced the concept in a more fundamental way, it could test its potential—and its potential audience appeal—in a more significant way. The driver behind the idea was Marissa Mayer of Google. She now heads Yahoo. It will be interesting to see if that company begins to experiment with the format in a larger way.

Memes and GIFs

Merriam-Webster defines a *meme* as "an idea, behavior, style, or usage that spreads from person to person within a culture." In the digital realm, a meme often comes in the form of a photo or set of photos with a funny caption that spreads virally on the Web. Memes usually make a sly reference to something that's currently top of mind in pop culture.

One well-known meme went viral after a few news organizations made factual errors in reporting on the U.S. Supreme Court ruling on the Affordable

Care Act. As the news was breaking, these organizations initially and incorrectly reported that the high court had struck down the act.

The meme, created by photojournalist Gary He, is a photo illustration of President Barack Obama holding up a digital tablet with CNN's incorrect Web headline on the ruling. No caption is necessary. The illustration is a direct visual reference to Harry Truman holding up the *Chicago Daily Tribune* edition with the wrong headline: "Dewey Defeats Truman." People who are familiar with the historic photo immediately see the parallel with President Obama's triumph.

Another popular meme involved Secretary of State Hillary Clinton. A photojournalist captured her image while in flight on a C-17 transport to Libya. She was wearing sunglasses and appeared to be texting on her BlackBerry. A pair of D.C. communications specialists set up a Tumblr blog and started posting images of Clinton texting others including President Obama, Vice President Joe Biden, Sarah Palin, Colin Powell, and celebrities like Ryan Gosling and Meryl Streep.

The "Texts from Hillary" folks kept the blog going for a week, accumulating 32 posts, 83,000 Facebook shares, 8,400 Twitter followers and over 45,000 Tumblr followers.[13] The meme-makers ended the blog when they received an actual text from Hillary and got to meet madam secretary. While it started as a

PHOTO 3-1 **After several news organizations wrongly reported the Supreme Court verdict on President Obama's health care reform law, photojournalist Gary He created an homage to the famous photo of President Harry S. Truman holding up a copy of the Chicago Daily Tribune bearing the erroneous headline: Dewey defeats Truman.**

Source: © Gary He. Reprinted by permission.

joke, "Texts from Hillary" sparked a public conversation about changing perceptions of Clinton. As Maureen Dowd wrote in a *New York Times* column: "Hillary Clinton cemented her newly cool image and set off fresh chatter about her future."[14]

I think of a meme as a visual idea that can range from the punch line of a joke to the wisdom of a fortune cookie. But do memes constitute a new form of storytelling? While memes don't have the scope or depth of a traditional story, they offer a new way of conveying ideas. They involve characters—often well-known people—and a snippet of a story line. As with many stories, it's helpful for the reader to understand a bit of history and current events in order to understand the context of the meme. And like any good story, a meme can change the way you look at something or someone; a meme can prompt debate and discussion.

At the same time, I would be hard-pressed to argue that memes, at least in their current form, add any significant clarity or nuance to a subject, and they rarely foster any empathy with the characters in the meme. (On the other hand, I suppose you could argue that we could empathize more with Hillary Clinton as we saw her consumed with texting, an act we can identify with.)

I'd like to add a note on GIFs here because animated GIFs often become memes. A GIF (which stands for Graphics Interchange Format) is a type of digital image format that allows for simple animation. GIFs have become popular because they are easy to share on the Web and can convey the information of a short snippet of video.

GIFs became a great format to use in showing athletes' feats during the 2012 London Olympics. The Atlantic Wire, for example, used a series of GIFs of U.S. gymnast Jordyn Wieber's performances to visually explain why she didn't make it to the finals of the all-around gymnastics competition.

Jenna Wortham, a technology reporter at *The New York Times*, called GIFs a form of storytelling:

> And over the past few weeks, the Games have highlighted the GIF as a particularly compelling storytelling format, an amalgamation of video and photo that despite its inherent succinctness is able to convey a narrative. It's a new medium for an era spent behind a browser, one that understands the impatience and fractured attention of people reading multiple things on a screen, the importance of grasping the takeaway within a matter of seconds.[15]

GIFs can be shared easily, and they can go viral quickly. At the same time, they have the quality of short videos, so they can convey the arc of a brief story. Wortham wrote:

> Whether they are used to capture a delectable moment on a show like *Mad Men*, an epic tumble down a flight of stairs or a bizarre facial expression, they are like the best bits of a conversation or a spectacularly good punch line, on repeat, for your entertainment, forever.[16]

GIFs have become so popular that *The Guardian* experimented with producing live GIFs from the first presidential debate between President Barack Obama and Republican nominee Mitt Romney in October 2012. *The Guardian's* Colin Horgan wrote:

> Used as it is as a multisecond snapshot of popular culture, [the GIF] is an expression of the hive mind at work, an all-knowing, all-seeing, all-creating collective brain self-referencing for only one reason: because it can. And, for better or worse, it might change how we see our politicians.[17]

Social Media

Journalists and writers are just beginning to explore how best to use social media for storytelling. But already they are trying to tell stories that transcend the short bursts of information typically conveyed by tweets and Facebook status updates.

One of the best examples of using Twitter for storytelling came when Alexandra Zayas, a reporter for the *Tampa Bay Times*, live-tweeted from a January 2011 rape trial in St. Petersburg, Fla. The alleged Bayshore rapist represented himself at trial without a lawyer and ended up cross-examining the victim. The exchange between the alleged rapist and the victim unfolded in a dramatic way. That drama was heightened because of the live, unfolding nature of the story.

Zayas later used Storify to present her tweets as a story of sorts. (Storify is a software tool, developed by a former AP journalist, that enables a user to compile tweets, Facebook updates, photos and other social media elements and place them into a meaningful order.) After that, Zayas wrote a full story for the newspaper, as well.

Twitter is a natural, powerful tool for covering breaking news. On Saturday nights, when I work as the front-page news editor for my news organization, I use my Twitter feed as a news wire. I'll often see breaking news alerts first on Twitter.

Some writers are recognizing that Twitter has the potential to be a storytelling platform beyond news alerts. Mallary Jean Tenore, managing editor of Poynter Online, pointed out:

> Twitter is a powerful tool for writers. With its 140-character limit, it's like an electronic editor that forces us to find a focus and make every word count. It's a verbose writer's friend and worst enemy—a constant reminder that it's often harder to write short than it is to write long.[18]

In an August 2012 Poynter column, Tenore presented several examples of compelling story-like tweets.

Xeni Jardin, a technology journalist at Boing Boing, is chronicling her battle with breast cancer on Twitter, Tenore wrote. Her tweets range from evocative descriptions of chemotherapy to arguments against the "Pink" campaign against breast cancer. She has built a community of more than 63,000 Twitter followers who care about what happens to her on a daily basis.

To be sure, some of this is due to the deep concern that many people feel about the topic of breast cancer. But a lot of it has to do with Jardin's strength as a storyteller. As Tenore notes, Jardin has the gift of evoking the underlying tension in a scene in just a few words. During one therapy session, Jardin tweeted: "Soft-rock radio in radiation waiting room. Mariah Carey's One Sweet Day. Bad track for room full of people possibly on way to heaven."

Another journalist, Joanna Smith of the *Toronto Star*, covered the aftermath of the Haiti earthquake via Twitter. In one scene, Smith tweeted: "Woman shrieking, piercing screams, 'Mama! Papa! Jesus!' as dressing on her wounded heel is changed outside clinic. No painkillers." Tenore notes that Smith employs the rule that all great storytellers know: Show, don't tell. Smith packs her tweets with action, dialogue and sensory details.

The storytelling that Zayas, Jardin and Smith present on Twitter reinforces all of the traditional values of storytelling. The brevity of Twitter enforces clarity and focus. The ability to cover a story as it unfolds, whether over minutes or days or months, enables the storyteller to capture the nuance of the subject. And the intimacy of the platform helps Twitter followers empathize with the storyteller and his or her characters.

What's harder to gauge is the power—and tension—that social media interaction will bring to this kind of storytelling. As journalists tell their stories via Twitter, they will certainly also receive questions and comments from their followers. Some of that interaction will no doubt interrupt and change the course of the storytelling.

For example, imagine readers asking Zayas to tweet a description of the defendant as the trial was going on, or asking Jardin to explain why Mariah Carey's song was a bad track that day, or asking Smith to take her reporting to another Haitian city. The storyteller may or may not respond. But there's an opportunity to elaborate or switch gears, right in the middle of telling the story. I see this as a positive development. As storytellers respond to their followers, there's a greater opportunity for clarity, nuance and empathy. At the same time, there's also a chance for greater confusion, as many voices could drown out the voice of the storyteller.

Facebook also has potential for new storytelling as a platform for gathering information and a venue for telling stories through other people's voices.

While I haven't seen many examples of this, Ian Shapira of *The Washington Post* produced a fascinating story based on Facebook status updates.[19] The story focused on a young woman who developed complications after childbirth and ultimately died. Shapira received permission from the woman's family to produce a story based on her Facebook updates, as well as those of her family and friends.

As a narrator, Shapira inserted his own voice sparingly and only when necessary to add context or move the story along. It was a successful experiment that shows how storytellers can use social media to tell stories through other people's voices.

Games

As part of the "serious games" movement, software developers are working with nonprofit organizations, advocacy groups and journalists to create games that help users understand complex issues. Players can "live" through complicated stories and current events by taking on the perspectives of the main actors. The players must make decisions and choices that the actors face, and they must understand the consequences of their decisions.

In some ways, a game is similar to an interactive graphic, in that the user has some control over the direction of the story and can learn about a topic in a nonlinear way. Games, however, can be an even more immersive experience than interactive graphics, transporting the user to another time and place. Like traditional stories, games tend to have beginnings, middles and ends; there's typically a larger narrative arc and a conflict to be resolved. When done well, games can bring clarity and nuance to a complex issue, and they can help the user empathize with some of the actors in the game.

In one remarkable project in 2007, veteran Bay Area journalist Paul Grabowicz worked with students at the University of California–Berkeley Graduate School of Journalism to create a game called "Remembering 7th Street." The game took players through a street known for its jazz and blues scene in the 1940s and 1950s. The journalism students used their wealth of research and reporting not to write stories but to build what amounted to a virtual street.

"A newspaper or other local news organization needs to be more than just a pipeline for informing people about current news and events," Grabowicz wrote in PBS's MediaShift Idea Lab blog. "It also should provide context for people to understand their community and its history. A video game can do that, by letting people re-live the history of their communities and understand not just what's happening today but what came before."[20]

CHANGING READING HABITS CAN REINFORCE STORYTELLING'S VALUE

Will the traditional long-form story survive in the digital age? Despite some of the hand-wringing that typically accompanies that question, I believe that the story will not only survive but thrive, as reading becomes easier on digital devices and as digital story clusters and streams encourage readers to explore related stories and other information that might interest them.

In recent years, many of us worried that the story was in peril. That's because the more we read online—on our desktop and laptop computers—the harder it seemed to read anything in-depth. We became accustomed to skimming and scanning stories for nuggets of information. And as we consumed more and more information on smartphones, our attention spans seemed to diminish.

But the iPad and other digital tablets are making reading more pleasurable. At the same time, the screens on smartphones are improving, and users seem to be adapting to reading longer stories on smaller devices.

If traditional storytelling is to survive, it must survive on mobile devices, as more and more people consume information on these devices. As of Fall 2012, nearly a quarter of U.S. adults owned a digital tablet, and another 23 percent planned to get one in the next six months, according to "Future of Mobile News," an October 2012 study by the Pew Research Center's Project for Excellence in Journalism in collaboration with The Economist Group. Meanwhile, 44 percent of adults owned a smartphone.

Many mobile users are "reading longer news stories—73 percent of adults who consume news on their tablet read in-depth articles at least sometimes, including 19 percent who do so daily," according to the study. "Fully 61 percent of smartphone news consumers at least sometimes read longer stories, 11 percent regularly."[21]

"And looking at the three-quarters of tablet news users who at least sometimes read in-depth articles, the majority read more than one article in a typical sitting," the report states. "About six-in-ten (61 percent) read two to three articles in a sitting and another 17 percent read four or more. And these are often articles they did not set out to read. Close to three-quarters, 72 percent, say they read in-depth articles that they weren't looking for at least somewhat often (including 17 percent who say that is very often the case)."[22]

The "Future of Mobile News" report presents another significant finding: Mobile technology appears to be increasing news consumption. While 55 percent of tablet news users say the news they get on the device is replacing news they'd get elsewhere, another 43 percent say the news they get on the device is adding to their overall news consumption. And for those who consume news across multiple platforms, 58 percent say their tablet news is adding to their news consumption.

Meanwhile, when we consider much longer-form storytelling, we find that one-fifth of U.S. adults have read a book, or e-book, on an electronic reader or tablet in the past year, according to an April 2012 study by the Pew Internet and American Life Project. The average reader of e-books has read 24 books in the past year.[23]

The growing popularity of websites like Longform.org and Longreads .com, sites that curate long-form journalism, reinforces the Project for Journalism Excellence's findings. The editors at these two sites bring a sharp eye for the best in-depth storytelling, as well as a savvy sense of how to present these stories in multiple digital formats. Their curated stories are available not just on Longform's and Longreads' websites, but also on their Facebook pages and via Twitter. Longform also has an iPad app, while both are available on Flipboard, the magazine-like aggregation app. Meanwhile, apps like Readability and Instapaper make it easy for readers to save stories, access them on multiple devices and enjoy them in a consistent and easy-to-read format.

Digital innovation is also reinforcing storytelling in several other ways. More and more people have the opportunity to tell their stories, and many more platforms are available to get their stories in front of an audience. Digital innovation has made it easier to publish one's work, via social media, on a blog or in an e-book.

With social media, the opportunity to share and recommend stories has significantly increased. For news stories in particular, the audience appears to be growing on social networks. From 2010 to 2012, the percentage of U.S. adults who read a news story or headline on a social networking site the previous day grew from 9 percent to 19 percent, according to a September 2012 study by the Pew Research Center for the People & the Press. One-third of adults under 30 got their news on social networks.[24]

Pressures on Storytelling's Values

While many of the new story forms are adding to journalism by expanding the avenues in which we can tell stories and by making it easier to share these stories, they are also applying new pressures to the values of clarity, nuance and empathy of good storytelling. I would argue that while it is getting easier to read long-form stories on digital devices, these digital devices are potentially driving us to distraction, diminishing our attention spans and our ability to focus. The research on this is still in its early stages. But our own personal experience would suggest that we are multitasking more and more on our digital screens.

Matt Richtel covered much of this subject in his *New York Times* series, "Your Brain on Computers." In June 2010, he wrote:

> At home, people consume 12 hours of media a day on average, when an hour spent with, say, the Internet and TV simultaneously counts as two hours. That compares with five hours in 1960, say researchers at the University of California, San Diego. Computer users visit an average of 40 Web sites a day, according to research by RescueTime, which offers time-management tools.[25]

In August 2010, Richtel cited research at the University of California, San Francisco, suggesting that human beings need downtime (time away from screens) to process what they have learned. Loren Frank, a physiology professor at the university, told Richtel: "Almost certainly, downtime lets the brain go over experiences it's had, solidify them and turn them into permanent long-term memories." Frank said he believed that when the brain was constantly stimulated, "you prevent this learning process."[26]

I bring up this issue because reading long-form stories requires time and focus. Today's storytellers must compete with a steady stream—some would say barrage—of information that we consume every day. That increases the pressure on storytellers to produce tales that are not only well told, but relevant, engaging and emotionally resonant.

While digital innovation is expanding the platforms on which we can get stories, it is also potentially creating a fragmented audience. Research suggests that our communities are already fragmented in the media that they consume for news and information. But I suspect that digital tablets and smartphones will only increase that fragmentation.

A May 2012 Nielsen report indicated that 67.3 percent of Asian Americans use smartphones, compared to 57.3 percent of Hispanics, 54.4 percent of African Americans and 44.7 percent of whites.[27]

The Project for Journalism Excellence's "Future of Mobile News" study found that while African Americans are less likely to own a tablet than are whites, those who do are more likely to get news on it daily: 56 percent of black tablet owners compared to 36 percent of white users. The percentage of Hispanics who own a tablet is comparable to that of whites, and they are just as likely to be daily news consumers on the device.

Overall, that's a positive trend for those of us who believe that, for democracy to thrive, news and information should be widely accessible to all. "Perhaps tablets and smartphones, which provide ready access to news from any source at lower cost of entry than desktop computers, may translate into a powerful news consumption tool for populations that felt underserved by the media in legacy forms," the report stated.[28]

I would like to raise a cautionary flag, though. If different demographic groups tend to have different access points for stories—say, one group primarily on tablets, another on smartphones and a third on several platforms—that increases the pressure on journalists to make sure that the quality of in-depth journalism and storytelling is consistent across all devices.

The deeper issue here is that we tell stories in order to make sense of the world, of ourselves and of our role in the world. We create master narratives about ourselves and about our collective societies. If we become fragmented by where we get our stories, our narratives potentially fragment, as well. If young people of color primarily get their news and information through short bursts of information (perhaps even with a sarcastic and cynical tone) on their smartphones, what narratives will they develop about themselves and their role in society? Whatever the answer is, it doesn't bode well for clarity, nuance and empathy.

Digital innovation is adding pressures to the values of storytelling in several other ways. Tweets, memes and GIFs, if they supplant traditional stories as the primary way people—particularly young people—share information, then clarity, nuance and empathy are diminished.

The day of the single narrator, who has control of a story through his or her authority and expertise, may be going or gone. There's nothing inherently wrong with that. We have the opportunity to add clarity and nuance to a story as more people, with different perspectives, contribute to the story. There's a benefit to having citizens contribute their photos and comments, especially if they are witnesses to a breaking-news story. But this is a double-edged sword. These additional voices can drown out the single narrator and bring confusion rather than clarity.

While there's great merit in allowing readers to see stories as they develop in real time, the strategy is less effective in the coverage of breaking news that features ambiguity and partial information. Consider the coverage of the shooting of Congresswoman Gabby Giffords, the imminent death of Penn State football coach Joe Paterno and the U.S. Supreme Court ruling on the Affordable Care Act. In the rush to get the stories first, journalists made factual errors. While such mistakes happen on any platform, social networks accelerate the spread of inaccurate information.

CONCLUSION

Jack Hart, the legendary editor and story coach, has argued that human beings are hard-wired for story. There's something in our DNA that compels us to find meaning in everything around us. We do so by telling stories.

Ultimately, we care about the future of the story because it has an ethical function, close to journalism's essential purpose. Sharing stories is also how we create bonds with one another. That's what I witnessed on my flight from Dallas to Chicago, as I watched the elderly man connect with the young mother and her 2-year-old son as he showed them videos of his granddaughter on his smartphone.

That is why I think that the traditional story will endure, even as digital innovation pushes and pulls and shapes the story into different forms. It's clear that the iPad and other digital tablets are making reading an even more pleasurable experience, and digital devices are making stories even more portable and sharable.

At the same time, I'm not naïve enough to think that advances in digital technology won't challenge the values that the best traditional stories can promote: clarity, nuance and empathy.

Now our traditional storytelling has to make room for other forms—interactive graphics, data centers, memes, GIFs and games—all of which convey information without necessarily telling stories in a linear way. Stories are becoming more like living organisms. Through story clusters and streams, readers can watch in real time as stories develop, expand and take on different paths. That's a messy process that can lead to confusion and, in some of the worst cases, the viral spread of factual errors.

Stories are becoming more like conversations. Especially through social media, readers can interact with storytellers and help direct the storytelling through questions and feedback. They can even add their own perspectives. In the best cases, those contributions can lead to greater nuance and empathy. In the worst cases, they can get in the way of the single narrator's clarity and turn a story into an endless argument, or even a game of "telephone" in which the original facts are lost and exaggerated in the retelling.

In a sense, every new form has its own strengths and weaknesses. As news moves from lecture to dialogue, it gains the energy and relevance of interactivity.

But it also loses the carefully constructed coherence of something that was prepared as a nuanced presentation.

Storytellers will have to bring their "A game" to their craft because their stories will have to compete for the time and attention of readers who are multitasking on their digital screens and woozy with information overload. And they will have to ensure that the quality of their stories is consistent across digital devices, as different demographic groups consume stories through different access points.

Despite all of these pressures and challenges, I remain optimistic that storytelling will flourish in the digital age, and I'm excited by the prospects for new forms of storytelling. As David Eagleman wrote in a review of *The Storytelling Animal* by Jonathan Gottschall: "The medium of story is changing, in other words, but not its essence. Our inborn thirst for narrative means that story—its power, purpose and relevance—will endure as long as the human animal does."[29]

Editors' Note: The Tampa Bay Times, *which operates PolitiFact, is owned by The Poynter Institute, the employer of this book's co-editor and several of its contributors.*

NOTES

1. Jon Franklin, *Writing for Story: Craft Secrets of Dramatic Nonfiction by a Two-Time Pulitzer Prize Winner* (New York, Atheneum, 1986), 48.

2. Bill Adair, "Let's Blow Up the News Story and Build New Forms of Journalism," *Poynter.org,* June 21, 2012, http://www.poynter.org/how-tos/newsgathering-storytelling/178038/lets-blow-up-the-news-story-and-build-new-forms-of-journalism/.

3. Joan Didion, *The White Album* (New York: Farrar, Strauss & Giroux, 1990), 11.

4. Jack Hart, *Storycraft: The Complete Guide to Writing Narrative Nonfiction* (Chicago, The University of Chicago Press, 2011), 9.

5. Ted Anthony, "In Campaign, a Battle over Owning America's Story," *Associated Press,* September 8, 2012, http://bigstory.ap.org/article/campaign-battle-over-owning-americas-story.

6. Jack Hart, *Storycraft,* 5.

7. Archie Tse and Ben Werschkul, "How Class Works," *The New York Times,* May 15, 2005, http://www.nytimes.com/packages/html/national/20050515_CLASS_GRAPHIC/index_03.html.

8. Edward Segel and Jeffrey Heer, "Narrative Visualization: Telling Stories with Data," IEEE Trans. Visualization & Computer Graphics (Proc. InfoVis), 2010, http://vis.stanford.edu/files/2010-Narrative-InfoVis.pdf.

9. Lee Hancock and Sonya Hebert, "Choosing Thomas," *The Dallas Morning News,* August 28, 2009, http://www.youtube.com/watch?v=ToNWquoXqJI.

10. "About Homicide Watch D.C.," Homicide Watch D.C., http://homicidewatch.org/about/

11. "Exploring a New, More Dynamic Way of Reading News with Living Stories," *Google Official Blog,* December 8, 2009, http://googleblog.blogspot.com/2009/12/exploring-new-more-dynamic-way-of.html.

12. "Our Mission," Sbnation, http://www.sbnation.com/about.

13. "TTYL," *Texts from Hillary,* April 11, 2012, http://textsfromhillaryclinton.tumblr.com/.

14. Maureen Dowd, "State of Cool," *The New York Times*, April 10, 2012, http://www .nytimes.com/2012/04/11/opinion/dowd-state-of-cool.html?_r=0.

15. Jenna Wortham, "Digital Diary: How GIFs Became the Perfect Medium for the Olympics," *The New York Times*, August 12, 2012, http://bits.blogs.nytimes.com/2012/08/12/how-the-gifs-became-the-perfect-medium-for-the-olympics/.

16. Ibid.

17. Colin Horgan, "The Presidential Election and the GIFs That Keep Giving," *The Guardian*, October 8, 2012, http://www.guardian.co.uk/commentisfree/2012/oct/08/gifs-giving-presidential-candidate.

18. Mallary Jean Tenore, "What Twitter Teaches Us about Writing Short & Well," *Poynter.org*, August 30, 2012, http://www.poynter.org/how-tos/newsgathering-storytelling/186371/what-twitter-teaches-us-about-writing-short-well/

19. Ian Shapira, "A Facebook Story: A Mother's Joy and a Family's Sorrow," *Post Local*, December 9, 2010, http://www.washingtonpost.com/wp-srv/special/metro/facebook-story-mothers-joy-familys-sorrow.html.

20. Paul Grabowicz, "Why Journalists Should Develop Video Games," *MediaShift Idea Lab*, February 6, 2008, http://www.pbs.org/idealab/2008/02/why-journalists-should-develop-video-games005.html.

21. Amy Mitchell, Tom Rosenstiel, Laura Houston Santhanam, and Leah Christian, "The Explosion in Mobile Audiences and a Close Look at What It Means for News, Future of Mobile News," *Journalism.org*, October 1, 2012, http://www.journalism.org/analysis_report/future_mobile_news.

22. Ibid.

23. Lee Rainie, Kathryn Zickuhr, Kristen Purcell, Mary Madden, and Joanna Brenner, "The Rise of E-reading," *PewInternet*, April 4, 2012, http://libraries.pewinternet.org/2012/04/04/the-rise-of-e-reading/.

24. "In Changing News Landscape, Even Television Is Vulnerable: Trends in News Consumption: 1991-2012," *Pew Research Center for the People & the Press*, September 27, 2012, http://www .people-press.org/2012/09/27/in-changing-news-landscape-even-television-is-vulnerable/.

25. Matt Richtel, "Attached to Technology and Paying a Price," *The New York Times*, June 6, 2010, http://www.nytimes.com/2010/06/07/technology/07brain.html?pagewanted=all.

26. Matt Richtel, "Digital Devices Deprive Brain of Needed Downtime," *The New York Times*, August 24, 2010, http://www.nytimes.com/2010/08/25/technology/25brain.html?page wanted=all.

27. Ingrid Lunden, "Nielsen: Smartphones Used by 50.4% of U.S. Consumers, Android 48.5% of Them," *TechCrunch*, May 7, 2012, http://techcrunch.com/2012/05/07/nielsen-smartphones-used-by-50-4-of-u-s-consumers-android-48-5-of-them/.

28. Amy Mitchell et al., "The Explosion in Mobile Audiences."

29. David Eagleman, "The Moral of the Story 'The Storytelling Animal,' by Jonathan Gottschall," *The New York Times*, August 3, 2012, http://www.nytimes.com/2012/08/05/books/review/the-storytelling-animal-by-jonathan-gottschall.html?pagewanted=all&_r=0.

Caitlin Johnston

In his essay on storytelling, Tom Huang argues that "digital innovation will bring profound changes and add new pressures to the values of storytelling." Homicide Watch is a data center that tells the story of crime through the use of public records, original reporting and user-generated information.

In the age of digital storytelling, Homicide Watch D.C. has distinguished itself as a leader in data presentation. Launched in 2010, the site aims to maintain records on every homicide in D.C.—from the day it occurred to the day of conviction or dismissal.

The tag line states: "Mark every death. Remember every victim. Follow every case."[1] Maps, videos, photo galleries, PDFs of court documents, interviews with family members—the site uses a range of storytelling tools to paint the most comprehensive picture possible of homicides in D.C.

The purpose of the site is clear:

> As DC residents, we believe that how people live and die here, and how those deaths are recognized, matters to every one of us. If it matters how someone is killed in Cleveland Park, then it matters how someone is killed in Truxton Circle, Ivy City, Washington Highlands or Georgetown. If we are to understand violent crime in our community, the losses of every family, in every neighborhood must be recognized. And the outcome of every trial—be it a conviction or an acquittal—must be recorded.[2]

Since its launch, Homicide Watch has been awarded the Knight Public Service Award by the Online News Association in 2012, and it was named an OpenGov Champion by the Sunlight Foundation.

Former beat reporter Laura Amico launched the site and runs it with journalist and Web developer Chris Amico, her husband. Together they gather, sort, visualize and present information on each crime. Entries include the victim's photo, biographical information, the date and cause of death, a map plotting the crime's location, stories written about the case and input from friends and family, when provided. Information is also included about suspects, along with names and phone numbers for detectives on the case.

While traditional journalism covers murders individually, in single stories sometimes accompanied by photos, Homicide Watch D.C. aggregates all the information in a common place, allowing for selective sorting and viewing based on the viewer's goals. The site design makes it easy for readers to choose how they want to sort through the information. Navigation includes links to "Latest News," "Victims," "Suspects," "Map," "Photos," "Documents" and "Calendar," which tracks court dates for the suspects.

The Amicos rely on a mix of traditional reporting and digital tools to fill the site. "It's a remarkable thing to behold—part database, part news site, it also serves as a kind of digital memorial for homicide victims in Washington," wrote David Carr, media columnist at *The New York Times*. "Their pictures are published, their cases are followed, and their deaths are acknowledged as a meaningful event in the life of the city."[3]

QUESTIONS

- What is the benefit of data sites such as Homicide Watch D.C. that allow readers to access and analyze information for themselves?

- Look at a week of cases and discuss what story the site collectively tells. What patterns do you see? What evidence—photos, documents, narrative—is most informative? What questions remain unanswered? Where might those answers come from? What role does narrative storytelling play compared to the other forms used on the site?

- When you view the data on Homicide Watch by victims, it tells one story. When you view it by suspects, it tells yet another story. And when you view it by the map, it tells still another. Briefly describe each story. What are the implications of allowing users to sort the data themselves without a "master narrative" to inform it? What context is emphasized and what context is lost?

CASE NOTES

1. Homicide Watch D.C. http://homicidewatch.org/.
2. "About Homicide Watch D.C." *Homicide Watch D.C.* http://homicidewatch.org/about/.
3. David Carr, "Innovation in Journalism Goes Begging for Support," *The New York Times*, September 9, 2012, http://www.nytimes.com/2012/09/10/business/media/homicide-watch-web-site-venture-struggles-to-survive.html?pagewanted=all&_r=2&.

Fact-Checking 2.0

Steve Myers

Back in 2007, when the fact-checking operation PolitiFact was just a baby, political campaigns tended to be befuddled when its reporters called. They spoke a different language than other journalists. They didn't want quotes, reactions or inside information but rather evidence to back up something the candidate had said.

"They were even more perplexed," said PolitiFact creator and contributing editor Bill Adair, "when we said it was false."

By 2012, five years later, campaigns knew the routine. They assigned staffers to respond to a growing list of fact-checking operations, including PolitiFact, FactCheck.org, *The Washington Post's* Fact Checker, the Associated Press and others. Some state and local politicians were growing accustomed to providing background material to back up their claims.

And the campaigns had gotten in the game, at least nominally. They sent out press releases and tweets purporting to fact-check their opponents. They trumpeted rulings that backed them up and distorted those that didn't, spurring a political-media *ouroboros:* Fact-checkers issued rulings; campaigns twisted their conclusions; fact-checkers issued more rulings.[1]

2012 was the year that fact-checkers rose to new prominence, bringing clarity to opaque political and policy debates in the Republican presidential primaries and the general election. It was easy to forget that a few years ago, such certainty was much more elusive—even though the movement of policing political dialogue was 20 years old.

That movement, which has taken on the shorthand name of fact-checking, began in earnest in 1992 when a number of news operations began "truth-squadding" political advertising. After stalling in the 2000 presidential election,[2] the movement was re-energized in the mid-2000s when a few organizations started full-time efforts—FactCheck.org in late 2003, *The Washington Post's* Fact Checker and the *Tampa Bay Times'* PolitiFact in 2007. When PolitiFact won a Pulitzer Prize in 2009, it was clear that the fact-checkers were on to something.

By 2012, those operations had moved out of beta, and they became a key part of campaign coverage. NewsBank catalogued more than twice as many stories with the term *fact-check* in 2012 than in 2008. News outlets published fact-checks of every major political event, often attempting to do them in real-time, tweeting links to previously fact-checked material as the candidates fell back on familiar, yet distorted talking points.

Fact-checking became one of the meta-themes of the election. There was discussion about whether campaign reporters should embrace the practice of disputing questionable candidate statements in their daily stories and whether debate moderators should have fact-checked President Barack Obama and Mitt Romney in real time. And the campaigns pushed back, even undertaking opposition research of PolitiFact reporters in Ohio and Virginia.

Truthfulness became an issue in a U.S. Senate race in Ohio, where Republican candidate Josh Mandel was attacked for racking up numerous Pants on Fire rulings[3] from PolitiFact. (In a meta-fact-checking moment, *The Columbus Dispatch* published an "ad watch"[4] for an ad that claimed Mandel "may be the most dishonest candidate in the country.")

Fact-checking seemed to be growing up at exactly the right time. Traditional newsrooms had contracted; the remaining journalists were under pressure to write more, faster, on a variety of topics. Traditional news sites shared the stage with those that put ideology before objectivity. And people were using social media to spread information quickly and widely, true or not. If the press couldn't be a gatekeeper, the fact-checkers reasoned, at least they could be a referee.

But along with the growth and promise of fact-checking came the other side of adolescence: awkwardness, misunderstanding, poor judgment. Fact-checkers sometimes let on that they hadn't quite figured out what they were doing. They knew what they wanted to do—validate truths, dispel untruths—but weren't sure how to get there. They found themselves doing a lot of defending and explaining.

Fact-checkers were criticized for rulings that seemed to defy common sense.[5] Conservatives charged that these journalists were trying to throw the game for Democrats; liberals accused the fact-checkers of being afraid to say that Republicans lie more. And no one could tell if all this fact-checking had any effect on the way politicians campaigned for office. (The fact-checkers said that wasn't even their goal.)

To an extent, the criticism was deserved. Some of these supposed fact-checks engaged in more argument than fact-checking; others checked things that were impossible to pass judgment on. The problems, and the pushback, signaled the growing pains of a maturing form of journalism.

It's hard to know exactly what this field will look like when it grows up. Will fact-checkers come to a common understanding of what they should check? Will they pursue the most elusive political untruths, those claims that are a mix of fact and fiction? What will happen when politicians triangulate their statements to pass muster? Will fact-checking raise public awareness of misstatements or make political rhetoric less distorted? And what do the fact-checkers want to achieve anyway?

It's equally hard to know how this niche will shape journalism. Will fact-checking percolate into all forms of journalism, with reporters routinely calling out untruths in their daily stories? Will journalists be comfortable being criticized for calling out untruths? Will this engender a more partisan media? The fact-checkers don't know the answers; they're figuring it out as they go. It will take time for them to establish conventions and standards and more time to spread them beyond political journalism.

In short, it's too soon to hand the keys over to this teenager. If given time to mature, perhaps this band of journalists will influence how the next generation practices the craft.

A GAP IN DAY-TO-DAY JOURNALISM

Not only did the rise of fact-checking incite pushback from political operatives in 2012, it spurred some soul-searching among journalists. What did it say about the news business if a specialty had been created out of something as Journalism 101 as checking facts? In January 2012, *New York Times* Public Editor Arthur Brisbane asked if journalists should become "truth vigilantes," as he called it: "I'm looking for reader input on whether and when *New York Times* news reporters should challenge 'facts' that are asserted by newsmakers they write about."[6]

Readers were dismayed that this was even up for discussion. "Isn't this your job as the news media?" asked one.[7] Brisbane was widely criticized for seeming to be unaware of the fact-checking movement and for worrying about whether such work jeopardized journalists' objectivity. But there was a kernel of truth in his post: If journalists devoted all their time to being truth vigilantes, they'd end up with very few bylines to demonstrate their crime-fighting.

Many reporters have reported catchy one-liners and assertions at political rallies without vetting them. Sometimes journalists don't know which claims are suspect, and they don't have the time to figure it out before deadline. (And these days, they're always on deadline.)

There are exceptions. Reporters who cover presidential campaigns for national news outlets become familiar with stump speeches and the facts behind them. Some local reporters learn which politicians are apt to stretch the truth. When in doubt, they stick to reporting well-known talking points.

But the tensions of 2012 over fact-checking are not entirely new. The fact-checking movement can trace its origins to columns by David Broder in 1988 and 1990.[8] After the 1988 election, he bemoaned the "negative, nasty, uninformative, disturbing, degrading, demagogic" advertising that dominated the presidential race between Vice President George H. W. Bush and Massachusetts Gov. Michael Dukakis. Broder suggested that campaigns be required to provide evidence backing up their ads and answer questions about them.

"Such accountability requirements might make the candidates think twice about what they're putting on the air—and maybe clear the air of the worst political pollution," he wrote. "At the very least, they would prompt the press to examine those ads more carefully and expose exaggeration and distortion more promptly than was the case this year."

In the late 1980s and early 1990s, several news outlets, including ABC News and a TV station in Austin, Texas, began to realize that TV advertising—which heavily influenced voters—was largely unmonitored by reporters. These outlets, and some others, realized that no matter how vigilantly they reported from the campaign trail, campaigns still perpetrated misleading messages in ads that reached millions of voters in their living rooms.

So a few news organizations developed ways to show TV ads without reinforcing their messages, and they started to call out the campaigns' misrepresentations in "ad watches." Brooks Jackson started doing this work for CNN in 1991. The project, originally called the "ad police," expanded to candidate debates and was well-received by the audience and the network's political director. For the 1992 election, CBS News created a feature called "Reality Check"[9] to check political rhetoric, headed by Eric Engberg. Glenn Kessler, who now writes *The Washington Post*'s Fact Checker, said in an interview for this essay that his first foray into the field was a 1996 story in which he debunked and added context to some of the claims in the Clinton-Dole presidential race.

News outlets still do those ad watches, but they haven't spurred nearly as much discussion and dissension as the modern-day fact-checking movement. What happened to ad watches? Perhaps first-generation fact-checking was subsumed by the quickening news cycle brought on by cable news and the Internet. CNN lost its monopoly on cable news with the arrival of Fox News and MSNBC in 1996; CNN grew less interested in Jackson's fact-checking and dismissed him in early 2003. (He went on to launch Factcheck.org.)

More and more, the news business was defined by speed and productivity, as news sites chased page views to grow audience and satisfy advertisers who paid by the click. Journalists learned that the Web audience rewarded repetition, reaction and rebuttal. Newspapers lost advertisers, laid off reporters and asked more of those who were left.

Those who produce the news are constantly on the hamster wheel, as *Columbia Journalism Review*'s Dean Starkman calls it.[10] Those who consume news are frustrated by the repetition and sensationalism of TV news and unsure whom to trust online. Those are the two sides of the modern news cycle, and the fact-checking counterculture addresses the dissatisfaction of both.

Back when information was scarce, a reporter's job consisted of maintaining connections to important people, attending newsworthy events, and telling others what they had seen and heard. People need that less now. The "what" of a newsworthy event is a commodity whose price rapidly drops to zero as news spreads via traditional and social media. Important people are Facebook friends with the people they want to reach, so they don't need journalists to get their messages out. Anytime something newsworthy happens, someone's there to post the video to YouTube.

Meanwhile, journalists have acknowledged that in the rush from one story to the next, they've missed opportunities to dig deeper. The Swift Boat Veterans for Truth skewered Sen. John Kerry's war record for weeks before a couple of news outlets found those claims to be false. No one found those weapons of mass destruction in Iraq.

Now that information is abundant, journalists must demonstrate their value by helping people filter through everything they see, hear and read. The fact-checkers are the vanguard of this shift in how journalism is practiced. People will hear about the applause lines in the State of the Union address but won't know if the president was telling the truth.

USED PROPERLY, A POWERFUL STORY FORM

Done right, fact-checks cut through the bramble of half-truths, oversimplifications, mischaracterizations and distortions that make up so much of political discourse. They speak directly to the reader: "Hey, you know that ad you keep seeing on TV? Well, it's not exactly true. We checked it out; here's what we found."

That's quite different from typical reporting, and it doesn't come easily to many journalists. Jackson described his initial reluctance at being asked to fact-check political ads for CNN in the early 1990s. "It called for reaching a conclusion and characterizing a statement. I'm an old AP reporter. I've never done that before," he said in an interview for this essay. Even if a reporter knew a statement to be false, he said, the tactic was to cite the offending statement, followed by enough evidence to enable the reader "to conclude that it was false. But you'd never say it was false."

Fact-checkers turn that inside out. Rather than gloss over a questionable point during a campaign stop—or ignore it, as they did when they controlled what information got out—they zero in on it. Fact-check stories read differently than others. They start off with the statement in question and describe the work the reporter did to authenticate it. Unlike traditional stories in which reporters try to be invisible, fact-checkers often refer to their own research, conclusions and previous reporting. They have to because, like investigative reporting, they must offer proof of their conclusions and prosecutions in order to be credible.

The stories end up "telling the story of your own reporting," said Lucas Graves, a University of Wisconsin journalism professor who spent a couple of weeks at PolitiFact as part of his dissertation research. "It's kind of liberating to say exactly what you did. Most journalists want to hide those seams."

At the AP, experienced beat reporters often do fact-checks in their areas of expertise. Those reporters "sometimes welcome the opportunity to break free of attribution at the end of every sentence and just say what they know," said Jim Drinkard, the editor who oversees that work. "When you've got someone who's covered the subject matter for 5, 10, 15 years, often they know more than some of the people they're fact-checking. There's no reason not to let them be the authority on this."

But even an informed, veteran journalist can misstep when writing a story that doesn't conform to the thousands she has written before. Some of these fact-checks start off badly by targeting statements that are uncheckable:

predictions of future events, claims about what someone thought or believed and expressions of political values. These stories fall short because the reporter chose an impossible task.[11]

Others fail because they contain little checking of actual facts. Such stories add context, explain political pressures and realities and assess the likelihood of something happening down the road. But they don't do what fact-checkers are supposed to do: examine an assertion and make a verdict.

Part of this stems from marketing; it's tempting to slap the "fact-check" label on a story to differentiate it from all the other analyses of the day. And some confusion is due to the use of a general term to describe a niche of journalism with unique practices and particular applications. There are fact-checkers at *The New Yorker*, but they don't do what the journalists at FactCheck.org do.

None of this excuses the stories that are grab-bags of contrarianism and counterargument, illustrated by a September 2012 AP story. In fact-checking former President Bill Clinton's contention that the Mitt Romney campaign was being untruthful, the story pointed out that Clinton had lied about his relationship with Monica Lewinsky.[12] Although true, that had no bearing on the accuracy of his statement about Romney. There is a place for a story that points out that Bill Clinton may not be the best preacher of truth-telling, but such a story is not a "fact-check."

At their worst, Graves said in an interview for this essay, such stories end up applying "he said, she said" journalism to the fact-checking realm. It's the worst of both worlds—barstool logic with a byline. If all political analysis is fact-checking, nothing is. Those mislabeled and poorly executed stories help critics of fact-checking argue that the niche is a spurious form of journalism.

FACT-CHECKING SHADES OF GRAY

Considering all the ways journalists can screw up a fact-check—and knowing that they hate being wrong—one pitfall is that they would check only the most elementary, noncontroversial facts. But fact-checking that focuses on the smallest building blocks of political rhetoric wouldn't address larger untruths composed of bits of fact and fiction. If fact-checkers constrain themselves to clearly defined facts, Graves said, "you very quickly wall off anything interesting or meaningful in politics."

Rarely does a politician mislead with a sweeping statement that can be disproven by a single, authoritative source. More typically, they do it by misusing facts: by taking things out of context, improperly blaming or taking credit, conflating, asserting cause or effect, and cherry-picking data.

Fact-checkers have pursued politicians into the dark corners of political truth, vetting claims like this:

- Was Obamacare a "government takeover" of health care?[13]
- Did Republicans seek to end Medicare?[14]
- Did Obama have a plan to gut welfare reform?[15]

Narratives like these can define policy debates and elections as candidates, their proxies and the media repeat them. These assertions are powerful because they seem clear-cut, but on examination turn out to be slippery.

This is where fact-checkers can do what other journalists can't (or won't). And it's where fact-checkers open themselves up to criticism that they're playing the same games as the politicians: taking things out of context, improperly blaming or taking credit, conflating, asserting cause or effect, and cherry-picking data.

The welfare debate in the summer of 2012 is a case study of fact-checking and pushback. It started with a Romney ad claiming that Obama was gutting work requirements for welfare recipients: "Under Obama's plan, you wouldn't have to work and you wouldn't have to train for a job. They just send you your welfare check." The Obama campaign responded by claiming Romney had supported regulations similar to what the Obama administration proposed. Some argued the Romney campaign was using coded language[16] meant to inflame racial division. Each campaign cited facts to back up their attacks, but the truth was not easily Google-able.

FactCheck.org, *The Washington Post*'s Fact Checker and PolitiFact weighed in in their customary detailed fashion. (FactCheck.org's story was 2,000 words, the equivalent of a long Sunday newspaper story.) They all reached similar conclusions: The Obama administration was in the process of changing work requirements of the 1996 welfare reform law, but the new rules wouldn't mean that the government would "just send you your welfare check."

Some journalists noted in their subsequent reporting that the Romney ad had been discredited. But this didn't end the debate; it just brought the fact-checkers onstage. The *Weekly Standard*'s Mark Hemingway, the fact-checkers' most vocal critic, picked apart their stories, added arguments the stories hadn't addressed, and generally indicted them:

> The result of all this is a textbook example of how "fact checkers" corrupt political discourse. Once they all came down on the same side of the issue, the mainstream media quickly calcified the conclusion that Romney was wrong to accuse Obama of gutting welfare reform. Rather than report on the policy details, the media simply made it a campaign story and acted as a megaphone for Democratic partisans eager to charge that Republicans were inflaming racial tensions merely for arguing that the goal of welfare policy should be self-sufficiency.[17]

Such criticism is unavoidable when the fact-checkers shine their flashlights into the murkiest political debates—even when the fact-checkers acquit themselves well, as they did in this case. The most pervasive political untruths are hard to pin down; if they were easy, they wouldn't spread so widely. A Romney adviser said as much during the Republican National Convention. "Our most effective ad is our welfare ad," said advertising strategist Ashley O'Connor.[18]

Romney pollster Neil Newhouse dismissed *The Washington Post*'s Four Pinocchios ruling on the welfare ad: "Fact-checkers come to this with their own sets of thoughts and beliefs, and we're not going to let our campaign be dictated by fact-checkers."[19] The last portion of what he said was widely quoted as evidence that the campaigns simply didn't care what the truth was.

That remains the most troubling question of this niche, one that fact-checkers have judiciously avoided: Does their work matter?

REFEREES WITHOUT AUTHORITY

In September 2012, the main players in the fact-checking movement gathered for an event at the National Press Club to predict which untruths they expected to hear during the presidential debates. During the discussion, Jackson asked if any candidate had "paid a price" for being untruthful. No one could cite an example.[20] So what's the point of these thousands of fact-checks?

Others had asked Jackson's question before. The fact-checkers have been remarkably on-message in their answers: Their goal is to tell people whether politicians are being truthful, not to make them more truthful. And yet fact-checkers are quick to cite ways—small ways, in the context of the overall campaigns—that their stories have influenced politicians. A couple times, they say, a politician modified his language or dropped a line of attack after being called out.

The two-pronged answer reveals a contradiction at the heart of the fact-checking movement: They want to affect political discourse, but they don't want to enter the fray. Despite their protests to the contrary, the fact-checkers are sending politicians a message through these thousands of fact-checks: You can color, you can hedge, you can exaggerate to a point, but we'll keep score. If your rhetoric goes beyond a certain point—a point that we determine, without your consent—then we'll call you out. Build your campaign on whatever messages you want, in service of any ideology, as long as they are grounded in verifiable truth.

It hardly seems a radical idea: that political discourse must be grounded in truth. But it is, among some people who run for office and make political ads and among a public that increasingly turns to ideological media. If everything is opinion, everything is debatable. It all depends on who's more convincing.

The fact-checkers won't acknowledge this overarching goal, and it's hard to blame them. That would put them in direct conflict with the political system. Politicians would tell their supporters that activist journalists were trying to dictate how politics should be played. Even the most stenographic reporters must deal with complaints of bias; why invite more?

Even so, the fact-checkers have found themselves part of the debates. In the summer of 2012, the Republican Party of Virginia compiled a report of PolitiFact Virginia rulings and concluded that the operation disproportionately issued unfavorable rulings for Republicans.[21] Around the same time, an unnamed GOP official said the party was looking into rulings, tweets and voting records of PolitiFact journalists, including one at its operation in Ohio.[22] The *National Review* anticipated PolitiFact's rulings about the Republican

National Convention by telling people to ignore the rulings[23] and to "resist the temptation" of citing PolitiFact when it ruled in favor of Republicans.

PolitiFact's Bill Adair has become used to such allegations of bias. He has taken to saying[24] that they are signs that PolitiFact has "disrupted the status quo" of politics. His response is one of the clues that fact-checkers aren't simply throwing flags for the benefit of the spectators. In effect, he's saying, "See, we are making a difference."

CHANGING THE FIELD?

There is another group that the fact-checkers could aim to evangelize: their colleagues. After all, fact-checking emerged in response to the inability of traditional journalism to hold politicians accountable. If fact-checkers don't want to change politics, then perhaps they aim to change how it's reported. On this point the fact-checkers also demur, saying they see their work as a companion to traditional reportage, not a replacement.[25] (There's probably genuine disagreement on this point, too.)

But the fact-checkers don't need to convert their colleagues in order to spread their values. They just need to get their rulings into other stories—and that happened more in 2012. It's ingenious: Rather than try to change "he said, she said" journalism, just become one of the voices in the story.[26]

Once the fact-checkers weighed in on Romney's welfare ad, other reporters didn't even feel the need to cite them. During the Republican National Convention, the *Los Angeles Times* ran the headline, "Rick Santorum repeats inaccurate welfare attack on Obama."[27] The story flatly stated, "In fact, Obama did not waive the work requirement." The *Atlantic's* James Fallows called it an encouraging sign "that the mainstream press is adjusting to the realities of 'post-truth politics.'"[28]

Fact-checking bubbled into campaign coverage in more subtle ways. Just before the Republican convention, *The New York Times* reported that the Romney campaign was shifting to a more aggressive messaging strategy.[29] It was exactly the sort of campaign tactics story that, by focusing on messaging, could have overlooked what was actually true. Instead the writers handled it deftly:

> Many of those voters are economically disaffected, and the Romney campaign has been trying to reach them with appeals built around an assertion that Mr. Obama is making it easier for welfare recipients to avoid work. The Romney campaign is airing an advertisement falsely charging that Mr. Obama has "quietly announced" plans to eliminate work and job training requirements for welfare beneficiaries, a message Mr. Romney's aides said resonates with working-class voters who see government as doing nothing for them.

In this case, the consensus among fact-checkers made such declarations relatively easy. But even in lesser-known cases, fact-checkers have been able to get the word out. They're cited in news stories. They appear on TV. People quote and link to them. Which brings us to the most innovative, and the most contentious, aspect of modern-day fact checking: the Truth-O-Meter and the Pinocchios.

SPREADING TRUTH THROUGH OVERSIMPLIFICATION

The Truth-O-Meter was part of Adair's original vision for PolitiFact; it was included in his first sketch of the idea. It represents PolitiFact's conclusion on any given statement, of course, but it's also the backbone of the site. Summary pages display statements and their corresponding Truth-O-Meter rulings, which can be browsed without clicking through to the underlying stories.[30] Who knows how many people cite PolitiFact rulings without understanding the reasoning?

That's the brilliance of the Truth-O-Meter: It's made to share, whether on TV or a Facebook status update. *The Washington Post's* Fact Checker has its Pinocchio ratings system.[31] Although the blog isn't built around it, it too spreads the word. These devices are a key reason fact-checking has taken off in the last few years, and they're fundamentally challenging to the credibility of fact-checkers. A journalist constructs a carefully weighted analysis of everything he thinks is important to evaluate a statement, and then he distills it to a one-dimensional, seemingly quantitative rating?

Those rulings are especially ironic considering how carefully fact-checkers avoid the word *lie*. (That word says something about someone's intent, and fact-checkers can't check what's inside someone's head.) But we all know the part of the children's rhyme that comes before "pants on fire," and we know what made Pinocchio's nose grow.

There are obvious and not-so-obvious reasons for the ratings systems. In the spirit of skepticism, let's start with the most commercial. By distilling a complex analysis to a single ruling, the fact-checkers make it more likely that their work will spread, even if people haven't read their stories. FactCheck.org's Jackson acknowledged such rulings help spread the fact-checkers' work, but his organization must uphold a stricter, more academic standard—and there's "obviously no scientifically valid way to measure the degree of mendacity" in a statement.

But such rulings are also perfect for social media. Want to knock down something a friend posted on Facebook? Post the link and note, "Four Pinocchios." Want to respond to something on Twitter? Retweet it and add, "PolitiFact: Mostly True." Instant credibility among your peers.

"It is a marketing gimmick," the *Post's* Kessler said, a "quick and easy way for people to understand what I'm getting at." Although he deliberately puts the Pinocchios at the end of his columns, he knows that the rulings spread well beyond the words that precede them.

The rulings also make it easier for other journalists to hold politicians accountable for their words—just cite PolitiFact or The Fact Checker. Same goes for the politicians.

It turns out that such rulings can aid the reporting process. Kessler described what he called the

> power of the Pinocchios . . . The interesting thing is, and this is the dilemma,
> is those Pinocchios are very powerful, and members of Congress in particular
> are fearful of them. So it gives a lot of credibility to my column. It gets people
> on the phone who want to explain themselves.

But this is not all marketing. These rulings also standardize the process—among reporters, politicians and individual stories. PolitiFact and the *Post's* descriptions of their rating systems are the sentencing guidelines of the fact-checkers. The process of coming to a ruling guards against bias and gradual shifts in thinking that are imperceptible from one story to the next. Those rulings tie all these stories together into a body of work—more than 6,000 in PolitiFact's case—with recurring characters.

Consistency is especially challenging for PolitiFact, which has franchised 11 state-level operations in 10 states. Those operations are editorially independent, but their stories appear on PolitiFact.com. The site has embraced lessons from the fast-food industry to ensure that a ruling in Wisconsin is comparable, as much as it can be, to one in Florida.[32] When a news organization joins PolitiFact, Adair trains the staff and distributes a *Truth-O-Meter Owner's Manual*. He teaches new users what kinds of statements are uncheckable, how to research fact-checks and how to write a PolitiFact story.

The ruling process has been standardized as well. After the journalist reports and writes a story, he recommends a ruling. Three editors, one of whom has edited the story, and the reporter discuss the ruling and come to a final decision. (The judgment process is called the "Star Chamber.") Of course, this is a judgment call; the goal is to make the judgments consistent.

The discipline created by those six Truth-O-Meter categories is one reason PolitiFact opted against creating a new one: "Unsubstantiated." The discussion came after people criticized its Pants on Fire ruling for Senate Majority Leader Harry Reid's statement that an anonymous source had told him Romney hadn't paid taxes for 10 years. PolitiFact's reporting showed that the claim was extremely unlikely, but there was no way to prove that it was false.[33] On the advice of a reader, Adair said, PolitiFact editors decided against the new category because they might end up using it too much.

When people criticize PolitiFact,[34] they're usually criticizing the Truth-O-Meter ruling,[35] not the story. In late 2011 and early 2012, PolitiFact was criticized for a few rulings, including one on a statement in Obama's 2012 State of the Union address: "In the last 22 months, businesses have created more than 3 million jobs. Last year, they created the most jobs since 2005."[36]

Both statements were correct, but PolitiFact issued a ruling of Half True. Editors then went back and revised it to Mostly True, explaining in an editor's note that the first ruling "was based on an interpretation that Obama was crediting his policies for the jobs increase. But we've concluded that he was not making that linkage as strongly as we initially believed." When MSNBC's Rachel Maddow attacked PolitiFact for its ruling on Obama's jobs claim, she noted that the story had said that both of Obama's statements were true. Maddow declared, "PolitiFact, you are fired. . . . You are undermining the definition of the word 'fact' in the English language by pretending to it in your name."[37]

That ruling and a few others spurred PolitiFact editors to look at their editorial process. Over time, they concluded, they had started to place too much emphasis on the implications and context of a statement rather than its literal truth, Adair said in an interview for this essay. An adjustment was in order. They came up with a new checklist for reporters to answer for every statement:

- Is the claim literally true?
- Is the claim open to interpretation? Is there another way to read the claim?
- Does the speaker prove the claim to be true?
- Did we check to see how we handled similar claims in the past?[38]

The challenge with these ratings systems is that when a fact-checker conducts a detailed examination of a statement that's in the gray area, the ruling will probably end up somewhere in the middle. And even if the fact-check describes the reasons, those stories don't get the attention that the rulings do.

So yes, the ratings systems are a marketing tool, but marketing that fulfills an audience need. For a journalism niche that runs counter to the culture of Web journalism, the Pinocchios and the Truth-O-Meter are the compromise, a way to meet the Web on its own terms. We can debate whether it's good for democracy to have people cite PolitiFact rulings in a semi-informed debate, but at least they're arguing informed conclusions and not distortions.

HOW CAMPAIGNS WILL ADAPT TO THE FACT-CHECKERS

After Obama won the 2008 presidential race, one would have figured that PolitiFact would go dark until the next campaign season. Instead, it unveiled the "Obameter," a way of cataloguing and measuring the president's progress on 500-some campaign promises.

Such promises are a key part of campaigning, but they were uncheckable in the Truth-O-Meter model. The Obameter provided a mechanism to hold the president accountable: Promise Kept, Promise Broken, Compromise, Stalled, In the Works, or Not Yet Rated.. Like the first version of PolitiFact, it wasn't a new idea—journalists have followed up on campaign promises before. But it did expand the fact-checking rubric to a new realm of political reporting. (The Obameter never did become as popular as the Truth-O-Meter.)

So what will be the next fact-checking innovation? The digerati have their eye on real-time fact-checking, perhaps done algorithmically. Imagine watching a speech on TV and seeing the Truth-O-Meter or the Pinocchio scale pop up on the screen. Instant context available to anyone watching TV, not just a small circle of news consumers seeking out the truth.

But after the fact-checkers demonstrated their heft in 2012—if they have truly disrupted the status quo—don't expect the campaigns to sit still. Perhaps they will figure out a way to triangulate their messages to fit the rules, something the AP's Jim Drinkard said, during an interview for this essay, has already happened in some cases.

The ideal situation for political campaigns is that they can twist the facts enough to deliver the message to the right people, without going so far that the inaccuracies draw too much attention. They're shooting for Half True. It's like football—if the referee isn't calling penalties on you, you're not playing hard enough. Imagine a world in which politicians aim for a Half True, and one in which fact-checking apps can display those rulings instantly on the TV screen. The fact-checkers will have been outfoxed. People may as well believe what they want; they'll be right half the time.

_____

Editors' Note: PolitiFact is operated by the Tampa Bay Times, *which is owned by The Poynter Institute, the employer of this book's co-editor and several of its contributors.*

NOTES

1. "Michele Bachmann Says `PolitiFact Came Out and Said That Everything I Said Was True' in Last Debate," *PolitiFact.com,* December 15, 2011. http://www.politifact.com/truth-o-meter/statements/2011/dec/15/michele-bachmann/michele-bachmann-says-politifact-came-out-and-said/.

2. "Newspaper Adwatch Stories: Coming Back Strong," The Annenberg Public Policy Center of the University of Pennsylvania, 2001, http://www.annenbergpublicpolicycenter.org/downloads/political_communication/factcheck/20071109_factcheckingjournalism/20071109_fcj_Newspaper_Report.pdf

3. John Celock, "Josh Mandel, Ohio Senate Candidate, Returns Birthday Gift from Ohio Democrats," *The Huffington Post,* October 10, 2012, http://www.huffingtonpost.com/2012/10/01/josh-mandel-returns-birthday-present_n_1929467.html

4. Jessica Wehrman, "Campaign Ad Watch: 'Pants on Fire'", *The Columbus Dispatch,* September 11, 2012, http://www.dispatch.com/content/stories/local/2012/09/11/adwatch10-art-gh8j91ci-1.html

5. "A Majority of Americans Are Conservative, Marco Rubio Says," *PolitiFact.com,* February 24, 2012, http://www.politifact.com/florida/statements/2012/feb/24/marco-rubio/majority-americans-are-conservative-marco-rubio-sa/.

6. Arthur S. Brisbane, "Should the Times Be a Truth Vigilante?" *The New York Times,* January 12, 2012, http://publiceditor.blogs.nytimes.com/2012/01/12/should-the-times-be-a-truth-vigilante/.

7. Brian, comment on "Should The Times Be a Truth Vigilante?" *The New York Times,* January 12, 2012, http://publiceditor.blogs.nytimes.com/2012/01/12/should-the-times-be-a-truth-vigilante/.

8. David S. Broder, "1988 Campaign Over, a Longtime Reporter Suggests Ways to Improve for '92," *Philly.com,* November 9, 1988, http://articles.philly.com/1988-11-09/news/26244270_1_vice-presidential-candidates-bush-dukakis-debates.

9. Frazier Moore, "Profile: Giving Washington a 'Reality Check': Eric Engberg's Reports on CBS News Raise More Than a Few Eyebrows," *The Associated Press,* July 02, 1995, articles.latimes.com/1995-07-02/news/tv-19351_1_eric-engberg.

10. Dean Starkman, "The Hamster Wheel: Why Running as Fast as We Can Is Getting Us Nowhere," *Columbia Journalism Review,* September 14, 2010, http://www.cjr.org/cover_story/the_hamster_wheel.php?page=all.

11. Calvin Woodward, "Fact Check: Misfires on Iran, China in Debate," *The Associated Press,* November 14, 2011, http://www.boston.com/news/local/massachusetts/articles/2011/11/14/fact_check_misfires_on_iran_china_in_debate/?page=full.

12. "Bill Clinton's DNC speech: Fact Check Finds Former President's Claims of Compromise a Stretch," *The Associated Press,* September 6, 2012, http://www.nydailynews.com/news/politics/bill-clinton-dnc-speech-fact-check-finds-president-claims-compromise-stretch-article-1.1153053.

13. Bill Adair and Angie Drobnic Holan, "PolitiFact's Lie of the Year: 'A Government Takeover of Health Care,'" *PolitiFact.com,* December 16, 2010, http://www.politifact.com/truth-o-meter/article/2010/dec/16/lie-year-government-takeover-health-care/.

14. Bill Adair and Angie Drobnic Holan, "Lie of the Year 2011: 'Republicans Voted to End Medicare,'" *PolitiFact.com,* December 20, 2011, http://www.politifact.com/truth-o-meter/article/2011/dec/20/lie-year-democrats-claims-republicans-voted-end-me/.

15. Glenn Kessler, "Spin and Counterspin in the Welfare Debate," *The Washington Post,* August 8, 2012, http://www.washingtonpost.com/blogs/fact-checker/post/spin-and-counterspin-in-the-welfare-debate/2012/08/07/61bf03b6-e0e3-11e1-8fc5-a7dcf1fc161d_blog.html.

16. Ron Fournier, "Why (and How) Romney Is Playing the Race Card," *National Journal,* September 1, 2012, http://www.nationaljournal.com/2012-election/why-and-how-romney-is-playing-the-race-card-20120829?page=1.

17. Mark Hemingway, "Obama's Palace Guard: How Media Fact Checkers Made Themselves of Service to the President in the Welfare Reform Debate," *The Weekly Standard,* October 1, 2012, http://www.weeklystandard.com/print/articles/obama-s-palace-guard_652895.html.

18. Ben Smith, "Romney Camp Bets on Welfare Attack," *BuzzFeed Politics,* August 28, 2012, http://www.buzzfeed.com/bensmith/romney-camp-bets-welfare-attack.

19. Ibid.

20. Michael Scherer, "The Frustrations of Fact Checkers," *Time,* September 26, 2012, http://swampland.time.com/2012/09/26/the-frustrations-of-fact-checkers/.

21. The Republican Party of Virginia, "To the Commonwealth of Virginia: A Comprehensive Analysis of PolitiFact Virginia's Questionable Objectivity," July 10, 2012, http://library.constantcontact.com/download/get/file/1103923423545-24/PolitiFact+Virginia+--+Political+Bias+--+Final+--+7-10-12.pdf.

22. "GOP Truth Squad Targets Bias in National PolitiFact Units," *The Washington Examiner,* July 19, 2012, http://washingtonexaminer.com/gop-truth-squad-targets-bias-in-national-politifact-units/article/2502623.

23. The Editors, "PolitiFiction," *National Review Online,* August 29, 2012, http://nationalreview.com/content/politifiction.

24. Neil Brown, "You Can Handle the Truth," *PoltiFact.com,* September 12, 2012, http://www.politifact.com/truth-o-meter/article/2012/sep/12/you-can-handle-truth/.

25. Glenn Kessler, "The Biggest Pinocchios of 2011," *The Washington Post,* December 22, 2011, http://www.washingtonpost.com/blogs/fact-checker/post/the-biggest-pinocchios-of-2011/2011/12/21/gIQAzbzFAP_blog.html.

26. Tom Cohen, "Obama, Romney tone down rhetoric, but campaigns don't," CNN, November 1, 2012, http://www.cnn.com/2012/10/31/politics/campaign-sandy.

27. David Lauter, "Rick Santorum Repeats Inaccurate Welfare Attack on Obama," *The Los Angeles Times,* August 28, 2012, http://www.latimes.com/news/politics/la-pn-santorum-welfare-obama-20120828,0,1255653.story.

28. James Fallows, "Bit by Bit It Takes Shape: Media Evolution for the 'Post-Truth' Age," *The Atlantic,* August 29, 2012, http://www.theatlantic.com/politics/archive/2012/08/bit-by-bit-it-takes-shape-media-evolution-for-the-post-truth-age/261741/.

29. Jim Rutenberg and Jeff Zeleny, "Romney Adopts Harder Message for Last Stretch," *The New York Times,* August 25, 2012, http://www.nytimes.com/2012/08/26/us/politics/mitt-romneys-campaign-adopts-a-harder-message.html?_r=1&.

30. "Statements from the National: 2012 U.S. President's Race," PolitiFact.com, http://www .politifact.com/truth-o-meter/elections/2012/us-president/.

31. Glenn Kessler, "About the Fact Checker," *The Washington Post,* March 1, 2011, http://www .washingtonpost.com/blogs/fact-checker/post/about-the-fact-checker/2011/12/05/gIQAa 0FBYO_blog.html#pinocchio.

32. Steve Myers, "PolitiFact Takes Lesson from Fast-Food Industry as it Franchises Fact Checking," *Poynter.org,* May 3, 2010, http://www.poynter.org/latest-news/top-stories/102422/ politifact-takes-lesson-from-fast-food-industry-as-it-franchises-fact-checking/.

33. "Harry Reid Says Anonymous Source Told Him Mitt Romney Didn't Pay Taxes for 10 Years," *PolitiFact.com,* August 6, 2012, http://www.politifact.com/truth-o-meter/statements/2012/ aug/06/harry-reid/harry-reid-says-anonymous-source-told-him-mitt-rom/.

34. Ben Smith, "The Facts About the Fact Checkers," *Politico.com,* November 1, 2011, http:// www.politico.com/news/stories/1011/67175.html.

35. Dylan Byers, "PolitiFact without the 'Truth-O-Meter,'" Politico.com, February 16, 2012, http:// www.politico.com/blogs/media/2012/02/politifact-without-the-truthometer-114704.html.

36. "Have Private-Sector Jobs Grown by 3 Million in 22 Months, with the Best Annual Totals Since 2005?" *PoliticFact.com,* January, 25, 2012, http://www.politifact.com/truth-o-meter/ statements/2012/jan/25/barack-obama/have-private-sector-jobs-grown-22-months-best-annu/.

37. Rachel Maddow, *The Rachel Maddow Show,* 6:04, MSNBC, http://www.nbcnews.com/ id/26315908/ns/msnbc_tv-rachel_maddow_show#50700479.

38. Andrew Phelps, "Inside the Star Chamber: How PolitiFact Tries to Find Truth in a World of Make-believe," *Nieman Journalism Lab,* August 21, 2012, http://www.niemanlab.org/2012/08/ inside-the-star-chamber-how-politifact-forges-truth-in-the-world-of-make-believe/.

Caitlin Johnston

In his essay, Steve Myers suggests that fact-checking is different from typical reporting and doesn't come naturally to all reporters. In this case study, three different organizations fact-checked the same issue, arriving at slightly different conclusions.

Republican presidential nominee Mitt Romney's campaign ran an ad in the summer of 2012 claiming that President Barack Obama was gutting work requirements for welfare recipients: "Under Obama's plan, you wouldn't have to work and you wouldn't have to train for a job. They just send you your welfare check." The Obama campaign countered that Romney previously supported regulations similar to the ones proposed by the president's administration.

Three organizations—FactCheck.org, *The Washington Post*'s Fact Checker and PolitiFact—ran detailed stories outlining the truths, half-truths and lies perpetuated by each side. Each organization came to a similar conclusion: Yes, the Obama administration was proposing changes to the work requirements, but there was no plan to send out welfare checks with no restraints, as the Romney camp had asserted.

The stories range in length from PolitiFact's 1,000 words to FactCheck .org's more than 2,000 words. Each starts by outlining Romney's claim, though the *Post* also outlined Obama's counterclaim. The fact-checking organizations then inform the reader that the rest of the story will try to answer the big question: Does the plan proposed by the Obama administration really mean the government will "just send you your welfare check"?

FactCheck.org, which dedicated the most space to this debate, tells readers immediately what is true and false:

> A Mitt Romney TV ad claims the Obama administration has adopted "a plan to gut welfare reform by dropping work requirements." The plan does neither of those things.
>
> - "Work requirements are not simply being "dropped." States may now change the requirements—revising, adding or eliminating them—as part of a federally approved state-specific plan to increase job placement.
> - And it won't "gut" the 1996 law to ease the requirement. Benefits still won't be paid beyond an allotted time, whether the recipient is working or not.[1]

While FactCheck.org negates Romney's claims right out of the gate, *The Washington Post* waits until the end of its analysis to present its conclusions. And even then, it finds blame on both sides, though more on Romney's.

The Washington Post Fact Checker calls welfare reform a "complex issue" and says neither campaign "necessarily conducts itself with glory."[2] After offering a condensed version of welfare reform history, the *Post*'s Fact Checker delves into Obama's counterclaim that Romney supported similar legislation. The Fact Checker was the only one to assess Obama's counterclaim that Romney once supported the same sort of rule changes as the Obama administration wanted. It calls that assertion "a case of apples and oranges."[3]

PolitiFact kicks off its story with an in-depth description of the Romney ad, an explanation of Obama's welfare plan, less history than the other two sites, and no mention of Obama's counterclaim that Romney previously supported a similar plan. Ultimately, PolitiFact finds that Romney's ad is "not accurate, and it inflames old resentments about able-bodied adults sitting around collecting public assistance."[4]

In the end, three organizations relying solely on facts, but using different processes, came to three versions of the same conclusion. FactCheck.org assertively states in the beginning and end that Obama's plan does neither thing Romney's ad claims; PolitiFact calls Romney's ad a "drastic distortion" of the plan; and *The Washington Post* Fact Checker finds that there's "something fishy about the administration's process" with the plan, but that Romney's ad is still "over-the-top."

QUESTIONS

- Which organization's analysis was most helpful to the audience and why?

- What actual facts did each organization check?

- Why might each of these fact-checking operations have come to slightly different conclusions?

- What do you consider the main goal of fact-checking?

- What skills does a reporter need to conduct a fact-check? How are those skills best developed?

- How much time should be devoted to fact-checking in the daily churn of journalism? Is it reasonable to assume a journalist should vet every claim, assertion and pithy one-liner a politician makes?

- What types of stories are best suited to this kind of journalistic policing?

Editors' Note: PolitiFact is operated by the Tampa Bay Times, *which is owned by The Poynter Institute, the employer of this book's co-editor and several of its contributors.*

CASE NOTES

1. "Does Obama's Plan 'Gut Welfare Reform'?" *FactCheck.org*, August 9, 2012, http://www
   .factcheck.org/2012/08/does-obamas-plan-gut-welfare-reform/.
2. Glenn Kessler, "Spin and Counterspin in the Welfare Debate," *The Washington Post*, August 8,
   2012, http://www.washingtonpost.com/blogs/fact-checker/post/spin-and-counterspin-in-the
   -welfare-debate/2012/08/07/61bf03b6-e0e3-11e1-8fc5-a7dcf1fc161d_blog.html.
3. Ibid.
4. "Mitt Romney Says Barack Obama's Plan for Welfare Reform: 'They Just Send You Your
   Check.'" *Tampa Bay Times: PolitiFact.com*, http://www.politifact.com/truth-o-meter/statements/
   2012/aug/07/mitt-romney/mitt-romney-says-barack-obamas-plan-abandons-tenet/.

chapter 5

Seeing Is Not Believing: Photojournalism in the 21st Century

Kenny Irby

In this age of online attraction, attention and engagement, photography remains a powerful reporting tool, yet it too is changing in at least two important ways. Photojournalism is no longer solely the pursuit of deeply passionate, highly skilled practitioners with an abiding zeal to shine light in dark places and offer a face to the faceless. Simultaneously, people are increasingly skilled at manipulating images and equally skeptical that what they see is real.

There once was a time when seeing was believing. Throughout the 20th century, photojournalism and photographic reporting played a vital role as a vehicle of democracy. A single photograph—or a series of images—captured the hearts and minds of a community, a nation, the world. History's photo album includes the dark Jim Crow South, war-torn Vietnam, brutalized apartheid South Africa, a solitary protester in Tiananmen Square, an American soldier being dragged through the dirt streets of Mogadishu. Immediately, we flip through the moments seared into our mental galleries. And in each instance, it was the photographs that ultimately touched our nation's conscience and moved us to action.

That once sacred trust between photographers and their audience is now vulnerable at every step of the process; we question each crucial choice from lens selection, camera angle, cropping alternatives, post-camera adjustments in the digital darkroom, photo selection and presentation choices: all arguably forms of manipulation.

With the advent of advanced digital technology and mass-market Internet delivery systems, seeing has become disbelieving for a large part of the audience.

IS EVERYONE A PHOTOJOURNALIST?

Digital cameras are everywhere—from the ubiquitous camera phone to affordable "pro-sumer" digital cameras, targeted toward the high-end amateur, blending professional and consumer elements. As the Sprint Unlimited iPhone 5 commercial, which targets "a billion roaming photojournalists, uploading the human experience," suggests, more people than ever before now participate in the photographic process thanks to these devices, and they share their images through email, text messaging, Flickr, Facebook, Twitter, Tumblr, Instagram and whatever is next.

Over the last 10 years, as traditional newspapers and magazines contracted—or shut down, like *The Rocky Mountain News* and *Newsweek*— photojournalists and picture editors have lost their jobs. At the same time, this flood of consumer images has become available to media outlets, which have created space for these images on their own websites. CNN, The Weather Channel and *The Huffington Post,* to name a few, lead the way in inviting citizens to submit photographs and videos of breaking news.

The publishing and broadcasting worlds have evolved dramatically since 1991, when George Holliday captured video of Rodney King being beaten by police officers in Los Angeles. That video was broadcast first by a local TV station and then picked up for the world to see. Although Holliday sold the video to KTLA for $500, he later sued CNN and other networks for unauthorized use of it (he lost).

In 2009, Janis Krums shared a photo via Twitter of U.S. Airways Flight 1549, just after an emergency forced it to land in the Hudson River. News organizations ran that photograph on the air and on their front pages. But Krums rejected requests to sell exclusive rights to it. He knew there was new value to images. When Krums' photograph surfaced on Twitter, news organizations credited it to him and offered supporting context: The Sarasota, Fla., resident captured the image from a ferry. This lent the image journalistic credibility.

PHOTO 5-1 **Janis Krums snapped this photo on his iPhone and posted it to Twitter moments after a plane made an emergency landing in the Hudson River.**

Source: © Janis Krums. Reprinted by permission.

Krums did not aspire to make media history, but his photograph, and others that record major moments—raises an important question: If everybody is a photographer, how do we maintain some credibility unique to photojournalism?

A photographer's intent can be journalistic—to inform an audience about meaningful events of the day. And expectations can be journalistic—if the audience and publisher believe what they are seeing accurately depicts what happened. When audiences are no longer sure what they can expect of a photograph (Is it an accurate representation or a manipulation?), trust erodes.

Seeing Is No Longer Believing

For the past 20 years, Adobe's powerful software program Photoshop has impacted the world of digital imaging in profound ways that have enhanced visual journalism but also threatened its integrity.

There have been countless embarrassing and regrettable examples that cast doubt on a photograph's authenticity: cases where visual elements were added or removed and cases in which totally fabricated situations were presented as real moments. All of these incidents have called into question the veracity and truthfulness of those photographic works and the integrity of the publications in which they appeared.

During the summer of 2012, MSN editor Tom Phillips launched the website "Is Twitter Wrong?" with the purpose of debunking inaccurate information being transmitted on the social network. In the universe of compelling photography, major weather events and natural disasters attract hoaxsters and Web traffic. As the monster storm Hurricane Sandy moved across the eastern seaboard of the United States, Phillips was early to debunk an image of lower Manhattan with an ominously cloudy sky looming. The image was shared on Twitter without sourcing or context, viewed by people who believed it was captured that day. Phillips filled in those information gaps when he revealed the photograph was actually captured in 2011 by a New York City finance professional, most likely through his tinted office window.

A second photograph that was widely distributed around the same time showed a rainy scene at the Tomb of the Unknown Soldier in Arlington National Cemetery. When the photo of vigilant guards was initially shared on Facebook by the First Army Division East, it was—again—presented without source information or context. NPR, *The Washington Post* and other news organizations published the photo as if it had been taken during the storms caused by Hurricane Sandy. Poynter Online reporters and others identified the photographer as a military wife who actually captured the image a month before the storm. Her husband is the regimental commander of honor guard at Arlington, which made the sourcing and attribution relevant as a way of assessing the image's credibility.

A third example comes from Iran: the disturbing case in 2009 of 26-year-old Neda Agha-Soltan, a protester whose death drew international attention and is considered an early stimulus to the Arab Spring Movement that followed a few years later in the region during the fight for democratic freedom. Neda's sudden death from sniper fire, documented on video by bystanders armed with cellphone cameras, was broadcast online, and the bloody video became a rallying point for further protest.

PHOTO 5-2 **This photo of soldiers guarding the Tomb of the Unknown Soldier in a rain storm, was taken a month before Hurricane Sandy made landfall on the East Coast. Still, it was passed around social media as a hurricane photo and published by several news organizations.**

Source: © Karin Markert. Reprinted by permission.

Initially, viewers did not know the source of the video, and the Iranian government questioned the context. Government spokesmen stated that images were a fabrication and unrelated to the protests, and because they were unsourced, people questioned their validity. That challenge foreshadowed what followed over the next several years as images spread widely without attribution or other context. That is a particular challenge internationally in places where people's own lives may be in jeopardy if they reveal they witnessed a certain event or documented it.

As images increasingly are created and distributed by individuals and organizations we don't recognize as credible journalists, we must demand greater transparency. We need to know who captured a photograph or video, who uploaded it and who is distributing it for what purposes. Transparency and context lead to credibility.

HOW TO THINK ABOUT VISUAL INTEGRITY

We live in a time of instantaneous visual imagery. Digital cameras, image-management software like Instagram and Photoshop, and advanced telecommunications devices such as satellite dishes and cellphones make the world a very different place for photojournalists, picture editors and viewers. As quickly as a photojournalist can capture an image, the image is transmitted for the world to see.

Countless people come to understand the world through still and moving pictures, which magnifies the responsibility of those who distribute photos and videos as purveyors of visual information. Part of that responsibility involves providing complete contextualization of photographs and video. Besides attribution making the image's source clear, information should also convey the traditional Five Ws of journalism: Who is in the frame, what is the image representing, when was it recorded, where and why? Providing that context is a central requirement of ethical photojournalism.

Your journalistic duty—as a photographer, as someone who shares photographs or as someone who edits them for publication—is to honestly and accurately represent the story at hand. Photographic images depict only a fraction of a given news event. So effective photographic reporting requires a sound, ethical decision-making strategy for deciding what goes inside the frame.

A photographic moment is not the "Truth" with a capital T; it is the sum of moral choices, news judgment and a series of technical considerations: exposures, cropping, color balance, camera angles and lens choice, to name a few.

Photographic reality is a matter of personal perspective; all journalistic reality is. Aesthetics can seduce us into subtly adjusting images away from their original reality. Native adjustments occur without our intervention as part of internal camera processing. For example, remarkably accurate computerized algorithms work inside digital cameras to measure lighting, distance and sometimes focus, predefined by the camera's brainlike computer processor.

But it is the other visual decisions that create ethical challenges and fierce debate about accuracy. The integrity of a photograph lies within the four borders of its composition. Therefore, when photographers or others add or subtract elements within the natural border of the photograph or create perspectives that do not naturally exist, we begin manipulation that raises credibility questions. That manipulation can happen along a wide spectrum, from staging events that appear inside the frame to adding a shadow in the digital darkroom that was not there in the original moment captured.

Forms of manipulation—the use of image filters and composites, for example—have existed in photojournalism and "wet" darkrooms for decades. But changing images in those days required planning and time. In the digital age, it is easy to make sophisticated changes quickly, with the click of a mouse.

Before you share a photograph—for publication on Facebook and Twitter or in a news publication—you should be able to answer questions about the context inside and outside an image's four borders.

- Check for a caption that offers attribution, credits and verifiable written context about the photograph and answers the Five Ws. If you are the source of the image, provide that information.
- Check or provide the same information in the photograph's metadata file.
- Check the image's shadows for consistent lighting direction.
- If you have access to one, check the file with a digital detection program.

- Remember: The authentic facts of a photograph reside within its pixels, and you can easily verify an image by examining those pixels for inconsistencies.

All the other ethical dimensions of journalism also apply to photojournalism. These dimensions include: weighing the public's right to know—and see—against an individual's right to be left alone; minimizing personal harm; avoiding conflicts of interest and creating a reliable portrait of the world. Photojournalists and picture editors need the competence and confidence to ask good questions about these things and make good ethical decisions with little time. To make sense of the vast volume of photographic images they are being bombarded with, citizens must acquire those same critical thinking skills.

Every time you share an image, you step into the picture editing process, which begins immediately after documentation. Seeking attribution and contextual information helps you validate the image, whether you are verifying it to share on Twitter or verifying it to publish in print. Whenever people share photographs through social media—like Twitter, Flickr, Instagram, Facebook—they are selecting the images they present to the world. Their purpose may not be journalistic, so as you mix all of these images in the same stream, how do you make a distinction between the journalistic photographs and the others? Attribution and context are the first step. There are several other key considerations:

- Remember to maintain your journalistic integrity inside and outside the frame.
- An excellent work of photojournalism is a blend of the accurate and the aesthetic.
- Know the news value of an image and story.
- Audience impact should always be one of your guiding principles.
- In an "always on" age, timeliness is critical but never an excuse.
- As you collaborate with other people—professionally or through casual crowd-sourcing—seek to understand the connection between the image and the larger narrative it represents.
- Maximize your journalistic responsibility while minimizing unnecessary harm to the individual(s) in the composition, those close to the individual(s) and the surrounding community.
- Continue to practice and evaluate your process for decision making. Asking good questions in advance will help you make better ethical decisions.

Photojournalism as a Tool of Democracy

To be the eyes of the community is a valued, sacred responsibility. That responsibility is threatened by three forces.

First, the media organizations that have been historically wedded to investing in the people and the procedures to maintain visual credibility appear to be abandoning their role by eliminating photojournalists and picture editors and by compromising photojournalistic standards.

Second, new visual reporters, emerging outside of newsrooms, may not value, recognize or promote journalistic accuracy.

Third, citizens who view and share images may value visual credibility less as there are increasing challenges to photographic authenticity and authority.

Yet amid these challenges, photographs remain critical visual facts. And we require a common set of facts to have productive conversations about what's happening in our streets, schools, sports stadiums and civic life. If we can't agree on the truth of what we see, it becomes powerless to influence what we say and do.

Caitlin Johnston

Kenny Irby suggests in his chapter that images are losing their authenticity. As we are exposed to distortions and fakeries and photographs whose origins and context are unclear, we become increasingly skeptical.

Chicago Tribune photojournalist Chris Sweda was capturing images of the newly opened Trump Tower from a nearby observation platform on June 24, 2010, when a massive storm broke over the city. So he started photographing it. And what he got was a rare photo of a double lightning strike: two lightning bolts simultaneously striking the Willis Tower and Trump Tower, two of the tallest buildings in Chicago.

It was a dream of a shot, perfectly documenting the supercharged storm and the city it overtook. Any Chicagoan would quickly recognize the iconic skyscrapers. The photograph was picked up by The Associated Press and took off worldwide. The *Chicago Tribune* ran the photograph on its site and in its print edition.

Almost immediately, online critics—who could be anyone from experienced photographers to a kid sitting at home—began questioning the authenticity of the photograph. The *Tribune* was flooded with calls and emails challenging

PHOTO 5-3 **The crowd questioned the authenticity of this double-lightening strike photo taken during a 2010 summer storm in Chicago.**

Source: Chris Sweda, Chicago Tribune / June 23, 2010.

the veracity of the image. Here are some examples of some such comments in one online forum at Fark:[1]

> Sigh . . . Long Exposure means that they didn't happen at the same time. See how bright the buildings are?

> Looks like a 'shop. And I haven't even seen that many in my time.

> Fake.

In response, *Tribune* photo editors conducted an internal investigation of the photo's authenticity. The main allegation was that the double lightning strike didn't actually happen in a single moment but was instead captured due to a long exposure time that made separate lightning strikes appear simultaneous.

There were several ways for the photo editors to validate the photo's accuracy. They started inspecting the internal clocks on the cameras carried by several of their staff photographers. Terrence A. James, another *Tribune* photographer, was also out shooting during the storm. James snagged a similar photo, showing both strikes, but from a different angle. And while Sweda's shot was taken at a four-second exposure—long enough for the critics to question—James' was shot at 1/80th of a second. Both of the cameras' internal clocks registered 7:45 p.m. for the lightning strike photos.

The *Tribune* went a step further. Moving the investigation outward, the staff did some crowdsourcing, which paid off when the staff discovered a video sent in by a reader that showed lightning striking not just two but three of Chicago's tallest buildings at the same time. Sweda was not able to capture this third strike, because it hit John Hancock Center, from where he was shooting.

While some readers continued to question the veracity of the photo, the *Tribune* staff came to the conclusion that Sweda's photograph was authentic and stood by it as an accurate depiction of the storm.

QUESTIONS

- Audiences often doubt the veracity of dramatic images. What could photograph editors do to anticipate these questions and provide answers?

- As the average citizen becomes more adept at the language of photo editing, what can editors do to stimulate conversation and engagement around images? What impact would that have on the audience's ability to trust images?

- What type of metadata is available with still photos? What about videos? How could editors use metadata to enhance credibility? Should publication of metadata be standard?

- Even if a photograph is authentic, if the crowd dismisses it as fake, what is the impact on a news organization's credibility?

CASE NOTE

1. "The Most Amazing Picture of a Double Lightning Strike Over Chicago You'll See All Day,"
    Fark.com, June 26, 2010, http://www.fark.com/comments/5448715/The-most-amazing
    -picture-of-a-double-lightning-strike-over-Chicago-youll-see-all-day.

PART 2

Learning the Transparency Habit

Kelly McBride and Tom Rosenstiel

Throughout the 20th century, as journalists wrestled with public trust, they often touched on the value of transparency, if not fully taking hold of the concept with both hands. In such practices as editor and ombudsman columns, descriptions of how many interviews were conducted to produce a story, or evidence of a TV correspondent's attempt to get answers on-camera, there was a clear sense that if we tell the audience how and why we do things, they won't assign spurious motives to our actions.

More often, however, we fell short rather than measuring up.

We underestimated what information would interest the audience. Some journalists assumed a stoic posture—the idea that good work should speak for itself and that saying too much might invite suspicion. Sometimes, we didn't have solid journalistic foundations for our actions, so we preferred to keep the doors closed. And sometimes we cut deals for access to information that required that we keep a few secrets, usually the name of a source.

Most often, perhaps, our efforts at transparency were hampered by capacity. There was only so much space in print and on the air, let alone time in the day. When the communication was limited and occurred in only one direction— from the journalist to the public—true transparency was hardly possible.

Instead of transparency, in the 20th century, journalism functioned on an industrial level that afforded publishers the luxuries of scale and neutral voice:

> Scale, because newspapers and broadcast news programs were distributed to the widest audience possible, thus generating advertising dollars to fund the news operations.

> Neutral voice, because news itself was generated from a distant or neutral point of view, as a way of suggesting it was nonpartisan to invite in the widest possible audience.

These two precepts, which grew out of both an economic and a democratic imperative, led to an ethical principle of *independence*: the notion that the organization and the individuals who create the news should not advocate for outcomes or slant the news in favor a particular point of view.

Much has changed about journalism in the 21st century to undermine the principle of independence. The advertising-based economic underpinnings of the profession have weakened substantially and will likely continue to decline. New channels and providers of news are popping up daily, including think tanks, partisans, social activists, entrepreneurial upstarts, social media and niche products. The demarcation between journalism and other forms of information have blurred so much that it is far more difficult to determine who is a journalist, let alone what types of information are acting as journalism.

With the dawn of the digital era, consumers also have many more opportunities to examine, question and critique the journalists and journalism organizations behind the news. All this leads some to conclude that independence—and with it the neutral voice style of presentation—are conventions of the past that no longer serve the profession or the public. Some go further and argue they never did serve the public—that at best they were commercial illusions and intellectual impossibilities.

We are not willing to go that far. We believe that journalism produced by people who strive to be independent observers, who allow the actors on different sides to make their best case—without "fear or favor," as Adolph S. Ochs described it more than a hundred years ago[1]—will continue to play a significant role in shaping our democracy and holding the powerful accountable. But two other forces are at play:

- It is clear that significant and substantial journalism can be accomplished through a point of view. *The Huffington Post,* founded in 2005 as a site for liberal political commentary, won a Pulitzer Prize in national reporting[2] for its 2011 series on wounded soldiers.[3] With that award, *Huffington Post* joined a rarefied group where the norm continues to be political independence.
- Among journalists and news outlets committed to independence, there is a mandate to speak with authority in order to cut through the noise and serve the public. Independence does not imply ambiguity when it comes to discerning truth.

With these changes in the market, transparency begins to supersede independence. Yet we believe this new mandate is closer to the original concept of objectivity as it was meant when it was introduced from social science into journalism in the early 20th century.

It is tempting to see transparency as a lower bar: We simply disclose our conflicts of interest, and we're good to go. In fact, true transparency is more than disclosure. It also requires producing the news in ways that can be explained and even defended. It becomes the key to a method. Transparency requires those who produce the news to anticipate how they will explain their actions before they act.

In a world in which an increasingly polarized public can choose from a wide array of sources for news, some consumers will demand this transparency. Who is this source you are interviewing? Why should I believe him? What biases might the guest on your program have that you aren't telling me about? Viewers can Google the source as they watch on TV or click a link in a story to the person's name to learn more.

These demands can also raise fundamental questions about the news operation. How does the business model that keeps an organization afloat impact news decisions? How do you make your staffing and hiring decisions? How do you decide what topics and issues (or beats) to cover? How do you decide which stories are important within those topics and issues? Why did you select those sources? What does your editing process look like? What mistakes have you made, and how will you disclose them and prevent similar mistakes in the future?

Most news organizations fall short every day answering these questions. We have yet to develop best practices for transparency on this level. It is far from a habit to be this open and communicative with our audiences. That is changing—most rapidly at new news operations that see disclosure and transparency as a way of establishing credibility in the first place.

As audience members demand more transparency, as technology allows for more communication, as news originates from a variety of sources, and as newsrooms develop better procedures, journalism of all kinds will become more transparent. Independent newsrooms will be able to describe how they create standards of objectivity and mitigate the inevitable conflicts of interest. News organizations with a point of view will create policies of accuracy and fairness, even when those values don't serve their agenda. As more newsrooms rise to this new level of accountability, the audience will come to expect it, and those organizations that lag behind will lose credibility.

In the chapters that make up this section, five voices muse over the meaning of this new transparency. Dan Gillmor begins by looking at the tensions between private platforms that host our social media and the public service that journalism is meant to provide. Gilad Lotan follows up with a challenge to our notions that algorithms are somehow objective, or even purely mathematical, and calls on those who produce news to use social media in ways that transcend the superficial and provide a meaningful understanding of the world.

Adam Hochberg looks at the ethical challenges that nonprofit newsrooms face as they attempt to establish policies that balance funding needs and editorial priorities. Ann Friedman looks at how newsrooms fulfill their obligation to serve a diverse audience.

Finally, Craig Silverman hones in on one of the most common ways that journalists fall short and lose credibility: inaccuracy and corrections. He looks at how journalists should rely on transparency to identify and fix their mistakes.

These chapters all rest on an assumption, one that a generation ago was controversial and even today can be challenging to fulfill: The most persuasive way to make a case for why audiences should trust you is to show your work, offer evidence to back it up and explain how you gathered it. In a world where so many people and organizations can create news and spread information, transparency becomes a mechanism that allows the public to sort the reliable from the suspect. When citizens can see how the work was created, how newsrooms are financed and who is in a position to influence editors and reporters, then they can judge the value of the news.

NOTES

1. "Without Fear or Favor," *The New York Times,* August 19, 1996, http://www.nytimes.com/1996/08/19/opinion/without-fear-or-favor.html, is a reprint of the original publication.
2. Michael Calderone, "Huffington Post Awarded Pulitzer Prize," *The Huffington Post,* April 16, 2012.
3. David Wood, "Beyond the Battlefield: From a Decade of War, an Endless Struggle for the Severely Wounded," *The Huffington Post,* October 10–21, 2011, http://www.huffingtonpost.com/news/beyond-the-battlefield/.

chapter 6

Do Private Platforms Threaten Public Journalism?

Dan Gillmor

Link TV, a small Web and cable news organization, launched an iPad app for its world news programming in November 2012. The app's appearance in the iTunes store meant that Apple had decided that the content provided by Link TV was acceptable under its somewhat vague standards. On Twitter, I asked the company whether a news organization really wanted to entrust a significant part of its future to the discretion of Apple, which has been known to ban apps—including, for a time, a political cartoonist—containing content it deemed objectionable?[1] As long as the iPad comprised 60 percent of the tablet market, there was no alternative, Link TV replied in a Twitter conversation: "We are trying to forge a new path for independent media. If most people have [the] iPad, so be it."[2]

The case of Link TV and its acceptance of Apple's rules demonstrated a growing dilemma news providers face in the digital age: More and more, they do not control the platforms on which they provide news. They have no choice but to use those platforms, which have become crucial choke points in the emerging information ecosystem. But, by ceding control to others, they are putting their futures at risk. The uncomfortable reality, which journalists need to confront before it's too late: Governments and businesses—with interests unfriendly to journalism—can create not just speed bumps on the fabled information highway, but outright barricades. A commitment to transparency ultimately requires explaining the systems that create and distribute journalism, including their weaknesses and their strengths. One could argue that fixing these faults is the responsibility of society at large. But journalists, who by nature ought to be dedicated to the ideals of free speech and democracy, bear the burden of leadership in the conversation.

HOW WE GOT HERE

In the 20th century, mass media achieved economies of scale that created significant barriers to entry. In most communities, journalism was dominated by newspaper monopolies and broadcasting oligopolies. For national broadcast news, there was a cartel of three networks.

Meanwhile, a small number of giant companies gained increasing owner-ship of media organizations, dominating what most Americans read, watched and listened to each day. This led to legitimate fears of consolidation, and while Congress allowed significant concentration, it didn't allow utter dominance by any single corporate entity.

With some exceptions, Federal Communications Commission rules for-bid the same company from owning local TV stations and the local newspaper, to ensure a diversity of viewpoints feeding the marketplace of ideas. (At the end of 2012, the FCC was considering relaxing or lifting those restrictions.)

In theory and, so far, mostly in practice, the Internet broke things open. We all came to own the equivalent of a printing press, we believed, and we could make what we created available to a potentially global audience. Yet a new kind of corporate oligopoly is emerging. In many cases, the consolidation is a consequence of natural network effects in digital technology. Coupled with increasingly controlling activities by government, often in concert with corpo-rate interests, we have reasons to worry.

The owners of the new control points fall under three broad categories: Internet service providers, typically cable and phone companies; software plat-form providers, such as Facebook, Apple and Twitter; and governments, prompted by security concerns and corporate interests. Individually and com-bined, they can be potent allies to journalists, or they can be adversaries. As usual with such things, they are both.

THE IMPORTANCE OF NETWORK NEUTRALITY

When it comes to Internet service, we have two main kinds of providers: wired-line and mobile. Among the former, in most American communities there are two broadband service providers: the cable and phone companies, and cable is rapidly becoming the dominant provider due to its fundamentally higher-speed architecture.[3] (In both cases, these companies at one time were monopolies established with government protection.) This duopoly-cum-monopoly is a far cry from the diverse and highly competitive nature of the Internet, which grew like wildfire in the 1990s, when data moved almost solely on phone lines (at much slower speeds) and multiple service providers competed for customers. The phone companies were required to serve all such competitors. A 1996 telecom law set in motion the rapid consolidation of Internet service providers (ISPs), because with broadband access, the phone and cable companies had an overwhelming advantage over any competitor and—unlike the same industries in some other nations—were given much more control over those lines. The number of ISP competitors dropped nearly to zero.

Because most phone companies haven't invested in fiber-optic lines to customers' homes, cable boasts vastly superior bandwidth in most places. DSL via phone lines is notably slower, and thus, cable is rapidly becoming the de facto broadband provider where it's available. Verizon is an exception with its fiber-optic connections, but Verizon has stopped expanding that network. No matter who provides it, American broadband service is slower and more expensive than the true broadband connections offered in many other countries. In the best-served places, the telecom companies provide platforms where ISPs compete. According to a 2012 survey by Pando Networks, the United States ranked 13th in average speed; South Korea's speed was about triple the U.S. rate.[4]

In the United States, the carriers insist that they should be able to decide what bits of information get delivered in what order and at what speed, if they get delivered at all, to the customer requesting them. This means, in effect, the right to play favorites in content. Most broadband carriers have instituted bandwidth caps. Comcast has even canceled the service of those who've used too much.[5] Carriers are also becoming content providers themselves, as Comcast did when it bought NBC Universal, creating a plain conflict of interest. What prevents Comcast from giving priority to its own content above all other content?

This is why a principle called *network neutrality* has emerged in recent years. It essentially says that the carriers should not favor one kind of content or conversation over another. The carriers have challenged the FCC's tiny moves toward network neutrality, and it's not hard to see why. If they can have a duopoly, with little incentive to truly compete, they can use that dominance to cut deals with big content companies at the expense of the smaller players, including startup media operations with different content to provide. And as the carriers become content providers themselves, the incentive to make these choices grows. Comcast says that its own streaming video service won't count against its bandwidth cap, unlike other streaming video services it doesn't own; a loophole in the FCC's already-weak regulations may give the cable giant cover. (Note: I own a small number of shares in Netflix, which offers a video streaming service that does count against the cap.) It is easy to imagine a time when carriers make all kinds of content-based decisions based on commercial or even political interests. One carrier, Verizon, has even said it has a First Amendment right to make decisions about content on its network.[6]

The serious potential for problems with wired-line broadband pales next to the actual situation with mobile carriers, who increasingly are becoming a primary means of Internet connection around the world. In the United States, mobile carriers have already won the FCC's approval to discriminate in their network practices, and they have bandwidth limits a fraction the size of wired-line carriers' limits. Clearly they cannot handle the kind of traffic that a cable or DSL line can bear, given the network limitations, but they're using relative scarcity to create customer-controlling business models.

Recently, AT&T's mobile arm declared its interest in charging some application developers for preferred connections to their customers. Who could afford that? Companies like Facebook, certainly, but smaller players would be hard-pressed to compete in such an environment. AT&T has also told customers that they will have to pay extra to use Apple's FaceTime video-chat application via their mobile phones (unless they're running data over Wi-Fi connections).

Do journalists recognize the potential threat? Some clearly do, although as of 2012 there seemed to be little institutional awareness or organized pushback from major journalism organizations. There has been sporadic coverage of network neutrality in recent years, meanwhile. But it's fair to speculate that most people wouldn't recognize the term or, even if they'd heard of it, know what it means. Yet this is a kind of consolidation and control that makes the corporate media giant of the past seem relatively insignificant. The biggest worry, especially for new entrants, is that the telecommunications companies will make deals with incumbent large media organizations to favor that content while making life harder, or at least more expensive, for competitors.

THE NEW "WALLED GARDENS"

In the 1990s, the Internet subsumed a company that wanted to be dominant in online service: America Online. AOL's approach was to create a "walled garden" in which customers would feel safe and comfortable. Some news organizations used AOL for their initial online presence. But as their audiences realized the greater value and variety of the wider Internet, the news providers also moved there.

We are witnessing what may be a return to the walled gardens, within which private companies, not the news organizations, have ultimate control. Facebook, Apple, Twitter and Google are among the many operators journalists are using as platforms for their work. Are journalists sufficiently aware of the potential risks? Do journalists have any power to advocate for free speech and minority viewpoints in these spaces? Can they hold the powerful accountable, when the powerful happen to be the very people who allow or disallow information to get to citizens? They can advocate, but they can't force.

Facebook, of course, is the giant, a company that has no precedent in global size and reach. Other companies, such as the old AT&T, Standard Oil and Microsoft, have dominated their own fields—and then faced pro-competition regulatory intervention. But to a degree never before seen, Facebook is the one network where you are likely to find almost everyone you know. It claims more than a billion regular users and has become more than the default home page for many of them. It is a place where users spend much—in some cases all—of their online time. And as Facebook makes deals with wireless carriers in some nations—the Internet is free as long as it's Facebook, but other data usage comes at a cost—it may literally become the only Internet that countless millions of new users can access. In this context, news organizations feel absolutely obliged to have a Facebook presence: It's where the audiences are.

But news providers need to understand that Facebook is not in business to help them. It's in business to help its own shareholders, period. The more that journalists use Facebook as a platform to show off their work and to engage with audiences, and the more that it becomes the default place online, the more they will be at Facebook's mercy—and they should recognize that Facebook is one of their most serious competitors for advertising in the long run. (Google is another.)

Moreover, some news sites have outsourced their article comments to Facebook. This is classic short-term strategy—using Facebook because the comments may be more controllable, as opposed to the rancid free-fire zones of the poorly moderated comments sections on most news sites. It's a high-risk strategy in the longer term, however, because Facebook, owning the platform, gets deep insights into the news providers' user bases. Even more worrisome, perhaps, is the way news organizations have encouraged their audiences to be part of third-party platforms that take great liberties with the data they collect. By encouraging audiences into these platforms, news organizations risk violating the audience trust they've built up over the years.

The same issues apply, to a lesser degree (so far), to Twitter and Google+, which compete for social-networking attention. Twitter's mostly exemplary approach to free speech—it has gone to court to keep information about its users out of overreaching prosecutors' hands—hasn't been perfect. During the London Olympics, Twitter blocked the account of a user who was harshly critical of a Twitter media partner. After a furious response from free speech advocates, the account was reinstated, and Twitter said it had learned a valuable lesson.[7] Even so, the incident made clear that Twitter users exist on the site at the sufferance of the company. Twitter is also becoming a media company in its own right and is likely to be yet another advertising competitor.

That competition clearly includes the search engines. Google, for example, has enormous power to decide who is visible, and it has collected staggering amounts of data on our individual preferences and how we use the Internet. So far, the company has behaved in mostly benign ways. But Google may not always be in the hands of people who take seriously the "don't be evil" mantra its founders established.

Apple occupies a different part of the ecosystem. The news industry's longstanding love affair with what has become the most valuable company on Earth only expanded with the death of Steve Jobs. But Apple has a long history of controlling behavior. Anyone creating a journalism app to be sold in the iPhone or iPad marketplace explicitly gives Apple the right to decide whether the journalism content is acceptable under the company's vague guidelines. Apple has used this to block material it considers improper, including, until the company came under fire for this, refusing for a time to allow Mark Fiore, who has won a Pulitzer Prize for his cartoons, to sell his own app.[8]

In a 2012 case, Apple rejected an app that tracked U.S. military drone strikes. According to Wired.com, the journalistic app was considered "objectionable and rude."[9] (Microsoft is moving in Apple's direction, while Google's Android ecosystem is much more open, at least so far.)

Apple's secretive ways have even led it to attack journalism itself. In 2004 the company tried to force several websites to disclose their sources in their

Apple coverage; the case was a direct challenge to fundamental business journalism practices.[10] (Note: I played a small role in that case, filing declarations on behalf of the websites that said they were engaged in protected journalism.)

Like Apple, Amazon exerts deep control over its own electronic publishing empire. The Kindle ecosystem is enormous and dominant in the ebook marketplace. Amazon has literally deleted books from Kindle owners' devices—including the beyond-ironic case of removing copies of George Orwell's classic, *1984*—and while the company acknowledged a major mistake, it offered no explicit promise that this wouldn't happen again under different circumstances.[11]

The purchasers of devices like the iPad and Kindle rarely realize that they own only the hardware, that the software, including content, is licensed, not owned, by the buyer. Since these devices are connected to networks, the hardware sellers (and telecom carriers) become arbiters of what exists on the devices. Similarly, in Facebook and other online platforms, the content exists only as long as the owner of the platform allows it. In his book, *The Future of the Internet and How to Stop It*, Jonathan Zittrain warned that walled gardens and restricted platforms threaten our freedom to use the devices we buy in the ways we, not the sellers, prefer.

Still another kind of platform journalists don't control is a financial one: the major payment systems. In December 2010, Mastercard, Visa and PayPal summarily cut off service to WikiLeaks, putting the controversial whistle-blowing site into deep financial trouble and further marginalizing an organization that had become an object of fear and loathing. While many in the new media world sounded an alarm, the response of journalists from legacy news organizations was mostly silence except to take note of what had happened. By ignoring the implications of what had happened—a financial blockade of an organization engaged in recognizably journalistic pursuits—traditional media people demonstrated a frightening disregard for their own futures. If this could happen to WikiLeaks, it could happen to them.

GOVERNMENT INVOLVEMENT IN INTERNET OVERSIGHT

Owning an Internet domain may not even be sufficient if the entertainment industry decides that a journalist's work is in some way contributing to copyright infringement. Working with the government, the movie and music companies have done everything they can to lock down the Internet. They haven't succeeded, but they are not giving up on this goal.

Hollywood and its allies have some rational worries, in particular the possibility that file-sharing sites beyond the reach of the law will destroy their businesses by making unstoppable infringement the rule rather than the exception. But it's worth noting that the major film studios have a longstanding loathing of technology they can't control—at least until it makes them money, as with videotape, once Hollywood's top object of paranoia.

In the Internet era, copyright holders have persuaded Congress to write increasingly restrictive laws designed to prevent infringement—but with dramatic side effects. You are not legally allowed to back up the DVD you purchased, for example, nor can you quote from it by "ripping" a small segment to another file. The copyright lobby failed to pull off its most brazen attempted coup early in 2012, when Internet users and companies rose up against the House of Representatives' Stop Online Piracy Act and companion Senate legislation.[12] These laws would have created outright Internet censorship in some cases, and a long-range effect, venture capitalists warned, would have been to slow innovation in any area where the entertainment industry felt threatened. These issues have received scant coverage from the major television news channels and networks, whose corporate parents have huge entertainment interests and have overwhelmingly supported harsh copyright laws.

Hollywood has persuaded President Barack Obama's administration on a number of occasions to use existing law against services it deems to be infringing. In a case that journalists covered, the administration confiscated the domain name of hip-hop website dajaz1.com in November 2010 and then stonewalled requests for information and redress, the site's attorney told reporters. Not until a year later did the government return the domain name, with no serious explanation and at best a minimal expression of regret for an act of outright censorship. It's difficult to imagine the American government taking a newspaper's website offline or preventing it from delivering its print copies; yet something like that happened in this case.[13] (Disclosure: The First Amendment Coalition, a nonprofit organization of which I am a member of the board, took an interest in this case.)

Government censorship itself is easier in the online world. With just a few phone calls to the key players in the Internet and mobile markets, Egypt's government essentially shut down online and mobile communications during the 2011 uprising. The ability to create Internet "kill switches" is no longer a theoretical concern.[14]

The Arab Spring—and anti-leak prosecutions in the United States—has also highlighted the dangers to journalists of using the Internet and some of the key platforms. Governments are getting increasingly sophisticated in their spying on dissidents and criminal suspects; journalists are easily caught up in surveillance even when they aren't the actual targets. Unfortunately, journalists are often technically unsophisticated, although the profession is starting to take this more seriously.

Plan B: Creating Options

The threats journalists face today may be varied and daunting, but we can make choices that minimize the risks or provide a way around the centralized control systems. Boiled down to essentials, this means having a Plan B for just about everything we do digitally.

News organizations' own websites are just that: their own, controlled by them and not subject—barring the ISPs' decision to interfere with content—to the whims of online app markets and stores. So it becomes essential, for example, to create a mobile service that doesn't require app approval. Similarly, journalists in nations that censor the Internet sometimes publish on servers located in other countries.

A nonprofit called the Freedom of the Press Foundation launched in December 2012 to help threatened journalism organizations, including WikiLeaks, by accepting donations and disbursing the funds to the organizations. In its first two weeks, the foundation raised more than $100,000. Whether the payment systems would target this entity remained to be seen. (Disclosure: I offered advice to the group before its launch and am a firm supporter.)

To avoid being spied on and inadvertently unmasking confidential sources, journalists are increasingly learning new kinds of tradecraft, including encryption. These new skills are no longer just a good idea, as the Committee to Protect Journalists and others have observed; in many parts of the world, they are becoming essential.[15]

But Plan B can get us only so far in the face of overwhelming power and control by centralized forces. For their own sake and for the public's, journalists will need to become more aware of threats to free speech and more active in protecting against those threats.

The promise of the Internet was profound: a radically decentralized, democratized medium where anyone could publish and anyone could be heard. But recentralization has become the trend of the new decade. This may simply be the nature of modern capitalism and government, which tend to accrete power when given the opportunity, but whatever the cause, the challenges are getting more powerful every day. Journalists are at long last starting to take note—and we can only hope it's not too late.

Editors' Note: Portions of this essay first appeared at the Nieman Journalism Lab *and in the* Columbia Journalism Review.

NOTES

1. Laura McGann, "Mark Fiore Can Win a Pulitzer Prize, but He Can't Get His iPhone Cartoon App Past Apple's Satire Police," *Nieman Journalism Lab,* April 15, 2010, http://www.niemanlab.org/2010/04/mark-fiore-can-win-a-pulitzer-prize-but-he-cant-get-his-iphone-cartoon-app-past-apples-satire-police/.

2. "LinkTV World News," *Twitter,* November 1, 2012, https://twitter.com/linktvnews/status/264067349299220480.

3. *Susan Crawford,* "Merger Made Comcast Strong, U.S. Web Users Weak," *Bloomberg,* December 25, 2012, http://www.bloomberg.com/news/2012-12-25/merger-made-comcast-strong-u-s-web-users-weak.html.

4. Ed Zitron, "Pando Networks Releases Global Internet Speed Study," *Pando Networks,* September 22, 2012, http://www.pandonetworks.com/company/news/pando-networks-releases-global-internet-speed-study.

5.   Dean Takahashi, "Who Will Pick Up Paying Customer That Comcast Dropped Because of High Data Usage?" *VentureBeat News,* July 29, 2011, http://venturebeat.com/2011/07/29/who-will-pick-up-paying-customer-that-comcast-dropped-because-of-high-data-usage/.

6.   Timothy B. Lee, "Verizon Called Hypocritical for Equating Net Neutrality to Censorship," *arstechnica,* November 16, 2012, http://arstechnica.com/tech-policy/2012/11/verizon-called-hypocritical-for-equating-net-neutrality-to-censorship/.

7.   Dan Gillmor, "Twitter's Guy Adams Ban: Is It Time for Users to Find a New Platform?" *The Guardian,* August 1, 2012, http://www.guardian.co.uk/commentisfree/2012/aug/01/twitter-guy-adams-new-platform.

8.   Ryan Singel, "Apple App Store Bans Pulitzer-Winning Satirist for Satire," *Wired,* April 15, 2010, http://www.wired.com/business/2010/04/apple-bans-satire/.

9.   Spencer Ackerman and Christina Bonnington, "Apple Rejects App That Tracks U.S. Drone Strikes," *Wired,* August 30, 2012, http://www.wired.com/dangerroom/2012/08/drone-app/.

10.   "Apple v. Does," *Electronic Frontier Foundation.* https://www.eff.org/cases/apple-v-does.

11.   Brad Stone, "Amazon Erases Orwell Books from Kindle," *The New York Times,* July 17, 2009, http://www.nytimes.com/2009/07/18/technology/companies/18amazon.html?_r=1&.

12.   Larry Magid, "What Are SOPA and PIPA and Why All the Fuss?" *Forbes,* January 18, 2012, http://www.forbes.com/sites/larrymagid/2012/01/18/what-are-sopa-and-pipa-and-why-all-the-fuss/.

13.   Timothy B. Lee, "ICE Admits Year-Long Seizure of Music Blog Was a Mistake," *arstechnica,* December 8, 2011, http://arstechnica.com/tech-policy/2011/12/ice-admits-months-long-seizure-of-music-blog-was-a-mistake/.

14.   Matt Richtel, "Egypt Cuts Off Most Internet and Cell Service," *The New York Times,* January 28, 2011, http://www.nytimes.com/2011/01/29/technology/internet/29cutoff.html.

15.   Frank Smyth and Danny O'Brien, "Journalist Security Guide," *Committee to Protect Journalists,* https://www.cpj.org/reports/2012/04/journalist-security-guide.php.

Caitlin Johnston

Dan Gillmor argues that as journalism moves onto a variety of third-party plat-forms, like Apple's iTunes store or Facebook, journalists are likely to face hurdles in delivering information to the public. Those hurdles have the potential to threaten free speech and the democratic marketplace of ideas.

Josh Begley designed his Drones+ app to send iPhone users a push notification every time there was a U.S. drone strike anywhere in the world. But in 2012, Apple banned the Drones+ app from the iTunes store, claiming "excessively objectionable or crude content," Begley told NPR.[1]

Begley found that hard to understand, considering the app worked as an aggregator, republishing information that was publicly available else-where. Drones+ relied on reports gathered by the London-based Bureau of Investigative Journalism, which tracked the use of unmanned CIA aircrafts, to send updates to the user's iPhone every time a strike occurred.[2] The app did not include graphic images of the attacks. Each update included relevant information about where and when the strike happened, the intended target, how many people died and how many were civilians.

It's easy to imagine an enterprising news organization trying to show some-thing similar on its website if it had the right resources. In fact, that's exactly what *The Guardian* did when it ran an interactive map in August 2012 plotting drone strikes in Pakistan. The map plotted more than 330 strikes with as many 3,247 casualties, including up to 852 civilians. It allowed users to click on indi-vidual strikes for more information, in the same way the app had done. And it was based on information from the London-based Bureau of Investigative Journalism, the same source as Drones+.[3]

The interactive map was featured on *The Guardian's* website and included in its iPhone app. Which means that while Apple allowed *The Guardian* to include the map in its app, it banned the exact same information from standing on its own in Begley's app.

Although organizations like Apple regularly partner with news media to disseminate information, that doesn't mean they agree with the journalistic val-ues that drive news production. As a private company, Apple has the right to sell (or not) whatever it wants. It has blocked porn and hate speech. It banned apps that take stances on gay marriage and another created by a Pulitzer Prize–winning cartoonist (although it reversed that decision).[4]

The media—the previous gatekeeper of information—now has a gate-keeper of its own. And as Begley learned, it doesn't have to give a clear answer as to why it lets some information through and not others. When Begley, at the time a graduate student at New York University, first submitted Drones+ to Apple, he was told that the app was "not useful" enough and didn't appeal to a "broad enough audience." Another rejection email told Begley that the app contained "content that many audiences would find objectionable, which is not in compliance with the app store review guidelines."

Apple has denied Drones+ three different times, effectively closing off an entire market to Begley and this information.[5] Apps rejected by Apple still have other options, such as the Android market, but Apple's refusal to sanction an app means that all iPhone, iPod and iPad users cannot get to the information through their devices.

QUESTIONS

• Apple allowed *The Guardian* to include the map of drone strikes in its app but banned Drones+, an app based solely on that information. What is the difference between a well-known, reputable news organization disseminating controversial material and a graduate student doing the same?

• What does Apple claim as its core values? How do those values compare to the values of journalism? To whom is Apple accountable, and how does this affect the work that it does?

• Should news organizations exert pressure on Apple to allow apps that exhibit a journalistic purpose?

• Do the media have a responsibility to act as an advocate for all disseminators of information, such as Josh Begley, or just established news outlets?

• Gillmor argues that journalists need a Plan B, when private organizations legally interfere with the dissemination of news. What's a logical Plan B for the Drone+ app?

CASE NOTES

1. Steve Henn, "Drone-Tracking App Gets No Traction from Apple," *NPR*, August 30, 2012, https://www.cpj.org/reports/2012/04/journalist-security-guide.php.
2. Jake Heller, "Josh Begley Tweets Entire History of U.S. Drone Attacks," *The Daily Beast*, December 11, 2012, http://www.thedailybeast.com/articles/2012/12/11/josh-begley-tweets -entire-history-of-u-s-drone-attacks.html.
3. Simon Rogers, "Drone Attacks in Pakistan Mapped," *The Guardian*, August 2, 2012, http:// www.guardian.co.uk/news/datablog/interactive/2012/aug/02/drone-attacks-pakistan-map.
4. Ki Mae Heussner, "'Anti-Gay' iPhone App Pulled from Apple Store," *abcNEWS*, November 30, 2010, http://abcnews.go.com/Technology/anti-gay-iphone-app-pulled-apple-store/ story?id=12274937#.UOxQPKzNnTo.
5. Spencer Ackerman and Christina Bonnington, "Apple Rejects App That Tracks U.S. Drone Strikes," *Wired*, August 30, 2012, http://www.wired.com/dangerroom/2012/08/drone-app/.

Networked Audiences

Attention and Data-Informed Journalism

Gilad Lotan

W hether you're an individual or organization, professional or amateur, social media provide an invaluable way to build an audience and to seek and disseminate information. Social network sites create compelling spaces where users are encouraged to respond, share and pass bits of information onward whenever it is most entertaining, insightful or relevant. These interactions generate a plethora of data, digital breadcrumbs left from people's searches, as well as likes, comments, thoughts and reactions.

While social media allow citizens to communicate directly with each other, media outlets and journalists have also capitalized on this data, integrating user-generated content into live streams and reporting. Some claim that amplifying user-generated content lessens the quality of publications, and many worry about the less rigorous fact-checking and source validation processes, which often happen only virtually and after the fact. Some question the credibility of media outlets in light of this type of behavior. Others question their bias.

The promise of data-driven journalism brings with it hopes of a more representative and unbiased media. In a perfect world, social networks would fully represent society, giving reporters the ability to easily plug into a wide array of on-the-ground local perspectives in response to events around the world. The true voices of people in the streets could be sourced and amplified as a part of the coverage curated by media outlets and journalists. Important information would spread in a hybrid manner, leveraging both the massive audiences who follow mainstream media and journalists but also taking advantage of the dynamically evolving networks formed amongst people. In this world, important information would come to light either via media entities or through citizens. The network would serve as a form of checks and balances, keeping those with disproportionate levels of power at bay.

But in reality, things are much more complicated.

The shift to a networked medium brings with it significant changes to our media ecosystem that we must take into account. We are no longer in a world where publishing content to an audience requires special connections or hefty resources. Anyone with an Internet-enabled device can easily upload a piece of media to the Web. The true bottleneck is no longer what gets published but rather what gets attention. In a networked media environment, neither the news media nor individual producers can effortlessly command attention. Nor can they determine when someone will notice their content. Authority is no longer institutional. Information spreads through friends, fans and followers. In order for a message to resonate, users along the way must be attentive at the right time and also must decide to pass it onward.

Data spread at an unpredictable speed within social network spaces, and most are seen only by a small number of people. To maximize the effectiveness of published content, journalists need to understand the networked nature of audiences: how fans and followers are interconnected, and how/what information tends to spread among them. The ability to attract attention is true power, and in this 140-character media ecosystem, understanding how people manage their attention is incredibly powerful.

This is not a new phenomenon. In the old system of exclusively industrial media, institutions were still competing for audience attention. CBS competed for viewers with ABC. Newspapers competed with television. To a large degree, however, the shifts in audiences were gradual. Media habits were ingrained, and the calculations about what might interest audiences were loosely based on ratings, circulation figures and focus group research. Today, as media compete with so many other options for attention, those calculations are much more sophisticated, and the civic implications as a result are arguably more important.

Mining data from social network spaces helps us gain insight into our audiences. This data can help us understand when people are active, and what topics users are coalescing around. In the same way that looking left and right before crossing the street helps us make a more informed decision, having a data-driven view of what conversations are taking place can help us better engage with our audience. Entities that once easily commanded an audience need to leverage data-driven methods to gain a better understanding of the topical and attention landscape. They must meet the challenge that those engaged in news have always contended with, trying to balance what will interest people with what editors consider important.

The proliferation of data also brings with it many challenges for both reporting and consuming information. Social networks themselves are biased by their constituents, which never exactly mirror the population at large.

Certain ethnicities are overrepresented, a significant challenge to social news as an equalizer. In addition, a growing number of algorithms make automated decisions on which content to recommend for people to read. Algorithms are generating top-news lists or hot trends and personalizing recommendations for readers. Algorithms leave the impression of being neutral, yet they are not. Algorithms are human creations. They encode political choices of their designers and have cultural values baked in. As curatorial power is enhanced by automated systems, we should understand the biases at play. Perhaps more important, we should work to make sure product engineers and designers are seeking to optimize the wanted outcome—an informed public—not just heightened traffic.

In the following section, three case studies are presented, each with a different take on how we can draw insight from data. The first highlights an incredibly fast information flow that took place right before President Barack Obama announced in May of 2011 that Osama bin Laden had been killed. The second discusses the implication of algorithmic curation on Twitter's trending topics list at the height of the Occupy Wall Street movement. And the third dissects the power of the network behind the spread of the Invisible Children's Kony 2012 campaign.

HOW NEWS OF OSAMA BIN LADEN'S DEATH SPREAD SOCIALLY

A full hour before the formal announcement of bin Laden's death, Keith Urbahn speculated on Twitter about the suddenly scheduled presidential address. Little did he know that his tweet would trigger an avalanche of reactions, retweets and conversations that would beat mainstream media as well as the White House announcement. Urbahn, chief of staff at the office of former Defense Secretary Donald Rumsfeld, wasn't the first to speculate about bin Laden's death, but he was the one who gained the most trust on Twitter. How did this happen?

Before May 1, not even the smartest of machine learning algorithms could have predicted Urbahn's potential to spark an incredibly viral information flow. While politicos "in the know" certainly knew him or knew of him, his previous interactions and the size and nature of his social graph did little to reflect his potential to generate trust from thousands of people within a matter of minutes.

On the evening of May 1, 2011, users on Twitter figured out that Osama bin Laden had been killed over an hour before the formal White House announcement. Within minutes of hearing about the presidential address, people were tweeting to figure out what it was about. Thirty-eight minutes after the announcement about Obama's address, a certain tweet confirming speculations posted by @keithurbahn started spreading like wildfire. Urbahn did not have a particularly influential presence on Twitter, with a following of 1,016.[1] But the right network effects came into play and enabled his post to generate enough trust among his followers, their followers and so on.

My colleagues and I at SocialFlow, a company that optimizes content for social media accounts, analyzed 14.8 million public tweets posted between 9:46 p.m. EST, the time at which an unplanned presidential address was announced, and 11:30 p.m. EST, when President Obama addressed the country. Figure 7.1 is a logarithmic, minute-to-minute detailed comparison of how frequently tweets were sent about bin Laden and Gaddafi (the two biggest topics of speculation) during the three-hour window. Before the announcement about an address, the terms were equally used on the network. However, as speculation about a connection to bin Laden strengthened, we see a clear rise in people's discussions and reposting of content about him. This spike occurs at just about the same time that Urbahn posted his valuable piece of information:

FIGURE 7-1   **In this chart, you can see that Twitter users were speculating evenly on whether the pending presidential announcement would involve Gaddafi or bin Laden, until 10:24 p.m., when a specific tweet changed the dynamic.**

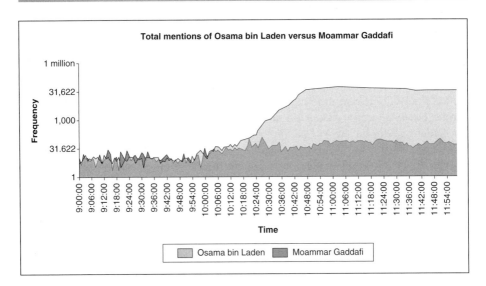

At 10:24 p.m. EST, Urbahn posted the following tweet (Figure 7-2), stating that a source he trusts claims bin Laden was killed.

The rate at which Urbahn's message spread was staggering. Within a minute, more than 80 people had reposted the message, including *The*

FIGURE 7-2

New York Times reporter Brian Stelter. Within two minutes, more than 300 reactions to the original post were spreading through the network. These numbers represent the people who either retweeted Urbahn's original message or posted a reaction to it. The actual number of impressions (people who saw Urbahn's message in their stream but didn't repost it) is substantially higher.

Here are two tweets posted by Jake Sherman and Brian Stelter, adding context to Urbahn's initial tweet:

- @JakeSherman: Rumsfeld chief, @keithurbahn, says he's told bin laden is dead. (10:24 p.m. EST)
- @brianstelter: Chief of staff for former defense sec. Rumsfeld, @keithurbahn, tweets: "I'm told by a reputable person they have killed Osama Bin Laden." (10:25 p.m. EST)

Both Sherman and Stelter vouched for Urbahn, adding their support and highlighting his connection to Rumsfeld. The network graphs in Figure 7.3 illustrate Twitter users who were critical in spreading Urbahn's post onto their networks. Stelter, who had over 50,000 followers at the time, yielded hundreds of retweets, furthering the spread of this message:

Authority, trust and persuasiveness play an important role in influencing others, but they are only part of a complex set of dynamics that affect people's perception. Connections are another important factor, along

FIGURE 7-3 **Keith Urbahn's tweet attributing bin Laden's death to a source was widely retweeted.**

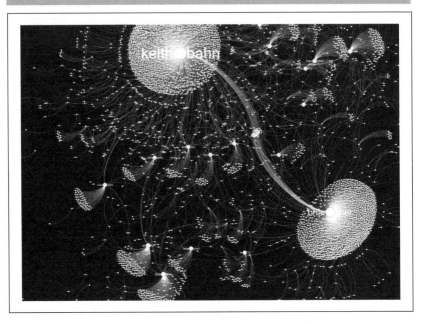

with timing and a dash of pure luck. But as humans, we are still incredibly irrational, tending to make decisions based on our intuition or our changing sentiment.

As we build out digital social spaces, we must remember that just because we have easily accessible data at our fingertips doesn't mean that we have the capacity to model and place a price tag on human behavior. Followers, friends or likes represent an aspect of our digital status, but they are only a partial representation of our general propensity to be influential. Urbahn wasn't the first to speculate about bin Laden's death, but he was the one who gained the most trust from the network. And with that, the perfect situation unfolded, where timing and the right social-professional networked audience, along with a critically relevant piece of information, led to an explosion of public affirmation of his trustworthiness.

ALGORITHMIC CURATION AND OCCUPY WALL STREET

An algorithm is a finite list of instructions that a machine performs in order to calculate a function. From simple counting operations to complex information sorting, a good algorithm is thought through and well defined to give the desired output in the least computationally complex manner. Algorithms are extremely good at scale. They can be used to efficiently classify text from millions of documents within microseconds, extract images of a certain type and identify complex correlations between multiple data points. Recommendation systems such as the ones used by Netflix and Amazon employ algorithms that learn about users' preferences through their actions, and personalize the information presented for every user, a task impossible to complete manually.

Algorithmically curated, personalized recommendations have become increasingly popular within digital media spaces. "Most-read articles" modules are based on simple math: the top 10 articles in terms of pageviews. On the other hand, "hottest articles" lists are more ambiguous and vary based on what the organization defines as "hot." Is it new content? Is it popular? Spiking? How far back is the data being compared? Are there white-listed or black-listed topics? What's hot is an intuitive and very human assessment of an ecosystem, yet a mathematically complex formula, if at all possible to reproduce.

Humans are still unbeatable for many types of tasks. Journalists and editors drive agendas, made up of qualities that are difficult to determine in a formula: trust, excitement, impression and intuition. Humans aren't always rational, and they may trust a source despite a bad reputation. The intuition that an experienced editor or journalist brings to the table cannot be replaced by automated formulas. The following case study highlights some of the unintended consequences of such automated systems.

Whether you're an activist, event organizer or marketer, trending topics bring tremendous visibility to the message that's being sent out. On Twitter, trending topics have become something of a status symbol: a signal of success for a cause, conference or newsworthy event. The list is controlled by an algorithm that publishes a constantly updating stream of phrases or hashtags across locations chosen by Twitter.

The precise algorithm for determining what topic is trending at any given point in time is private, but the basic thrust is that it's not exclusively about volume. If it were, Justin Bieber would be forever trending. The algorithm adapts over time, based on the changing velocity of the usage of terms in tweets. If we see a systematic rise in volume, but no clear spike, it is possible that the topic will never trend, as the algorithm takes into account historical appearances of the observed phrase (TFIDF: Term Frequency Inverse Document Frequency). The implications are clear:

1. The longer a term stays in the trending topic list, the higher the velocity required to keep it there.
2. It is much easier for a term never seen before to become a Twitter trend.
3. It is extremely important to understand what else is happening in the region or network (if Kim Kardashian's show is airing, you can forget about trending!).

As the Occupy Wall Street movement gained momentum in terms of visibility, media coverage and number of participants throughout the fall months of 2011, it had a difficult time "occupying" Twitter's Trending Topics list. #OccupyWallStreet, the movement's dominant hashtag, never once hit New York City's trending topics list. Some blamed Twitter for censoring content from the list. In fact, the reasons the hashtag never became a trend were purely algorithmic.

FIGURE 7-4

George Reese
@GeorgeReese

👤▾   🐦 Follow

Interesting. #takewallstreet is trending. #occupywallstreet is not. Pretty strong evidence of censoring.

↩ Reply   🔁 Retweet   ⭐ Favorite

8
RETWEETS

1
FAVORITE

10:54 PM - 17 Sep 11 · Embed this Tweet

The plot in Figure 7.5 shows the number of tweets per hour that included one of six chosen hashtags since September 15, 2011 (the start of the physical manifestation of the movement). We see the diurnal patterns of tweets including the #OccupyWallStreet hashtag consistently appearing since the initial Wall Street occupation. All other hashtags in the plot had appeared on New York City's trending topics list at some point during the observed time period. Note that all other hashtags had clear spikes along with a very fast decline.

Even though a significant number of people were posting about the Occupy movement, this plot makes it crystal clear that other events easily took precedence. We see unquestionable differences in velocity between the consistent, slowly accelerating #OccupyWallStreet curve and the other hashtags that draw more than four times the participation at their peak. When we look at sheer numbers of participants in hashtags, such as #WhatYouShouldKnowAboutMe

FIGURE 7-5   **When we compared different trending hashtags, from New York City with #OccupyWallStreet, we discovered that they all had a similar shape - a rapid period of sharp acceleration, hinting at the embedded bias within Twitter's trending topics algorithm.**

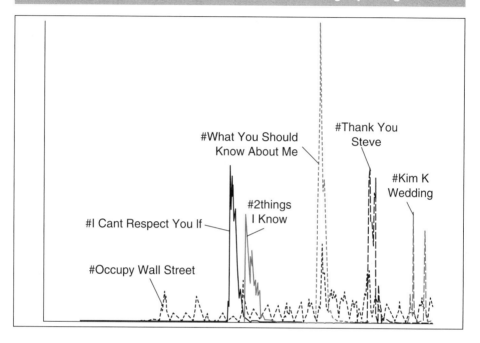

or #ICantRespectYouIf—both of which trended in New York City—it is clear that they're extremely difficult to compete with.

When analyzing why a topic did or did not trend, it is important to understand what it's competing against. An intuitive example: It is much harder to make a topic trend during the day than at night in major U.S. cities.

In this day and age, when the slightest algorithmic tweak can shift the scale of attention given to one topic over another, how transparent should we expect services like Twitter to be with regards to the way they calculate, adapt and manage what bubbles up to the top? Should we be instituting algorithmic regulation? Perhaps it's time that companies exposed information about their ranking algorithms, striking a fine balance between exposing just enough information to enable users to make smarter decisions. Or perhaps we should be thinking more deeply about the relationship between editorialized and algorithmically generated content? *Techmeme* and *Mediagazer* use a hybrid approach. What would it mean for trending topics to be part algorithmic, part editorialized?

ALGORITHMIC BIAS VERSUS PERCEPTION OF NEUTRALITY

As soon as digital information providers add any form of curation and recommendation mechanisms (a common practice within social network spaces), the technology loses its neutrality. In some ways, "Twitter's trending topics algorithm acts like a lot of human news editors, who are more interested in the latest news rather than ongoing stories," says Tarleton Gillespie of Cornell University.[2] Values are coded into recommendation systems such as Twitter's trending topics and Google search, which constantly tweak their algorithms, most recently to promote newer content. As these recommendation systems grow, a single engineer or product designer may not fully understand the logic behind all of the pieces that make up the whole.

A number of examples have already surfaced, where unintended consequences of algorithmically generated results led to awkward outcomes, such as Amazon's $23,698,655.93 book about flies, the result of algorithmic pricing used by vendors to ensure that their product prices change based on a competitor.[3] In this case, the two booksellers who used algorithmic pricing to ensure that they were generating marginally more revenue than their main competitor ended up pushing the price of a book on evolutionary biology to $23.6 million.

Remember Siri's inability to find abortion clinics in New York City?[4] The fact that Siri, Apple iOS's "intelligent personal assistant," couldn't find abortion clinics in New York City is not because Apple is pro-life. Many abortion clinics don't necessarily use the word *abortion* in their description, hence the search algorithm powering Siri's results couldn't match these answers. Siri's designers didn't test to make sure there were proper results, even though mundane questions such as where to bury a body had answers—dumps, swamps. This alludes to an innate bias, built into Siri's mechanism, defined by what its designers and engineers deemed important or funny.

Another example where algorithms have unintended consequences is search engine optimization, the process of affecting a website's visibility so that it appears more frequently in search results. Search engine optimization has become somewhat of a science, where people game the system by placing parameters that the search-ranking algorithm looks for, increasing the score of their website and raising the likelihood that it will appear higher on the search results page. Whenever changes to the search algorithm are made, it affects millions of businesses that make a living due to traffic coming in from search.[5]

These are not Google, Apple, Amazon or Twitter conspiracies, but rather the unexpected consequences of algorithmic recommendations being misaligned with people's value systems and expectations of how the technology should work. The larger the gap between people's expectations and the algorithmic output, the more user trust will be violated.

Blogger Liz Strauss eloquently describes why she quit Klout, feeling cheated by an algorithm that constantly changes under her feet.[6] Klout tries to measure a user's influence across his or her social networks by giving them a score. The score changes based on Klout's algorithm, which has also changed multiple times over the past two years. Strauss wanted to trust the algorithm, even though she initially doubted it, but she broke down and quit after multiple algorithm changes, because scores changed abruptly with little to no information from the company itself.

Designers and builders of these technologies need to strike a fine balance between making sure users understand enough about the choices encoded into their algorithms, but not too much to enable them to game the system. People's perceptions affect trust. And once trust is violated, it is incredibly difficult to gain back. There's a misplaced faith in the algorithm, an assumption that algorithms accurately represent objective truth.

THE SPREAD OF KONY 2012

The networked nature of social media gives it unique properties, where some pieces of media spread at phenomenal rates and others die quickly. At times, a joke made locally in one region of the network may spiral out of control and jump to another section of the network, where it will completely lose its context and possibly even offend readers. A good example of context collapse is a sarcastic joke told by a 19-year-old Muslim student in the United Kingdom, who created the hashtag #BlameTheMuslims, aggravated at how Muslims were immediately accused for causing the 2011 Norway attacks that killed 77 people.[7] This meme quickly spread worldwide, drawing harsh criticism from users around the world, who didn't necessarily understand the initial sarcastic undertone of its creator.

By analyzing network structure we can get a better understanding of how certain pieces of content are likely to spread. There's evidence that dense clusters of users generate a fertile environment for certain types of information to spread. The following case study details one of the most viral information flows we've ever witnessed. Our findings highlight the way in which Invisible Children activated a pre-existing community of users who were already affiliated with the organization.

If you spent any time at all on Twitter or Facebook in March of 2012, you undoubtedly heard about Kony 2012. The campaign by the nonprofit advocacy group, Invisible Children, centered around Joseph Kony, the Ugandan warlord and leader of the Lord's Resistance Army, a guerrilla group with a long and violent history that includes the kidnapping of children. With striking dramatic imagery and Hollywood-style editing, the campaign video presents an utterly compelling message for the age of social media: By simply clicking "share," the viewer can make a difference in the world.

And "share" the world did. The video racked up more than 100 million views on YouTube within six days (Susan Boyle, the woman who sang "I Dreamed a Dream" on *Britain's Got Talent,* had 100 million views in nine days, and Lady Gaga in 18 days). The campaign's seemingly overnight success brought with it a wave of criticism.[8] We were curious about the volume and spread of the message from a data perspective. How and why did the message spread so fast? Was it truly out of nowhere?

In looking at the data, we detected that a pre-existing networked infrastructure was already in place, triggered at the start of the campaign. Invisible Children had already been building an on-the-ground network of young supporters across the United States, activating them all at the same time, as the campaign began. The data makes this clear.

Figure 7.6 represents the initial 5,000 users who posted to the #Kony2012 hashtag. Each node represents a Twitter user, while the edges represent their connections, effectively who follows whom. The darker a node, the earlier it participated in using the hashtag. The graph is organized using the OpenOrd layout algorithm, which places highly connected users in close proximity, identifying major clusters within the graph.

The data reinforces what we suspected about the organization. Its formal profile (@invisible) is central to its activity, also represented in the graph. In the top center are Invisible Children founder Jason Russell (@JasonRussell) and other employees of the organization. Also present is actress Kristen Bell (@IMKristenBell), who was very involved with the organization early on. The most interesting aspects of this graph are the other clusters that appear. These are highly connected groups of users who were posting to the cause from the beginning.

Looking more closely at the profiles that comprise the clusters, some fascinating characteristics emerge. Each cluster represents users from different

FIGURE 7-6 **Tweets about Kony 2012 originated in a few key locations, suggesting an organized campaign, as opposed to a spontaneous trend.**

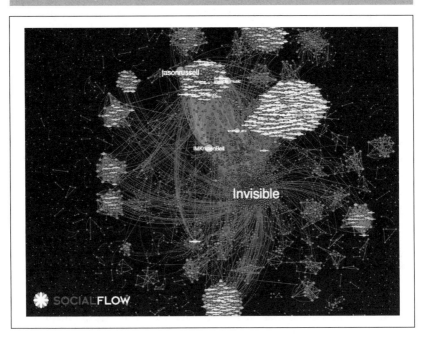

locations. The large cluster on the top right includes users from Birmingham, Alabama, who were some of the earliest to publicize the video. The cluster is substantially larger than the others, leading us to believe that Invisible Children had strong roots in Alabama. In addition, the hashtag #Kony2012 initially trended in Birmingham on March 1, a few days before the video was even published online. Other clusters in the graph include Pittsburgh; Oklahoma City; and Noblesville, Indiana (see Figure 7.7).

This movement emerged not from the big cities, but rather from small- to medium-size cities across the Unites States. It is heavily supported by Christian youth, many of whom post biblical psalms as their profile bios. When looking at their user bios, we identified commonly used words such as: *Jesus, God, Christ, University* and *Student*.

Contrary to the way the media portrayed the spread of this video, it didn't just come out of nowhere. Invisible Children had been carefully planning the campaign, traveling to various schools across the United States, gathering supporters. The launch of the video was also carefully planned, so that all affiliated youth shared the video on exactly the same day. Different parts of the network lit up at exactly the same time, making it easier for the content to trend and thus gain much higher visibility.

FIGURE 7-7   **The tweets that first mentioned Kony2012 were concentrated in a few geographic locations, first in Birmingham, Ala.**

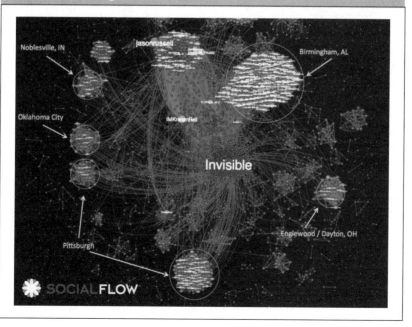

UNDERSTANDING NETWORK PATHWAYS IS POWER

The Internet democratizes publishing. Anyone with a message and limited access to the Web can easily publish content to a publicly accessible page. Social networked spaces bring the promise of mass distribution, yet as we've seen with the case studies above, their networked nature complicates matters.

Social networks tend to be highly interconnected; groups of friends connect to other groups through a web of shared relationships. Facebook flaunts that, on average, there are four degrees of separation across its one billion user base. Yet the fact that we're all interconnected doesn't mean that information will necessarily spread. The distance between people may seem short, but finding the right route for a message to be passed along is contingent on a wide array of variables. Be it timing, topic, network structure, trust, authority, algorithmic recommendation or pure luck, social networks offer the promise of going viral, yet the majority of messages die very fast. As James Gleick notes: "When information is cheap, attention becomes expensive."[9]

In our networked information landscape, understanding what people are willing to be attentive to and the pathways that information spreads is true power.

Networked actors such as journalists and media outlets may hold this power to decide what message to amplify and spread. But in many cases, such as Keith Urbahn's Osama bin Laden tweet, an important message has the capacity to reach a massive audience even when its source has a limited following. A combination of the right message, the right time, an eager audience and a powerful network may accelerate the spread of information. As we saw in the case of Kony 2012, the pre-existing networked structure held the power to seed a message across the board, giving it extraordinary velocity in sharing and thus visibility. By manipulating the networked nature of social sharing, Invisible Children orchestrated a campaign that reached levels of visibility we'd never previously seen.

Finally, the onslaught of information brings the need for automated filtering mechanisms. It is common for algorithms to decide what content people are following. From hot lists to personal recommendations, algorithmic curation and filtering helps us all deal with massive amounts of data. But this comes with a consequence. As seen in the Occupy Wall Street trending topics case, there's an innate bias to algorithmic systems, many times promoting the novel and "spiky" content over any slow-growing trend. Journalists must come up with the right vocabulary to define algorithmic attributes, and work with engineers, product designers and news editors to identify their biases and limitations.

The job of a journalist and editor is to maintain an informed public. Can we design and implement algorithms that optimize for an informed public, rather than pageviews and traffic? How do we even start to quantify a person's level of "informed-ness"? What is the right balance between automated news personalization and curated, editorialized feeds? What would the augmented journalist or editor look like? And how can technology and algorithms be used effectively in the newsroom to inform both journalists and the general public?

Contrary to common belief, social networks are not meritocratic. Networks are hierarchical, and certain positions hold power over others. In an age where our media ecosystem has become truly networked, we need to discern the consequences of this shift and use data-driven methods to inform our understanding of our audience.

NOTES

1. Keith Urbahn, Keith Urbahn Twitter Stats, http://twittercounter.com/compare/keithurbahn/month/followers.

2. Laura Sydell, "How Twitter's Trending Algorithm Picks Its Topics," *NPR*, December 7, 2011, http://www.npr.org/2011/12/07/143013503/how-twitters-trending-algorithm-picks-its-topics.

3. Michael Eisen, comment on "Amazon's $23,698,655.93 Book about Flies," April 22, 2011, http://www.michaeleisen.org/blog/?p=358.

4. Danny Sullivan, "Why Siri Can't Find Abortion Clinics, and How It's Not an Apple Conspiracy," December 1, 2011, http://searchengineland.com/why-siri-cant-find-abortion-clinics-103349.

5. Drew Hendricks, "Everything You Need to Know about the Latest Google Algorithm Update," October 18, 2012, http://www.examiner.com/article/everything-you-need-to-know-about-the-latest-google-algorithm-update.

6. Liz Strauss, "Klout, My Story, and Why Opting Out Was My Only Choice," *Successful Blog*, December 5, 2011, http://www.successful-blog.com/1/klout-my-story-why-opting-out-was-my-only-choice/.

7. Gilad Lotan, "United Kingdom: #BlameTheMuslims Twitter Hashtag Spins Out of Context," August 1, 2011, http://globalvoicesonline.org/2011/08/01/united-kingdom-blamethemuslims-twitter-hashtag-spins-out-of-context/.

8. Ethan Zuckerman, "Unpacking Kony 2012," March 8, 2012, http://www.ethanzuckerman.com/blog/2012/03/08/unpacking-kony-2012/.

9. James Glieck, "How Google Dominates Us," *The New York Review of Books*, August 18, 2011, http://www.nybooks.com/articles/archives/2011/aug/18/how-google-dominates-us/?page=2.

Caitlin Johnston

Gilad Lotan suggests that news is not only what gets published but what gets noticed. Yet some information gets a lot of attention because of a pre-existing network, not because the crowd suddenly embraces the content. That challenges journalists to develop expertise in audiences and how they connect on social media.

In the digital age, garnering 100 million views in six days is an impressive feat. When Invisible Children, a nonprofit advocacy group, achieved this in March 2012 with its Kony 2012 video, the social media community went wild. The Kony 2012 video campaign convinced journalists that its viral explosion was a matter of chance, a serendipitous event that occurred because thousands of people stumbled on the video and were all moved at the same time. The reality pointed to years of carefully planned marketing.

The campaign from Invisible Children centered around Joseph Kony. A Ugandan warlord, Kony was the leader of the Lord's Resistance Army, a guerrilla group with a long and violent history that includes the kidnapping and conversion of children into soldiers. But the video, with its dramatic imagery and high-end editing, compelled viewers to believe in the power of social media—to believe that if they shared it with enough people, they could make a difference.

News organizations jumped on the story, posting about the viral video and its inspiring take off. For instance, check out Michael Geheren's lede for a blog on *The Huffington Post* about the video's viral nature: "You always hear that change cannot happen overnight. One man by the name of Jason Russell proved that statement wrong."[1]

Despite what the headlines said, the Kony 2012 video was anything but a sudden sensation. "While the video was a huge catalyst, 'Kony 2012' was not an overnight success," StayClassy CEO Scott Chisholm told Pam Baker of TechNewsWorld.[2] "This success happened over five years, with the last two years spent making sure each campaign feeds the next."

So why not report on that aspect? Did journalists simply not know of the planned marketing behind the video? Or was it a choice to favor the romanticized narrative of people being so moved by these children's plight that they had to share it? Is there something less inspirational about watching years of hard work pay off as opposed to watching something explode out of nowhere?

"Personally, I have never seen an outpour of support from people on my Facebook news feed like this. Close friends, co-workers, and friends from across the globe all started posting it last night," Geheren wrote. "Maybe America will prove me wrong, but the viralness of the video is amazing. I don't think I have ever seen something spread so fast, with so many people bought into the cause."

But Geheren, like so many others, was misinformed. People all started posting the video that night because Invisible Children had, for years, been building a network of young supporters across the United States. After the group had cultivated enough of a base, it signaled to the supporters to start posting the video at the same time, triggering the campaign.

The initial movement was heavily supported by Christian youth clustered in Birmingham, Ala.; Noblesville, Ind.; and Oklahoma City. The campaign had traveled to schools in these cities and others gathering supporters. Because they were spread across the country, when the network lit up at the same time, it made it easier for the content to trend and gain higher visibility.

While mainstream media were swept up in the overnight success story frame, the tech industry caught on a little quicker. Baker of TechNewsWorld wrote a 1,700-word story explaining the actual nature of the video's success. "Before the video was made, thousands of young people were on standby, ready to click, like, retweet and otherwise promote it," Baker wrote. "And the website was designed to make sharing super easy for these kids. With such a pent-up groundswell behind it, 'Kony 2012' almost couldn't help but be an 'instant' success."

Shama Kabani, CEO of The Marketing Zen Group, said it took off "because it had all the elements of a great story—background on the founder, a plot, a resolution, a call to action." In an interview with TechNewsWorld, Kabani said: "It told a story which was compelling and impactful. Any nonprofit with a mission they believe in can do the same!"

It might not be a fairy tale narrative, but the reality of Kony's success was still a gripping one. It showed that high production values enhance credibility and that careful planning and professional marketing can be powerful. The truth may have been a more interesting story than the more mythical version of sudden viral notice. And yet in the days and months following its release, media outlets continued to cover the video as an instant, unplanned phenomenon.

"The group, Invisible Children, sprung to fame when its video Kony 2012 went viral with nearly 80 million people watching the 30-minute production," said a March 14 Associated Press story in *The Australian*.[3] "The overnight success earned the San Diego-based nonprofit organization widespread praise and heightened scrutiny."

"It's not exactly the typical formula for a viral video, but the film became the most viral video of all time," wrote Nick Carbone of *Time* in a roundup of 2012 viral videos, giving Kony 2012 the No. 1 spot.[4] "It's undeniable that *Kony 2012* set a new bar for all things viral."

Social media site Mashable wrote, in an article entitled "How Social Media Fueled the Most Viral Video of All Time," that the success of the video, according to research by the Pew Internet and American Life Project, was tied to shared links on Twitter and Facebook among 18- to 29-year-olds.[5] One of Pew's takeaways was the importance of social media for spreading news to young readers.

"No matter how you feel about the controversial documentary about Ugandan general Joseph Kony, you've got to admit its reach is remarkable," said Gizmodo.[6]

All of these articles focused on the instant success of the video, with little or no mention of the active marketing campaign that fueled that popularity.

QUESTIONS

- What is the news value of covering viral videos? What obligation do journalists have to understand the forces at play behind social media trends?

- What questions should a news organization ask itself when reporting on viral social media? Reporters are suspicious of press releases and positive angles. Should the same suspicion inform reporting on viral content? Does the arranged nature of the Kony video disqualify or diminish its significance?

- Does it matter whether a video or other piece of content goes viral spontaneously or because of a well-coordinated marketing campaign?

- Coordinated campaigns have always been used by activists to get the attention of society and journalists. Think of a march on Washington or a letter-writing effort. When does the success of the campaign itself become newsworthy?

CASE NOTES

1. Michael Geheren, "Kony 2012: Changing the World, One Tweet at a Time," *The Huffington Post*, March 7, 2012, http://www.huffingtonpost.com/michael-geheren/post_3074_b_1326942 .html.
2. Pam Baker, "How and Why Did 'Kony 2012' Go Viral Overnight?" *TechNewsWorld*, April 11, 2012, http://www.technewsworld.com/story/74835.html.
3. "Kony Video Activists Defend Their Expenses," *The Australian News*, March 14, 2012, http:// www.theaustralian.com.au/news/world/kony-video-activists-defend-their-expenses/story -e6frg6so-1226298612675.
4. Nick Carbone, "Kony 2012," *TIME Entertainment*, December 4, 2012, http://entertainment .time.com/2012/12/04/top-10-arts-lists/slide/kony-2012/#ixzz2F2mR8p2H.
5. Zoe Fox, "KONY 2012: How Social Media Fueled the Most Viral Video of All Time," *Mashable*, March 16, 2012, http://mashable.com/2012/03/16/kony-2012-pew-study/; Lee Rainie, Paul Hitlin, Mark Jurkowitz, Michael Dimock, and Shawn Neidorf, "The Viral Kony 2012 Video," Pew Internet, March 15, 2012, http://pewinternet.org/Reports/2012/Kony-2012-Video.aspx.
6. Mario Aguilar, "Kony 2012 Is the 'Most Viral' Video of All Time," *Gizmodo*, March 12, 2012, http://us.gizmodo.com/5892541/kony-2012-is-the-most-viral-video-of-all-time.

Centers of Investigative Reporting

New Model, Old Conflicts

Adam Hochberg

The downfall of North Carolina politician Stephen LaRoque followed a familiar trajectory.

LaRoque, a powerful Republican state legislator, found himself the target of an aggressive investigative reporter. In a series of stories, writer Sarah Ovaska raised questions about two charities LaRoque managed in his hometown. Ovaska's investigation concluded that the legislator accepted millions of dollars in federal loans, directed much of the money to his relatives and political associates and paid himself a generous salary.[1]

LaRoque denied the allegations and claimed to be the victim of "tabloid" journalism. But almost two years after the stories ran, a federal jury convicted him of fraud and other crimes,[2] determining that he used government money to buy cars, a house for his stepdaughter and Fabergé eggs for his wife. Court records suggest a grand jury issued subpoenas shortly after Ovaska published her findings. LaRoque resigned his legislative seat following his indictment.

Of course, LaRoque is hardly the first politician to be brought down by an intrepid investigative journalist, but his situation illustrates a relatively new trend. Ovaska doesn't work for a mainstream newspaper or broadcaster but rather for a liberal-leaning nonprofit organization known as N.C. Policy Watch, which publishes her work online.

As traditional news organizations scale back on investigative and in-depth reporting, N.C. Policy Watch is among dozens of nonprofits that increasingly are taking on that role. "We've seen such a decline in the number of media doing that kind of work," said Ovaska, who spent six years covering courts and government for the (Raleigh) *News & Observer*. She said she left the newspaper in 2010 because N.C. Policy Watch gave her the opportunity to do bigger stories. "I get to do the work that I thought I was going to be doing when I went to journalism school," Ovaska said.

Nonprofit investigative reporting isn't a totally new trend. Publications such as *Mother Jones* and *Consumer Reports* have been doing it for decades, as have some public broadcasters. But in recent years, the number of nonprofits that employ investigative journalists has mushroomed.

The groups defy easy description. Some primarily are advocacy organizations that use investigative journalism as a tool to promote philosophical agendas. Human Rights Watch and the Natural Resources Defense Council are among the better-known national and global groups that have incorporated journalism into their missions, while the trend is slowly growing among state and regional groups such as N.C. Policy Watch, the Institute for Southern Studies and a network of state capital reporting organizations affiliated with the Franklin Center for Government and Public Integrity.

More commonly, journalism nonprofits adopt an independent, nonpartisan, nonideological focus and are modeled after traditional media organizations' investigative units. Some of these investigative reporting centers are affiliated with universities, such as Columbia, Brandeis and the University of Wisconsin. Others are stand-alone operations. A few of the centers—like ProPublica and the Center for Public Integrity—have national influence and employ dozens of journalists. But a significant number are local one-person operations. Almost all depend on foundations and individual donors for financial support.

"These non-profits are an oasis in the desert of the current journalism scene," Chuck Lewis, who founded the Center for Public Integrity and now directs the American University Investigative Reporting Workshop, said in an interview. His 2010 report, "The New Journalism Ecosystem,"[3] identified more than 70 investigative reporting centers around the country, most of them formed in the past decade. At least a third of them have won awards for their reporting, including Pulitzer Prizes and Peabody Awards.[4]

But as this new journalistic model grows, it raises new questions about ethics, accountability, transparency and trust. "The ethical issues are even more acute in non-profits than in more mainstream types of journalism," Stephen Ward, at the University of Wisconsin Center for Journalism Ethics, said in an interview. He identified several challenges for investigative non-profits:

- Because nonprofits rely on different funding streams than do traditional profit-based media, they face constant decisions about whom to solicit for money and whether such contributions could endanger their journalistic independence.
- The small size of many nonprofits erodes the journalistic profession's traditional firewall between the newsroom and the fundraising or advertising department. At some nonprofits, journalists raise money to support their own work. A few, such as the Maine Center for Public Interest Reporting, have found themselves in the uncomfortable position of investigating their own donors or board members.
- Funders may expect more for their money than just independent journalism. As a condition of their grants, they might seek news coverage built around their areas of interest or demand tangible "deliverables," such as specific public policy reforms.

- As advocacy groups incorporate investigative reporting into their mission, they may pursue only stories that promote their ideology. Groups with overt philosophical agendas are likely to face questions about their journalistic integrity, while even nonideological organizations may face collateral questions about their motives or the political leanings of their funders.

"These are the issues that are going to make or break the credibility of these organizations," Ward said. "If too many of these organizations become suspect as to their independence, that's really going to hurt the movement."

A KEY QUESTION FOR NONPROFITS: WHOSE MONEY SHOULD WE TAKE?

At first glance, nonprofits may seem relatively immune to outside pressure. Unlike their counterparts at traditional media organizations, most nonprofits don't have to tangle with advertisers—the car dealer who threatens to pull its newspaper ads to protest a story about automobile safety or the local hospital that agrees to sponsor TV health segments only if reporters interview its doctors.

But relying on foundations and individual donors for support is no guarantee of editorial freedom. Those kinds of backers often have pet issues and may offer money with the expectation that the nonprofit earmark it for coverage of certain topics. Many independent reporting centers struggle with the question of whether to accept such restricted funds and where to draw the line on donor demands.

Generally, centers take contributions earmarked for coverage of broad subjects, such as education or transportation. For instance, the California-based Center for Investigative Reporting accepted a grant[5] to create a community health-reporting beat, while Buffalo, N.Y.'s Investigative Post received a dedicated grant for environmental reporting.[6] In both cases, the organizations accepted donor earmarks with the understanding that funders won't be allowed to dictate specific investigation topics or story angles.

More troublesome are potential funders who not only earmark money for a particular topic but also request that the stories promote a particular conclusion or viewpoint. Not uncommonly, journalistic nonprofits are forced to choose between accepting such funder involvement or walking away from lucrative grants.

"We have been told that if we would write about health care in the state and the need for everyone to have it, we would have the doors opened to potential funding," said Naomi Schalit in a phone interview. She runs the Maine Center for Public Interest Reporting with her husband, John Christie. "I've talked to foundation funders who said that if we'd write about the potential of solar energy, they'd be willing to look at a grant proposal," she said, adding that her reaction to those potential funders was, "No freaking way."

At the Common Language Project, an investigative reporting center at the University of Washington, co-founder Jessica Partnow once accepted a grant from a local civic organization for coverage of election issues, only to find out later that the group expected her to cover all of their events. "We had different expectations of what would happen with that money," Partnow said in a phone interview. "Based on that experience, I don't know that we would accept a topically focused grant again."

Schalit and Christie also experienced another potential pitfall of nonprofit journalism. On two separate occasions since they founded the Maine Center in 2010, they angered funders with investigations that struck close to home. One donor was a university president who became a key figure in a center investigation of state hiring practices.[7] The other was a politically connected attorney who objected to the center's probe of a state energy agency.[8]

Complicating the situation further, both donors also served on the Maine Center's board of directors. Schalit said the attorney contacted other board members in an effort to push back against the energy stories. "It was starting to be a degree of interference that was completely intolerable," she said. Both donors ended up resigning from the board, and Schalit said neither the pressure nor the donors' resignations affected the center's investigations. "You have to be prepared to lose (funding) when you do this kind of work," she said.

Indeed, one of the first challenges that face the founders of independent journalistic organizations is deciding on some fundraising ground rules. While virtually none of the centers tolerates direct editorial interference from funders or board members, there's less agreement on other dicey questions, such as whether it's ethical to accept money from corporations, labor unions, current and former office holders or other people whose political views are well-known.

"You have to think about who you're going to go to for money," Robert McClure said in an interview. The former *Seattle Post-Intelligencer* reporter co-founded InvestigateWest, a three-person nonprofit. "As a reporter, you're supposed to be squeaky clean and not take a cup of coffee, and then all of a sudden you're going to people and asking them outright for money."

When Lewis founded the Center for Public Integrity in 1989, one of his first actions at the fledgling organization was to put together a blacklist of potential funders. "It was about twenty pages of companies, labor unions, and others that I would not want to take money from because they all had done things I didn't like at one time or another," he recalled. "With a name like the Center for Public Integrity, I was very conscientious of how I would look."

It didn't take long, however, for Lewis to realize his constraints were unrealistically harsh and impractical. He and his board members decided to throw out the list and evaluate each potential funder individually, rejecting only those that posed obvious conflicts of interest, such as political parties or government agencies. "We all realized that if we were completely pristine and perfect, there would not be an organization," he said. "There simply wouldn't be any money."

BALANCING JOURNALISTIC ETHICS
WITH FUNDERS' GOALS

While Lewis built the Center for Public Integrity into a large enterprise with dozens of journalists and a multimillion-dollar budget, Brent Gardner-Smith is a more typical purveyor of nonprofit journalism. The former newspaper and public radio reporter is the sole employee of Aspen Journalism, a Colorado reporting center.

More than half of the centers in the Investigative Reporting Workshop's 2010 survey had four or fewer full-time employees. The survey found that those groups' budgets rarely top $250,000 a year; some operate on as little as $20,000.

At his one-man operation, Gardner-Smith personally researches and writes most of the investigative reports. He also raises money, nurtures relationships with his board members and responds to complaints from public officials.

"When I worked at the *Aspen Daily News* and wrote an article a major advertiser didn't like, the advertiser might pull his ad campaign and complain to the publisher and editor, but generally the firewall was very firm, and I didn't have to deal with them directly," Gardner-Smith said.

Now, Gardner-Smith has no such buffer, and as he conducts investigations in a relatively small town, he's found himself navigating through ethical and political thickets. For instance, his reporting about a proposed city-owned hydropower plant was attacked by Aspen's mayor, who observed that some of Aspen Journalism's donors and board members are on record opposing the plant.[9]

"Part of my complexity is that I'm one person," Gardner-Smith said in a phone conversation. "I don't think I was influenced in any way by my board or my donors on the story, but I can see someone saying it appears that I might have been." He said a local newspaper that had been reprinting Aspen Journalism's stories about the plant became less enthusiastic about doing so after the mayor complained.

"We've got a new generation of community publishers," Brant Houston, the Knight chair in investigative and enterprise reporting at the University of Illinois, said in an interview. "Suddenly you have a lot of people dealing with what it's like to be a small-town publisher."

Gardner-Smith, who relies on only about a half-dozen major donors to fund Aspen Journalism, said he goes out of his way to avoid discussing stories with them. Although some are prominent local leaders from whom he occasionally mined story tips when he was a newspaper reporter, his relationship with them changed once they became his financial supporters. "I had to tell them that ironically they had a lot more influence over me before they decided to give me $50,000," Gardner-Smith said, adding that he's refrained from reporting certain stories to avoid the appearance that he was influenced by donors. "It's awkward to tell them, but I can't do their bidding for them."

Again, however, this is an area where some investigative nonprofits have found it impractical to maintain a hard line. Especially in smaller communities, the people who are most interested in funding nonprofit journalism may also be the most engaged and knowledgeable news sources. In Buffalo, Investigative Post founder Jim Heaney considers it acceptable to use a funder as an information source, as long as the funder has no say in how the information is used. McClure at InvestigateWest said he sometimes kicks around potential story ideas with funders and once published an investigative piece based on a tip from an official of a foundation that supported his organization. "We know where these guys are coming from; we know what their agenda is," McClure said about the foundation, which promotes environmental issues. "But it's a really good story."

Houston, the Illinois professor, complimented journalists for trying to maintain a sturdy firewall between reporting and fundraising, but he said they also must remain realistic. "To their credit, good journalists tend to overcompensate," Houston said, noting that a nonprofit reporter getting a tip from a funder isn't a whole lot different from a small-town newspaper publisher hearing something newsworthy while chatting with an advertiser. "You've got to keep dealing with people," Houston said.

Another common challenge among investigative nonprofits is raising money from foundations, which may not be accustomed to supporting journalism. Before handing over a check, those funders may seek a more tangible "deliverable" than just a news story. They may want assurance that a proposed journalistic investigation is likely to result in some measurable impact that relates to the foundation's goals, whether that's cleaner water, better schools or a specific public policy change. Rarely can journalistic organizations predict that such reforms will result from their investigations, and few would consider it ethical to try.

"When it comes to solutions or reforms, we try to be careful to understand our limits as journalists," Andy Hall of the Wisconsin Center for Investigative Journalism said in an interview. "I'm comfortable with us helping bring an issue to the public's attention, but when it comes to determining the actual fixes that ought to be implemented, that's a job better left up to the public and the policymakers."

Hall, who helped convene a 2010 roundtable report on "Ethics for the New Investigative Newsroom,"[10] said he's turned down money from foundations whose goals for grants conflict with the Wisconsin Center's journalistic mission. In the report, he noted that while foundation support sometimes comes with strings attached, it's incumbent on the news organization to assure that the strings match the organization's editorial mission.

ADVOCACY, JOURNALISM OR BOTH?

Among investigative journalists, few questions are as controversial as a deceptively simple one: "What is an investigative nonprofit organization?"

Some journalists favor a narrow definition. They confer the title only on organizations that are independent and nonpartisan and that have no agenda other than producing thorough, accurate reporting. These organizations adhere to standard journalistic ethics and carry out their work largely in the same manner as mainstream newspapers and broadcast outlets.

But others criticize that definition as too restrictive because it doesn't make room for advocacy groups and nongovernmental organizations (NGOs) that practice journalism as part of their agendas. One such group, Human Rights Watch, earned a 2012 Peabody Award for its reporting in Russia and Papua New Guinea. Another, the International Crisis Group, produced groundbreaking stories widely cited by mainstream media on such issues as the Rwandan genocide. "Some of the best investigative research and writing is actually being done by NGOs," said American University's Lewis. "They're hiring journalists. They're using all the practices and sensibilities of traditional journalism."

A 2011 study by the Pew Research Center's Project for Excellence in Journalism documented the extent to which ideologically oriented nonprofit organizations are producing journalism. It found more than 20 such organizations operating in state capitals, many under the auspices of two national organizations. The liberal American Independent News Network funds a group of state organizations with *independent* in their names, such as the New Mexico Independent, while the conservative Franklin Center finances local groups that share the name *watchdog,* such as the New Hampshire Watchdog.[11]

The challenge for news consumers, policy makers and others is assessing whether these organizations' passion for their ideological philosophy dilutes their journalistic credibility or results in investigations that are more political than journalistic. Would an environmental group investigating pollution near a factory seek information and comments from the plant's owners? If the group advocates tougher government regulations, would it present a thorough and fair analysis of those proposed regulations, or would its reporting consist of cherry-picked data that reinforce the group's views?

By the standards of traditional journalism, which considers detachment a core value, any work authored by an advocacy organization is immediately suspect. According to conventional journalistic thinking, no organization that has a stake in a particular issue can report on that issue fairly. "I've worked in advocacy groups before," said Schalit of the Maine Center, "and when I produced a report, while everything in it was fact, my job was not to give a whole lot of credence to the other side. I was writing advocacy; I was not writing journalism. That doesn't mean it didn't have integrity of its own, but it was a different animal."

The concerns are especially strong when the advocacy group is involved in highly charged political issues. While Lewis notes that "most people in the world are generally supportive of human rights," organizations that are more easily pigeonholed as conservative or liberal are likely to find their journalism extensively questioned.

The Franklin Center, which calls itself a libertarian, free-market think tank, is among the organizations that have found themselves in the middle of these questions. Some of its local organizations have been denied membership in state capital press corps, while the national group has not been permitted to join the Investigative News Network (INN), an association of nonprofit journalism organizations. "We operate under professional journalism standards," Franklin Center Vice President Steven Greenhut said in an interview for this book. "We just admit the fact that we see the world from a free-market perspective, and I don't see how that makes us any less real journalists."

Indeed, we're well past the era when trustworthy journalism was exclusively the domain of traditional news organizations that maintained a veneer of impartiality. (To be sure, even those mainstream media organizations face growing public skepticism about their independence and balance.)[12] "Pretty good journalists can work for biased organizations," said Ward, the University of Wisconsin journalism ethicist. "It's not like we can say *ex cathedra* that if you're not perfectly pure in your organization, then all of your journalism is a piece of crap."

Rather than attempting to enforce a strict definition of what makes an organization *journalistic* (an effort that's likely to fail), it's more useful to educate the public about the values of various organizations and provide tools to help readers evaluate an organization's agenda. In its 2011 report, The Pew Research Center listed several criteria consumers might use to assess the credibility of news sources.[13] Among the most useful were these:

The Organization's Transparency

While groups with ideological agendas can produce fair and credible journalism, they also should be upfront about their motives, organizational mission and funding. A clear and honest description of the group should appear on its website, as well as in the text of any stories that it distributes to newspapers, broadcasters or other media organizations.

Many of the nonpartisan investigative reporting organizations follow this standard. For instance, when Gardner-Smith distributes his stories to local newspapers in Colorado, they include the tagline, "Aspen Journalism is an independent nonprofit news organization working in the local public interest. For more, visit AspenJournalism.org." Readers who visit that website can see the names of the group's funders, board members and even its attorneys and accountants.

But such openness is not always seen among ideological organizations that produce journalism. Some of the Franklin Center's local watchdog websites fail to mention their parent organization's free-market ideology, and the center does not reveal its donors.[14] Professor Houston, who chairs the Investigative News Network board of directors, said that lack of donor disclosure is what keeps the Franklin Center from being welcomed into INN. And he advises readers to be skeptical of organizations that fail the test of transparency. "People need to know where your funding is coming from and that (your organization) has not been set up as a front for a political party or special interest," Houston said.

Depth, Quality and Fairness of Individual Stories

The Pew Center study found that many of the ideologically driven nonprofits fail to follow one of the basic tenets of journalism: balance. In Pew's examination of the watchdog sites and American Independent News Network sites, a majority of stories cited only one point of view when reporting on controversial issues.

A critical reading of such stories should include an assessment of who served as sources and whether those sources' views are presented fairly. In addition, it's not unreasonable to expect journalists to "show their work," with links to source documents, transcripts or audio/video of raw interviews, and other background information that can attest to the story's credibility.

Ovaska, the N.C. Policy Watch reporter, said she's aware her stories face more scrutiny because she works for a left-wing group, and she takes extra steps to help readers evaluate her reporting. Her online story about LaRoque, the embattled North Carolina politician, included links to a variety of government documents and detailed her efforts to balance the story by attempting to interview LaRoque, his family members and his business associates.[15] "I take time to show my sources a lot more than I would have done in a newspaper setting," Ovaska said in an interview. "When you're in the mainstream media, you've got years of reputation there, and I simply don't have that."

Themes throughout an Organization's Stories

Even if a particular organization produces individual stories that are fair and credible on their own, its entire body of work may reflect ideological biases. The group may, for instance, choose to investigate only scandals involving Republicans or highlight wasteful government spending only in programs championed by Democrats.

Not surprisingly, the Pew study found the statehouse reporting sites funded by the conservative Franklin Center tended to produce more stories that scrutinized government spending, and those affiliated with the liberal American Independent News Network tended more toward traditional progressive issues such as labor, the environment, and gay and lesbian equality.[16]

While both group's issues are valid topics for journalistic investigations, the public should be aware of the extent that an organization's philosophy or funders affect its news agenda. By skimming several stories on the organization's website, readers can get a sense of whether the group's work is tailored to promote a particular point of view.

DEVELOPING FORMAL POLICIES IS DAUNTING, BUT ESSENTIAL

Despite the myriad of ethical challenges that surround the work of investigative nonprofits, Lewis found that only half the organizations he surveyed in his 2010 report had formal ethics or editorial policies. Smaller groups with one- or two-person staffs were slightly less likely to adopt policies, often for the simple reason that the founders were so busy writing stories and raising money that they hadn't time. "Just to get up and running was a lot of work," said McClure, who co-founded InvestigateWest in 2009, "and an ethics policy is another thing we still need to think about."

Like a number of other small investigative reporting centers, InvestigateWest follows the Society of Professional Journalists Code of Ethics,[17] a seminal set of standards that's served as a journalistic guidepost for decades ("Seek truth and report it, minimize harm, act independently, be accountable"). But the SPJ code hasn't been updated since 1996 and doesn't contemplate the unique ethical issues of investigative reporting centers. For instance, it speaks to relationships with advertisers, but not with donors or foundations.

"The SPJ guidelines are great as far as they go," said Hall at the Wisconsin Center for Investigative Journalism, "but they don't specifically address some of the circumstances that arise when a small crew is founding and operating a nonprofit news organization." Hall's center has developed a far more extensive set of rules, which he offers as a model to his counterparts at other nonprofits. Among its contents:

- **Donor transparency:** As the dust-up with the Franklin Center demonstrates, funder disclosure is a core ethical value to many in the investigative reporting center movement. The Wisconsin Center follows INN transparency guidelines,[18] accepts no anonymous contributions and lists all donors' names[19] on its website.
- **Editorial independence:** The Wisconsin Center accepts gifts and grants[20] to support particular investigations or specific areas of interest, such as the environment or the economy. But the center retains full editorial control of its content. It also requires funders to transfer their money prior to the start of the investigation, and it does not issue refunds to disgruntled donors.
- **Firewall between journalism and fundraising:** Only board members and designated staff members are authorized to raise revenue.
- **Conflicts of interest:** Center staff members are expected to immediately report "any real or apparent" conflict of interest with funders or subjects of investigations. The center's board of directors is charged with studying the situation and taking appropriate action to protect the organization's interests and credibility.[21]

Those guidelines not only set clear standards for nonprofit journalists but also provide funders with a realistic idea of what they can and can't expect for their contributions. Investigative reporting centers that show their potential donors explicit written ethics policies might help avoid misunderstandings. "You've got to draw lines well in advance," said Ward, who worked with the Wisconsin Center on its policy. "You've got to spend time with funders explaining to them how journalists think about what they do. And it's got to be upfront."

The Wisconsin Center also has a formal "facilities use agreement" with the University of Wisconsin–Madison, where its offices are located. Although the center gets no direct university financial support, the school provides it with rent-free space in a campus building, and center journalists deliver guest lectures and agree to employ student interns.

While it's easy to understand why overworked nonprofit journalists aren't eager to develop extensive ethics documents (the Wisconsin's Center's various policies fill 17 pages), Hall calls the guidelines an "absolute must" for news organizations. Besides providing them to potential donors and members of the public, he used them on one occasion to help answer the concerns of a state legislator who questioned the center's relationship with the state-funded university. (The inquiries came after the center reported a controversial story about the Wisconsin Supreme Court.)

"A nonprofit news organization can't afford not to find the time to adopt ethical standards," Hall said. "It puts its own credibility and even survival at risk." Hall adds that his ethics rules remain a work in progress. His financial support policies, barely two years old, were revised in 2012 to add several new sections. Likewise, Chuck Lewis recalled that even though the Center for Public Integrity had a formal ethics policy, virtually every board meeting during his 15 years there included discussions of some new ethical issue.

Indeed, the same traits that make investigative reporting centers one of the few vibrant outposts of in-depth journalism—their aggressiveness, versatility and entrepreneurial innovation—also make them a breeding ground of uncharted ethical challenges. It's difficult to predict the exact kinds of dilemmas the organizations may face in the future. Unlike the traditional media, which coalesced around one set of familiar journalistic values, the nonprofit investigative reporting universe seems destined to remain diffuse, with universities, advocacy groups, non-ideological organizations, and even intrepid individuals engaging in investigative journalism.

Some will find themselves perpetually trying to balance their goal of producing independent journalism, their need to raise money and their funders' efforts to influence content. Some will see their reporting as a tool for promoting an ideology; others will recoil at the idea of mixing journalism and advocacy.

But the investigators most likely to survive—and see their work have significant impact—are those who anticipate the ethical challenges and address them in an upfront manner. Those organizations will freely disclose information about their own motives, funding and reporting techniques, and they will empower their audience with the tools it needs to fairly assess the investigative work. In this more diverse journalistic environment—with less separation among journalists, funders and advocates—there's likely to emerge a direct correlation between an organization's transparency and its credibility.

NOTES

1. Sarah Ovaska, "NC Lawmaker Gets Big Pay While Loaning Friends Federal Money," *NC Policy Watch*, August 3, 2011, http://www.ncpolicywatch.com/2011/08/03/nc-lawmaker-gets-big-pay-while-loaning-friends-federal-money/.

2. *United States of America v. Stephen A. LaRoque* legal indictment, http://www.wral.com/news/state/nccapitol/document/11912791/.

3. Charles Lewis, "New Journalism Ecosystem Thrives," *Investigative Reporting Workshop: American University School of Communication*, October 29, 2010, http://investigativere portingworkshop.org/ilab/story/ecosystem/.

4. Ibid.

5. "Investigative Reporting Center Wins $440K Grant for Community Health Coverage," *San Francisco Business Times*, April 14, 2010, http://www.bizjournals.com/sanfrancisco/stories/2010/04/12/daily37.html?page=all.

6. "Knight Foundation Funds Investigative Post," *Investigative Post*, September 5, 2012, http://www.investigativepost.org/2012/09/05/knight-foundation-funds-investigative-post/.

7. John Christie and Naomi Schalit, "University System a Haven for Former Top State Staffers," *Pine Tree Watchdog*, May 3, 2012, http://www.pinetreewatchdog.org/university-system-a-haven-for-former-top-state-staffers/.

8. Naomi Schalit, "Energy Program Shut Down after Questions Raised about Politics, Effectiveness," *Pine Tree Watchdog*, January 31, 2011, http://www.pinetreewatchdog.org/energy-program-shut-down-after-questions-raised-about-politics-effectiveness/.

9. Brent Gardner-Smith, "City Report on Hydro Riddled with Errors," *Aspen Journalism*, April 10, 2012, http://aspenjournalism.org/2012/04/10/city-report-on-hydro-riddled-with-errors/.

10. "Ethics for the New Investigative Newsroom," The Center for Journalism Ethics, http://www.npjhub.org/wp-content/uploads/2010/07/2010_roundtable_report.pdf.

11. Jesse Holcomb, Tom Rosenstiel, Amy Mitchell, Kevin Caldwell, Tricia Sartor, and Nancy Vogt, "Assessing a New Landscape in Journalism," *Journalism.org*, July 18, 2011, http://www.journalism.org/analysis_report/non_profit_news_1.

12. "Press Widely Criticized, But Trusted More than Other Information Sources," *Pew Research Center for the People and The Press*, September 22, 2011, http://www.people-press.org/2011/09/22/press-widely-criticized-but-trusted-more-than-other-institutions/2/.

13. "Navigating the News Consumer through New Terrain," *Journalism.org*, July 18, 2011, http://www.journalism.org/analysis_report/navigating_news_consumer_through_new_terrain.

14. "About," Watchdog.org, http://watchdog.org/about/.

15. Sarah Ovaska, "How the Investigation Was Done," *NC Policy Watch*, August 3, 2011, http://www.ncpolicywatch.com/2011/08/03/how-the-investigation-was-done/.

16. "Story Topic," Journalism.org, July 18, 2011, http://www.journalism.org/analysis_report/story_topic.

17. "SPJ Code of Ethics," Society of Professional Journalists, http://www.spj.org/ethicscode .asp.

18. "INN Membership Standards & Application Procedures," *Investigative News Network, April 25, 2012,* http://investigativenewsnetwork.org/about/inn-membership-standards.

19. "Funding," WisconsinWatch.org, http://www.wisconsinwatch.org/about/funding/.

20. "Wisconsin Center for Investigative Journalism Policy on Financial Support," *WisconsinWatch.org,* August 31, 2012, http://www.wisconsinwatch.org/about/funding/ fundraising-policy/.

21. "Ethics and Diversity at the Wisconsin Center for Investigative Journalism," WisconsinWatch .org, http://www.wisconsinwatch.org/about/ethics/.

Caitlin Johnston

Adam Hochberg examines the ethical challenges that nonprofit news organizations face as they replace some of the investigative work that was once conducted by newsrooms. One pressure point: Small operations have less division of labor.

With budget cuts and layoffs continuing to slim down once robust news operations, investigative reporting in many cities has been pushed out to nonprofit organizations. In Aspen, Colo., former newspaper and radio reporter Brent Gardner-Smith runs a one-man, investigative operation called Aspen Journalism. As the only employed member of Aspen Journalism, Gardner-Smith is responsible for writing, photography and editing, in addition to securing funding for the non-profit.

For months, Gardner-Smith reported extensively on a controversial city plan to build a proposed hydro plant. On January 4, 2012, Aspen Journalism published a 4,300-word story breaking down the key players, both for and against the hydro plant, and detailing a lawsuit challenging the proposed plant.[1] Members of the Aspen community were aware of Gardner-Smith's ongoing investigation into the hydro plant. But it wasn't until April 2012 that some people, most notably the mayor, started airing complaints about Gardner-Smith's work.

On April 9, 2012, Gardner-Smith published a story examining a new report that estimated the new hydro plant would produce less electricity than the city had suggested. The report, filed the week before, said that the net annual amount would likely be 5.4 million kilowatt hours compared to the 6.2 million previously promised.[2] The report Gardner-Smith was quoting turned out to be wrong. The mayor in his criticism pointed out that two members of Aspen Journalism's board of directors were on record being opposed to the project. The mayor was furious. At a meeting that night, he railed against Gardner-Smith and Aspen Journalism, accusing him of catering to the interest of his board and his funders instead of reporting the truth, no matter which side it supported.

As it turned out, the mistaken conclusion in the report—and thus in Aspen Journalism's story—was the result of erroneous information city officials had put into a public filing, not a deliberate effort to accommodate an investor's bias. Aspen Journalism published a new story the following day clarifying the error: "City of Aspen officials are working to correct several mistakes in a report submitted last week to the Federal Energy Regulatory Commission regarding its proposed hydropower plant on Castle Creek," read the story.[3]

Several days later, on April 13, the *Aspen Daily News* ran a letter to the editor from the mayor in which he apologized for his attacks against Gardner-Smith and Aspen Journalism. "I accept full responsibility for erroneously attributing those errors at a recent meeting to the reporter," the mayor said, "and therefore apologize to Brent Gardner-Smith and the *Aspen Daily News* for assigning those errors to anyone other than the city."[4]

So Gardner-Smith, Aspen Journalism and its donors weren't to blame. But the incident still raises important questions: What responsibilities do nonprofits have to disclose their sources of funding, those sources' political biases, and any impact that might or might not have on the reporting?

For the most part, this isn't a problem for traditional news outlets. Advertisers and subscribers continue to fund most mainstream journalism, although some news organizations are experimenting with foundation funding and other new revenue sources. Large news organizations have different individuals in charge of finding advertisers and others in charge of producing the news. But at community newspapers, some radio stations and nonprofits like Aspen Journalism, that luxury doesn't exist. So Gardner-Smith and other players have to take certain precautions.

For example, Aspen Journalism included an editor's note in later stories about this subject:

> And we have this disclosure note: Tim McFlynn, a board member of Aspen Journalism, served as a co-convener of a community mediation effort at the Aspen Institute on Aspen's proposed hydro facility on behalf of Public Counsel of the Rockies. He also, in his role as chair of Pitkin County's Open Space and Trails board, urged Pitkin County to hire a team of experts to independently review the city of Aspen's assumptions and consultant reports on the hydro project.[5]

Also, when Gardner-Smith distributed his stories, he included a tagline explaining that Aspen Journalism is an independent nonprofit and invited readers to visit the website for more information. The website lists the names of the group's funders, board members, attorneys and accountants.

QUESTIONS

- How could Gardner-Smith have anticipated the mayor's accusations of bias? Why are smaller operations particularly vulnerable to such perceptions? What can small nonprofit newsrooms do to counter the appearance of bias?

- What best practices can news startups embrace at their very inception to foster credibility?

- What, if any, influence or involvement should funders or board members have over the content of an investigative nonprofit?

- Many funders have agendas. What should a model policy say regarding the interests of funders?

CASE NOTES

1. Brent Gardner-Smith, "A Look at Who Is Suing Aspen over Water Rights for Hydro," *Aspen Journalism,* January 4, 2012, http://aspenjournalism.org/2012/01/04/a-look-at-who-is-suing -the-city-over-water-rights-for-hydro/.

2. Brent Gardner-Smith, "New Report Drops Net Power Estimates for City Hydro Plant," *Aspen Journalism,* April 9, 2012, http://aspenjournalism.org/2012/04/09/new-report-drops-net -power-estimates-for-city-hydro-plant/.

3. Brent Gardner-Smith, "City Reports on Hydro Riddled with Errors," *Aspen Journalism,* April 10, 2012, http://aspenjournalism.org/2012/04/10/city-report-on-hydro-riddled-with-errors/.

4. Mike Ireland, "Apologies," *Aspen Daily News Online,* April 13, 2012, http://www.aspendailynews .com/section/letter-editor/152731.

5. Brent Gardner-Smith, "Aspen's Water Rights for Hydro Questioned," *Aspen Journalism, July 10, 2011,* http://aspenjournalism.org/2011/07/10/aspens-water-rights-for-hydro-questioned/.

chapter 9

A New Pathway
toward Sourcing

Ann Friedman

W e've all heard the good old-fashioned case for diversity. Journalistic outlets have a civic (and, most would argue, ethical) obligation to reflect in their content the interests and concerns of the breadth of their audience. While we all agree on its validity, that reasoning hasn't proved to be a great motivator in changing the makeup of newsrooms across the country. In the 1970s, lawsuits prompted some of the pillars of the news media to diversify their staffs. And while in the intervening years, notable women and people of color have advanced to some of the most powerful positions in media, most of America's news broadcasts, home pages, mastheads, tables of contents and blog rolls remain largely white and male.

Forty years after those seminal lawsuits, it's clear media diversity won't be pushed forward in the courts. Instead, the diverse makeup of professional newsrooms will progress and regress with economic prosperity, never becoming a true mandate, but never falling completely away either. Like saving for retirement, it's important, yet easy to put off.

But now digital culture is changing the dynamics of diversity. Successful journalists and media outlets will embrace diversity not because of lofty ethical ideals but because those who don't will be left behind. With the explosion in the number of news sources and ways of accessing them, it's more necessary than ever for outlets to build a dedicated audience. Including diverse perspectives, sources and angles are all ways of doing this.

At the same time, consumers have more diverse media options, which creates audience fragmentation. So there is also a new social imperative for media: to fight against the splintering of audiences into narrow niches, which poses a threat to democracy. Social media provide an excellent portal to the multiple, overlapping conversations occurring at any given time about any given news story and also provide a great check on media decision-making. Having better tools for ensuring diversity, however, doesn't mean we know how to use them. Thus any contemporary discussion of diversity for the new century should concern itself not only with the *why* but also with the *how*.

In the digital era, all consumers have access to a much wider array of media, forcing traditional outlets to compete for readers and viewers with startups, general-interest sites to compete with niche blogs, and individual journalists to compete with each other. No longer an idle goal, diversity has emerged as a way for journalists and outlets to offer their audience something more. With so many media makers scrambling to tell similar stories, there are distinct advantages to tapping diverse sources, networks and angles. Journalists with diverse networks—and newsrooms with diverse staffs—have the means to report and tell stories that are of interest to a wider array of consumers and, in so doing, prove they deserve to survive and thrive.

In the past, *diversity* has been used as a shorthand for racial or gender parity. While that is still critically important to journalism, we'll use a broader definition, courtesy of Merriam-Webster: "the condition of having or being composed of differing elements: *especially* the inclusion of different types of people." The idea is to ensure that a range of perspectives is reflected, a wide variety of curiosities are sated, and a broad spectrum of interests is represented in the work journalists produce. The point of our newsrooms and outlets is not that they *look* like America, it's that they think like and accurately reflect America.

The best part? In the digital age, when every viewer and reader can be counted and sources are accessible at the stroke of a key, diversity has never been easier to attain. For individual journalists, drawing on a deeper and broader pool of sources means higher-quality reporting and fresh angles, which can mean the difference between rising to the top of the most-read list or languishing at the bottom. For media outlets, appealing to a more diverse audience means being able to target different market segments, which is of great interest to potential advertisers.

"The digital world has changed the revenue dynamics for publishers," writes analyst Matt Shanahan on his blog, Digital Equilibrium. "In the print world, a publisher's shipment of physical media was the basis for generating revenue. In the digital world, consumption of media is the basis for revenue. . . . In other words, engagement is the unit of monetization."[1]

If outlets are quoting and catering to the same tiny group of people, it seems highly unlikely that they'll be able to achieve a level of engagement that's worth monetizing. Diversity has made the transition from an ethical—or sometimes a legal—imperative to what its advocates said it was all along: good business. It's essential to the financial and professional viability of professional journalists.

THE PARADOX OF FILTER FAILURE

In a highly competitive era when people might be as likely to get their news from a friend's Facebook status as they are from a Pulitzer Prize winner, diversity is one way for professionals to stay relevant and also rise to the top.

Yet digital technology has also added new challenges to diversity. Access does not guarantee audiences are getting a fuller range of information. As

Eli Pariser writes in his book *The Filter Bubble*, we're increasingly siloed by personalized search results on Google and self-selected networks on Facebook and Twitter. Users tend to follow people who are like them, folks who read similar things and have similar opinions and are of the same race and socioeconomic status, making it harder and harder to connect with those who think differently and act differently. When we miss news stories or overvalue others, tech types refer to it as *filter failure*. By consistently serving only certain segments of the population, media organizations—especially those that aim to attract a broad swath of the population—can suffer their own casualties.

The line between *producer* and *consumer* of media has been all but erased, just as the overall amount of content produced has skyrocketed. For those of us who make media for a living, this means diversity is a mandate for survival. In the age of social media, police department Twitter feeds and corporations and advocacy groups producing news, we're competing with a truly diverse group of media makers. If we're not serving our diverse audience, they'll serve themselves.

Even though filter failure is common, it is not universally desired. Indeed, it might even be considered a paradox of diversity. Filter failure is a case of diverse options leading people to move farther apart rather than closer to a shared understanding.

But filter failure is also not necessarily universal. There is evidence of an appetite for diverse perspectives. Take an old-media example, *The Week*, a CliffsNotes compilation of the week's news that deliberately provides snippets of a range of opinions. That magazine saw its circulation increase 127 percent between 2004 and 2012, a time during which other print newsweeklies were tanking.

Diversity—of sources and story ideas—is a way for professional journalists to provide value beyond social media and other crowd-sourced channels through which a growing percentage (19 percent in 2012, up from 9 percent in 2010)[2] of people now get a large portion of their news. Professional journalists can offer consumers a chance to go beyond their Twitter and Facebook streams and get a wider view of the world—one that is broader, deeper and more accurate than what is provided by media amateurs, who offer their own opinions or those of people like them.

For smaller media outlets, diversity also offers an opportunity to beat big-time competitors who are still going back to the same three sources (and rehashing the same tired narratives). Tapping a more diverse group of sources can give reporters an advantage over those who aren't looking broadly enough.

Besides additional incentives to prioritize diversity, the digital era also provides the methods for diversifying our networks of both sources and fellow journalists. But it doesn't happen without intention. Journalists must develop and use those networks to find story ideas, unearth unexpected angles and check our pre-standing assumptions to create better journalism with a wide impact.

"THE NOISE FROM AMERICA"

My alarm goes off in the morning. Before I flip on CNN, before I tune in to NPR's "Morning Edition," before I open up nytimes.com, what do I do? I reach for my phone and check email, Facebook and Twitter. My first points of contact with the outside world are all with self-selected networks. Friends and colleagues bring me the first news of the day. Of course, because I'm a journalist, some of these people are also sources or experts I keep up with precisely because I like how they filter the first news of the day. I've curated a list.

Like everyone else in the digital age, journalists now have a plethora of ways to visualize the intellectual feeding chain that is made up of their personal and professional connections. The Twitter stream, the LinkedIn relationships, the Facebook feed, the Tumblr dashboard: These are now a primary way by which story ideas flow to us. And this network—the fellow journalists, sources, industry experts and friends we follow on various platforms—can have a large bearing on how we determine what stories are worth telling or reporting. (For an idea of just how crucial Twitter has become to most working journalists, peruse the Media Diet feature at *The Atlantic*.)[3]

It's become hard for me to even imagine an era in which it wasn't possible to have a broad source list at my fingertips. It's now practical, through my daily networks—Facebook, Twitter, smaller sites I read—to lay the groundwork, so that I have a bigger, better idea of what's happening in the world that I am covering. And when that network fails or falls short, with a few search queries I can get a range of perspectives I might have otherwise missed. It makes intuitive sense: If my ideas are shaped by the people in my network, a more diverse network will yield more ideas.

In the past, diversifying source networks was a much more arduous task. A Minnesota Public Radio project, the Public Insight Network, marshaled listeners to catalog lists of sources and how to reach them. Gannett newspapers used to have databases where reporters were asked to input sources who weren't white, so the paper could reflect a broader sample of the community on its pages. Today, this is not so much a newsroom-wide task as it is an individual task. Reporters can take it on themselves to curate their social streams and strategically search for underrepresented points of view, without sharing their sources with their colleagues.

Of course, some journalists rightly caution that not all social media networks provide an accurate glimpse into the public psyche. Each platform, like each individual source, has its own biases built in. Brian Stelter, a media reporter with *The New York Times*, has carefully constructed his Twitter feed "with a balance of political viewpoints, geographic locations, and gender distribution," he told me in an interview. "It's not always conscious, but if I sense during a debate that I'm getting too many conservatives but not enough liberals, I will over time seek out more liberals." He follows more than 2,600 people.

However, political leanings are just one of Stelter's factors. "I worry more about geographic and class biases," he says. "I find myself following what I would complimentarily call 'normal people,' not just political reporters. I like having the noise from America in my feed. Twitter is largely an East-West Coast thing, so I seek out people from places in the middle."

To get around some of the inherent biases in Twitter, Stelter also uses Facebook's public search function. He can search *presidential debate* and see what users with a profile set to *public* have written about the topic. Whether it's because most people see Facebook as a more private platform or whether it's because more Americans use it, he finds these status updates to be even more telling than tweets. During the first presidential debate in 2012 between President Barack Obama and Republican nominee Mitt Romney, "the comments were so much more cynical and angry and blunt than they were on Twitter," Stelter says. "Twitter is a bunch of nerds and people who do this for a living. Whereas on Facebook everyone's like, 'These are all a bunch of liars and hacks.' It was a reminder of how many Americans are dispirited by the whole system. But I couldn't sense it on Twitter, and I certainly couldn't sense it on TV."

For his book on morning television, Stelter has found his diverse social-media network invaluable as he attempted to go beyond the ratings to tell the full story about what's happening. The reactions from those "normal people" on Twitter and Facebook guided his reporting. "All reporters who cover TV have been really, really slow to accept and embrace the fact that *Good Morning America* is now the No. 1 morning show," he says. "We all thought it was sort of a blip, and *Today* was going to come back, and we shouldn't blow it out of proportion. But viewers in my feed said it louder and more clearly than any reporters that they like *Good Morning America* now. The collective preference of the country had changed."

This knowledge allowed Stelter to cover the story in a way that set him apart from every other expert and ratings-obsessed journalist on his beat—and probably more accurately reflect to viewers what they were already sensing about the state of morning television. He continues, "I could sense that from tweets earlier than I could from executives or producers. The great thing about normal citizens is that they don't mince words the way that experts do. I think sometimes you get a more "pure" read that way. Those sources gave me more confidence that I was covering the story the right way."

Twitter and Facebook are not primary sources, he stresses. But they are points of entry to a very wide pool of various points of view and a great way to gut-check what your other sources are telling you, and to see which stories are of interest to the public beyond the insiders you consider core sources.

This is a two-way street. Just as journalists use social media as an entryway to sources and ideas, many readers use them the same way. They may see a fact or personal blog post from a friend on Facebook, then go to a trusted journalistic outlet to check its veracity. Friends have told me that they love to read the headlines on the home page of *The Huffington Post,* for example, but they always follow up with *The New York Times* to get a more complete picture. If you can see a growing interest in a particular story on niche sites, you can apply your reportorial skills to it and not only capitalize on the interest in that news but also increase the value of your news organization to that interested community.

The agenda can shift very quickly when more diverse perspectives are taken into account. Take, for example, the story of the Susan G. Komen Foundation's decision to pull funding from Planned Parenthood in January 2012.

On January 31, the Komen foundation announced it would no longer provide grants to Planned Parenthood to provide breast-cancer screenings. This immediately became the biggest story of the day in a few niches of the Internet: among those who are interested in abortion politics and, to a lesser extent, in the nonprofit and foundation world. Reporters who were plugged into those networks, such as the folks at *The Washington Post*'s Wonkblog, picked up the story the following day and began asking questions about why the funding had been pulled. They also added reporting, noting the shaky research behind the supposed link between abortion and breast cancer. Meanwhile, pro-Planned Parenthood activists began circulating petitions to reinstate the funding, and the scope of the story grew. By February 2, the story had made headlines and broadcasts around the country, and Komen's top official had resigned.

In the past, it would have taken weeks for this story to bubble up. Even if Planned Parenthood officials had sent a press release to a health reporter at *The Washington Post,* that reporter might have had no sense of the strong appetite for information about the incident. In 2012, all it took was a glance at Twitter conversation to realize that this was a story of great importance, not just to a segment of the population concerned with abortion and public health but to a wide swath as well. And it took only a few days for it to go from that conversation to a major news story. A diverse source network can lead to faster, better, more relevant reporting.

JUST "DUDES BEING DUDES"

What about the stories that aren't clear-cut breaking news? As the amount of content created has grown exponentially, so has the amount of opinion writing and magazine-style trend reporting. In an age where success is measured in clicks, opinion and trend stories have moved out of the style and op-ed sections to bleed into all beats. As journalists try to tie together disparate cultural threads and draw broad but meaningful conclusions, diversity offers an opportunity to fact-check the theses and, rather than merely cycle through a familiar set of nut grafs, actually add a new slant to the ongoing narrative.

While no trend is universal, some of these pieces ring truer than others. And while social media provides one avenue to uncover such trends, they also have many pitfalls. One cautionary tale—especially given that it's about journalism—cropped up in 2008[4] and again in 2011,[5] when *The New York Times* profiled a set of young, up-and-coming bloggers in Washington, D.C. The initial profile, published in 2008, described a tight-knit group of post-college pundits, many of whom lived together in what they affectionately called "the Flophouse." While they had attained some professional success in the form of paid blogging gigs at local news sites or niche political magazines, they were by no means household names. While many young female journalists were also gaining prominence in Washington at the time, only a few were mentioned in the piece. They were outnumbered by at least 2 to 1. Their exclusion from that initial trend story became a repeated oversight in the narrative.

Three years later, when *The Times* ran a piece checking in on the young blogger scene in Washington, women were even more conspicuously absent. The men profiled in 2008 had moved on to more prestigious jobs at *The Washington Post* and *The Atlantic.* "In only a few years," reporter Sridhar Pappu wrote, "these young men and others like them have become part of the journalistic establishment in Washington." The article mentioned, almost as a footnote, that one of the bloggers' girlfriends was also a journalist. She was quoted not about her own career trajectory, which had followed a similar path, but about the professional advancement of her male friends. Headline: "Washington's New Brat Pack Masters Media." Sample quote: "Everyone's gotten a little bit older and a little more boring."

I'll say. The follow-up piece was published at a time when there had been a spate of navel-gazing profiles about prominent men in media, including a *Women's Wear Daily* piece about "dudeitors," a handful of young men with extremely powerful editing jobs in New York. (Quote from the piece: "Just a night of dudes being dudes, bros being bros, but there's a lot of this going around Manhattan media these days.") Some critics, myself included, decided we'd had enough. I knew firsthand dozens of female journalists who were working just as hard and innovating in all corners of the profession. Yet they never seemed to merit an article.

So I wrote my own: "Washington's Lady Journos Have Been Here All Along."[6] The parody pointed out that plenty of women who had toiled as editorial assistants and underpaid bloggers were rising through the professional ranks as well—it's just that their success wasn't linked together and highlighted as a trend in a national publication. I made a point of naming names, creating a long list of the women that the previous *New York Times* pieces had overlooked. I quoted myself: "Everyone's gotten a little bit older and a little more tired of being constantly rendered invisible."

The stories that we journalists tell about any ongoing narrative require a constant checkin to make sure that the original premise wasn't flawed. If we don't recheck the original premise (in this case, that the best up-and-coming political bloggers are a handful of young white men who live in Washington, D.C.), we'll reach the same conclusions over and over (like the story about a "brat pack" growing up). Trend stories and narratives like these matter because they have a tendency to shape outsiders' perceptions and become self-fulfilling prophesies. They also alienate audience members who don't see themselves or those like them reflected in the content, they distort the truth, and they often cause direct harm to those who are left out.

This example is also useful because it speaks directly to the question of diversity within the profession. For magazines looking to hire staff writers who already have a following, a mention in a *Times* trend story is good proof that you're a known quantity. In the years between the 2008 and 2011 male-pundit trend pieces, the bloggers went from jobs at *The American Prospect* to *The Washington Post*, from *Reason* to *Slate*, from *The Washington Independent* to *Wired*. While it's undoubtedly true that this was primarily due to their own hard work, in modern journalism, the ability to prove you have an audience is one surefire way to gain a promotion. And having *The New York Times* describe you as an up-and-coming writer to watch is certainly one great way to build that audience. And on the flip side, when it comes to women hoping to build their careers in a similar fashion, exclusion from such a story is not a death knell, but it certainly doesn't help.

In the case of these trend stories, the oversight was even more inexcusable because the reporters were writing about journalism. Journalists' individual networks—the people we turn to when we have a freelance assignment or a staff job to fill or an award nomination to make—also have a dramatic effect on the diversity of the profession. Yes, we all have easy access to a more diverse set of sources than in decades past. But to go back to the maxim about newsrooms reflecting the way America *thinks*, the best way to do that is to employ a diversity of thinkers: people who are embedded in a variety of communities with a range of interests.

Thankfully, the strategy for hiring a diverse newsroom is similar to the strategy for finding diverse sources for a story. The Internet leaves a breadcrumb trail. If you look around your newsroom and see mostly white faces, ask yourself to think about the handful of nonwhite journalists you know. Look at whom they follow on Twitter. Add them on Facebook or LinkedIn and see whose work they're promoting. Add those people to your network, too. The professional colleagues you see in your feeds day in and day out are a window into different corners of the industry. This is also a fantastic way to facilitate cross-platform collaboration, as photographers tend to follow other photographers, producers other producers, editors other editors, and so on.

Just as news organizations have a business imperative to diversify, individual journalists also stand to gain by appealing to different audience segments. *The Times'* Stelter was so adept as sussing out unexpected sources as a self-employed blogger at TVNewser that he was hired as a media reporter by *The New York Times*. Nonjournalists provide some instructive lessons here, too. Maria Popova, the curator of BrainPickings, has built a formidable Web empire based on her ability to sniff out links that are off the beaten path. Popova describes her site as "a kind of Rube Goldberg-like machine of curiosity and discovery"; few modern media outlets might claim to aspire to that description, yet it undoubtedly lends itself to incredible levels of audience engagement.

Many journalists have come to consider omnivorous curators like Popova the enemy. "News relevant to a particular audience can be assembled cheaply and easily, with significant benefit for readers seeking divergent and even competing points of view," explained a 2011 report from the Columbia University Graduate School of Journalism, "but low-cost aggregators compete with content creators for pageviews, and often win."[7]

Relevant, competent media outlets will meet that demand for divergent perspectives. Successful newsrooms will do it by encouraging diverse thinking, experience and sources and by prioritizing those factors in their hiring. Successful journalists will take these lessons to heart on an individual level, thinking more broadly about their reporting, sourcing and story selection. With digital tools for building personal networks, assessing story ideas and engaging wider audiences, it seems entirely possible that meeting the age-old diversity imperative could result in a considerable professional payoff for both individual journalists and the publications that employ them.

NOTES

1. Matt Shanahan, "The New Discipline in the Subscription Economy: Recurring Revenue Management," *Scout Research*, January 24, 2013, http://blog.scoutanalytics.com/revenue-optimization/engagement-as-the-unit-of-monetization/.

2. "In Changing News Landscape, Even Television Is Vulnerable," *Pew Research Center for the People and the Press*, September 27, 2012, http://www.people-press.org/2012/09/27/in-changing-news-landscape-even-television-is-vulnerable/.

3. "The Media Diet," The Atlantic Wire, http://www.theatlanticwire.com/posts/media-diet/.

4. Ashley Parker, "Washington Doesn't Sleep Here," *The New York Times*, March 9, 2008, http://www.nytimes.com/2008/03/09/fashion/09bloghouse.html?_r=1&.

5. Ridhar Pappu, "Washington's New Brat Pack Masters Media," *The New York Times*, March 25, 2011, http://www.nytimes.com/2011/03/27/fashion/27YOUNGPUNDITS.html.

6. Ann Friedman, "Washington's Lady Journos Have Been Here All Along," http://annfriedman.com/post/23450575655/washingtons-lady-journos-have-been-here-all-along.

7. Bill Grueskin, Ava Seave, and Lucas Graves, "The Story So Far: What We Know about the Business of Digital Journalism," Columbia Journalism School, http://cjrarchive.org/img/posts/report/The_Story_So_Far.pdf.

Case Study 9: The Danger of Unidentified Bias

Caitlin Johnston

Ann Friedman argues that individual journalists are primarily responsible for overcoming the blind spots that result from their own biases. And newsrooms, she says, are primarily responsible for hiring diverse thinkers. In this case, both of those systems appear to have fallen short.

While journalists trumpet the importance of diverse newsrooms and sources, that didn't stop *The New York Times* from being decidedly nondiverse when describing a development within the journalism profession.

In 2008[1] and 2011,[2] *The Times* published feature stories about up-and-coming bloggers in Washington D.C. Two different authors both marveled at the success of these young journalists, holding them up as examples of the best and brightest in the new wave of the industry.

"In only a few years, these young men and others like them have become part of the journalistic establishment in Washington," wrote Sridhar Pappu in a 2011 *New York Times'* article. "Once they lived in groups in squalid homes and stayed out late, reading comic books in between posts, as more seasoned reporters slogged their way through traditional publications like The Hill and Roll Call. Now the members of this 'Juicebox Mafia,' as they were first called by Eli Lake of *The Washington Times,* in a reference to youth, have become destination reading for—and respected by—the city's power elite. Indeed, arguably they are themselves approaching power-elite status (as well as, gasp, age 30)."

While there is nothing wrong with pointing out new talent, many people raised questions about the method each of these stories used when selecting which bloggers to highlight. All the bloggers featured as primary characters in both stories were white men, except for a cameo appearance by a woman blogger.

The Juicebox Mafia coverage highlights a diversity problem magnified by repetition. In today's journalistic climate, much is made of the ability to riff off information that is already out there. However, if the pre-existing information lacks diversity, so does the content that grows from it. Although written by a different reporter, the second story was a follow-up to the first.

Social media have made it infinitely easier to narrow our exposure to different views. People follow others with similar beliefs, reinforcing the same points and counterpoints. The same is true for how journalists pick what they write about and the sources they include. Pappu, the author of the 2011 *New York Times'* story, neglected to mention that he used to work with many of the bloggers mentioned in his story.

Furthermore, by focusing exclusively on these bloggers, *The New York Times* reinforced a narrow understanding of the current media climate. In an article for Mediaite,[3] Frances Martel wrote:

> *The New York Times'* understanding of a younger generation of bloggers still consisting of the same group of writers as those they chose to highlight here–or their complete neglect of early-20s writers in opting to call those with more experience in the business the younger ones–demonstrates a lack of understanding of just how quickly a young consumer of media can become a young producer of media on the Web, and how those young producers of media can quickly find themselves shifting roles from protégés to role models.

Perhaps if the writers of the articles had a more diverse group of sources and information, they would have known that the rise of these bloggers wasn't unique to white men, and that many modern journalists follow the same trajectory.

The rise of digital media allows readers to access more news outlets than ever before, but it doesn't mean they're getting more diverse information. Just as the reporters who wrote about the Juicebox Mafia limited their sources to a narrow, homogenous range of people, readers limit the material they take in to their personalized search results on Google and self-selected networks on Facebook and Twitter. The Juicebox Mafia stories made it clear how easy it is to get trapped in a media bubble.

QUESTIONS

- Diversity of sources and information has always been a concern for journalists. In today's digital landscape, how can reporters best diversify their sources? How do social media outlets such as Twitter and Facebook make diversity more or less attainable?

- Analyze your own social media spheres. How diverse is your circle of friends? What about the actual feed that you see? How diverse is that? What could you do to ensure more diversity?

- The rise of the Juicebox Mafia showed not only a lack of diversity but a problem with the digital echo chamber. Because the first story didn't include many women or minorities, it was easier for the subsequent content to repeat the same mistake. In an Internet era defined by riffing off pre-existing material, how can a reporter safeguard against this?

- Does the fact that consumers can more easily find diverse content change the responsibility of news organizations to provide diverse content to their audience? What is their responsibility?

CASE NOTES

1. Ashley Parker, "Washington Doesn't Sleep Here," *The New York Times*, March 9, 2008, http://www.nytimes.com/2008/03/09/fashion/09bloghouse.html?_r=1&.

2. Sridhar Pappu, "Washington's New Brat Pack Masters Media," *The New York Times,* March 25, 2011, http://www.nytimes.com/2011/03/27/fashion/27YOUNGPUNDITS.html.

3. Frances Martel, "The *NYT* Ignores Shortening Generation Gaps In DC 'Brat Pack' Profile," *Mediaite*, March 26, 2011, http://www.mediaite.com/print/the-nyt-ignores-shortening-generation-gaps-in-dc-brat-pack-profile/.

Corrections and Ethics

Greater Accuracy through Honesty

Craig Silverman

Major news organizations planned for and hyped June 28, 2012, like it was the hard news equivalent of the Super Bowl. That was the day the Supreme Court of the United States handed down its decision about President Obama's Affordable Care Act. The stakes were high: Would a core component of the law—the individual mandate requiring citizens to have health insurance—survive? Or would it be struck down, gutting one of Obama's signature initiatives at the height of his bid for re-election?

Some news organizations put together teams, played out scenarios for different decisions and planned how the news would be shared in real time. There was a lot of attention dedicated to getting it first and being ready to analyze the decision and its social and political implications. It's fair to say few journalists imagined a scenario in which they got the decision wrong. We rarely prepare for failure. It's therefore no surprise we do such an inconsistent, and often inadequate, job of correcting our errors.

When the decision was handed down, AP, Bloomberg and Reuters correctly reported the news. CNN and Fox News, however, stumbled badly. The journalist that each of those organizations installed at the courthouse to read and interpret the decision failed to read all the way through the relevant section. They told their teams the individual mandate had been struck down. That information was relayed and went live on air, to email alerts, websites and mobile devices.

Although they made the same mistake on the same big story—and attracted the same scrutiny and ridicule—the responses by CNN and Fox News to their mistakes were strikingly different.

"CNN regrets that it didn't wait to report out the full and complete opinion regarding the mandate," reads part of that network's statement. "We made a correction within a few minutes and apologize for the error."[1] The correction was distributed to its website, mobile devices and Twitter; an email alert was issued.

Fox News, on the other hand, denied it made a mistake. "We gave our viewers the news as it happened," reads a statement it issued to reporters and posted to its website. "When Justice Roberts said, and we read, that the mandate was not valid under the Commerce clause, we reported it." The network also pointed out mistakes made by others and concluded with another assertion of its accuracy: "Fox reported the facts, as they came in."[2]

How is it that two major media organizations made the same error at almost the same instant and subsequently issued such remarkably different responses? This divergence in the handling of mistakes is not a cable news issue. It has nothing to do with any real or perceived political leanings of Fox News and CNN.

News organizations of all kinds, the world over, have different, sometimes contradictory correction practices. (Not wanting to admit an error is, unfortunately, one of them.) This scattershot approach leads to public confusion and frustration, enables errors to live on and may also contribute to the erosion of trust in the press. This state of affairs would be understandable if corrections were a new practice. But they've been a part of news and publishing for hundreds of years. The problem is that journalists and news organizations fail to recognize the profound role that admitting our errors plays in maintaining trust with the public. This leads to corrections that are often inadequate or even compound the damage.

A few weeks after CNN and Fox News' Supreme Court errors, ABC News followed with its own breaking-news mistake and questionable correction. Reporter Brian Ross said live on air that the man behind a mass shooting in an Aurora, Colo., movie theater may have had connections to the Tea Party movement. Ross was wrong and was soon called out for the error. But ABC News' initial reaction was to issue a public statement that was more deflection than correction. It read:

> An earlier ABC News broadcast report suggested that a Jim Holmes of a Colorado Tea Party organization might be the suspect, but that report was incorrect. Several other local residents with similar names were also contacted via social media by members of the public who mistook them for the suspect.[3]

The network eventually issued a more sincere correction:

> An earlier ABC News broadcast report suggested that a Jim Holmes of a Colorado Tea Party organization might be the suspect, but that report was incorrect. ABC News and Brian Ross apologize for the mistake, and for disseminating that information before it was properly vetted.[4]

The second correction is more honest about ABC News' failure. It's a correction that helps repair the damage.

Rather than viewing corrections as a necessary evil, news organizations should treat them as a means to help create a strong connection to the people they seek to inform. With that connection comes trust and a more honest relationship. That, in turn, should encourage the public to support journalists' efforts by consuming what we create. Each error that we admit fully and sincerely brings us closer to the public. The practice of correction is even more essential now that it's possible for anyone to easily bring a mistake to the attention of others. Refusing to acknowledge an error and offer a forthright admission today borders on the absurd and further destroys trust.

THE CONTRACT OF CORRECTION

Benjamin Harris came to America looking for a fresh start. As a publisher in England, he'd been jailed for printing a seditious pamphlet. Harris arrived in Massachusetts in the late 1600s and was soon planning his new venture, the first newspaper published in what would become the United States, *Publick Occurrences Both Forreign and Domestick*.

Before launching the new publication, Harris had set out a vision for the paper in a prospectus published in 1690. It contained what may be the first news corrections policy recorded on paper, a legacy that connects a central element of modern journalistic transparency to the origins of American journalism. Harris wrote that, "nothing shall be entered, but what we have reason to believe is true, repairing to the best fountains of our Information," according to an excerpt of the prospectus quoted in Walter Lippmann's *Liberty and the News*. "And when there appears any material mistake in anything that is collected, it shall be corrected in the next."[5]

Those two sentences contain a promise news organizations have made to the public ever since: We will use quality sources and do our best to get things right; but when we are wrong we will own up to it publicly, and as soon as possible. This is what I call the Contract of Correction, and it has been in place for hundreds of years. It's designed to instill and build trust by making it clear to readers that the press is accountable, that we acknowledge our mistakes and do so publicly.

Even in Harris' time, publishers recognized that trust was critical to the success of their enterprise. They went to great pains to declare their allegiance to truth and accuracy. One early English paper of the time even called itself the *True Informer*. But these boasts about accuracy and trust were largely empty promises.

In one notable example from 1624, the celebrated early publisher Thomas Gainsford took to the pages of his publication to thank "a reader for correcting a previous erroneous story that located the Antichrist's birth in Babylon," wrote journalism ethicist Stephen J. A. Ward in his book, *The Invention of Journalism Ethics*.[6] There was no Antichrist, of course, but issuing a correction about the location of its birth lent an air of credibility to the erroneous claim.

Early publishers had no codes of ethics, no best practices for gathering, verifying and communicating information. Although people were clearly doing the work of journalists, no one was called a journalist until later in the

18th century, long after newspapers were born. Still, men like Harris and Gainsford saw the necessity of corrections. "Publishers started producing weekly or biweekly newssheets on sale from a public office where people could come back and say, 'That report doesn't jibe with reality,'" Ward told me in an interview for my 2007 book, *Regret the Error*. "They had to try and retain the reader's confidence."

A corrections policy was a responsible act, and it was also good business. Accountability and transparency were a selling point to convince the public that a publication was worth reading. Worth paying for. Worth coming back for again and again. Corrections helped build a trusted relationship with readers. Trust was good business then, as it is today in an information and publishing environment that is characterized by abundance rather than scarcity.

"The philosophy of news ethics—tell the truth to the degree that you can, 'fess up when you get it wrong—doesn't change in the switch from analog to digital," Clay Shirky writes in Chapter 1 of this book. "What does change, enormously, is the individual and organizational adaptations required to tell the truth without relying on scarcity and while hewing to ethical norms with reliance on a small group of similar institutions that can all coordinate around those norms."

Along with a change in the way they tell the truth, news organizations must also change the way they fix their errors. To gain true value, corrections must now flow over various networks and reach people who have long since left a website or app, perhaps never to come back. Corrections must prove as viral as the errors that spawn them. They must also be clear and honest and offered with sincere regret.

This is not the current state of corrections.

THE PROBLEM WITH CORRECTIONS

The first problem is there are far too few corrections. A 2007 study by accuracy scholar Scott Maier, an associate professor at the University of Oregon's School of Journalism and Communication, found that American newspapers corrected less than 2 percent of the factual errors they made. Yet over seven decades, research has found between 40 and 60 percent of news articles in American newspapers contained factual errors.[7] In other words, journalists make errors at a steady pace but correct only a few of them, and even these haphazardly. We have broken the contract of correction.

The second problem with corrections relates to the ones that do get published. They are often written to minimize the damage of the error, rather than communicate the correct information and express regret for the mistake. They are rarely shared and promoted the way other content is in today's networked world.

This may be partly due to the longstanding practice at some news organizations to avoid repeating the error in any resulting correction. The motivation is understandable: Why compound a damaging assertion or mistake by repeating it?

But it leads to some awful, and awfully confusing, corrections, such as this 2012 online correction from Canada's *Globe And Mail*:

"Editor's note: An earlier headline on this story was incorrect and was changed."

And that's all they had to say.

In his introduction to *Kill Duck Before Serving,* a collection of *New York Times* corrections, former *Times* standards editor Allan M. Siegal explained why corrections must be complete and include the original error:

> Editors once feared that if the specifics of an error were detailed in a correction, the repetition would somehow heighten the damage. They have come to understand that readers want to know just how wide of the mark the story fell, and how the misstep affected the wider point.[8]

In some cases, news organizations are only willing to correct a potentially actionable error. Broadcasters have traditionally fallen into this category. When every second of a newscast is measured out (and fought over), it often takes a truly egregious mistake for an anchor or reporter to take the time to correct a mistake on air. There are, however, exceptions. After *This American Life* realized that a monologue about Apple by performer Mike Daisey included fabrications and false claims, it set to work creating an entire episode dedicated to its retraction of the previous work and an investigation into the issue itself.[9] In the end, the retraction episode was downloaded more than the original, highly successful "Mr. Daisey and the Apple Factory" show.

Journalists must do everything we can to prevent mistakes. But when they do occur, we must treat errors as an opportunity to assert our ethics and principles, to show our dedication to truth and accuracy and our willingness to be accountable for our work. Many news organizations fail to understand that by publicizing their failings, they demonstrate they're worthy of trust. Their failures are in fact one of their best opportunities to forge a stronger connection with the public they seek to serve.

A 1999 study of newspaper readers by the American Society of News Editors found that 78 percent of people "felt better" about a newspaper when they saw corrections. "Stress accuracy," said one respondent. "If there's a mistake, admit it. People are more likely to believe you. Don't hide it in small print. Let them know you want them to know your mistakes."[10]

Yes, failure builds trust—but only if handled properly. The respondent's comment includes a sentence that every journalist should take to heart: "Let them know you want them to know your mistakes." News organizations and journalists have always struggled with the idea that they should promote their mistakes. Why emphasize your failings? The natural human reaction is to hide them, to move on and try to pretend they don't exist. Isn't that a better way to create trust?

It's not. How we admit and fix our mistakes transcends journalism and speaks to a basic truth about the human experience and condition. This truth provides the explanation for why respondents to that ASNE survey saw corrections as positive rather than negative.

THE TRUST PARADOX

Organizations that seek to be trusted must first understand what makes humans trust and connect with each other. Humans are connected by imperfections. To deny their existence, to cover them up, or refuse to engage about them is to deny something fundamental about journalism. It makes institutions seem less human.

A world of clichés is available to express this: Something is too good to be true; to err is human; nobody's perfect. These casual phrases flow from the core of human experience. They are expressions of vulnerability, embraces of failure. They are profoundly true on a human level, and this translates to key aspects of life, work, society and, of course, the press.

"The truth is that we are actually drawn to people who are real and down-to-earth," wrote Brené Brown, a researcher and the author of books such as *The Gifts of Imperfection* and *Daring Greatly*, in an article for CNN.com. "We love authenticity and we know that life is messy and imperfect."[11] Admitting failure is at the core of how humans create connection and trust. Brown's research into vulnerability and shame became widely known after a TEDx talk she gave in 2010 went viral. As of this writing, it's been viewed more than 7 million times on the TED website.

Her talk, "The Power of Vulnerability," shared what she learned from years of qualitative research into human connection and the role shame plays in our lives. "Connection is why we're here," she said. "It gives purpose and meaning to our lives." In order for connection to occur between people, we "have to allow ourselves to be seen—really seen," according to Brown.[12] That means showing imperfections and flaws. People feel more connected to each other when they share the things that cause them shame and make them feel vulnerable. To show these things is to truly be seen. It is the key to building connection.

It naturally follows, then, that when journalists share our flaws and errors, we become more worthy of trust and connection. In the vulnerabilities of each other, we see ourselves. We see a human face. The paradox at the heart of corrections—admitting failure in order to gain trust—speaks to the core of human experience and interaction. Corrections are more than just good practice and good business. They're a powerful tool for building trust and connection with the public. Corrections help make journalism more human and therefore more deserving of trust.

Brown said the people in her research who lived fulfilling lives with strong relationships "believe that what made them vulnerable made them beautiful." This is the spirit with which we journalists must embrace corrections. Preventing error is paramount, but when we fail—and there will always be mistakes—we must see the act of correction as an opportunity, rather than a walk of shame or something to be hidden: *Let them know you want them to know your mistakes.*

Unfortunately, this isn't possible when the first reaction of so many news organizations is to minimize a mistake, to bury a correction. Or refuse to admit an obvious error. This extends even to the worst of offenses in the profession.

When a staff reporter for Hearst's *New Canaan News* in Connecticut was found to have fabricated sources and quotes in at least 25 articles, the paper offered nothing more than a 152-word brief for readers, published late on a Friday afternoon. "A newspaper's credibility is its most important asset," said David McCumber,[13] who was then the editorial director of the Hearst Connecticut Media Group.[14] "This is a gross violation of our standards and of the *New Canaan News'* well-earned reputation."

And yet the paper refused to offer any additional detail to its readers, and McCumber declined all press requests. In the end, reporter Paresh Jha was found to have fabricated other work, but the paper never updated its statement or listed any of the compromised work.

When journalists fail to be accountable for errors, when we stonewall, when the worst happens in our newsrooms, and when the industry as a whole can't agree on basic best practices, we squander the opportunity presented by corrections and transparency.

It's therefore time for a reaffirmation, a redrafting of the Contract of Correction. We should keep Harris' top-line declarations that we work hard to prevent error and correct our mistakes publicly and quickly. In addition to those, I propose five other key elements of effective correction that should guide the way the press fixes its errors. These elements ensure corrections are adapted to our networked world and, more important, position the press to seize the opportunity to foster a new level of trust and connection.

FIVE KEYS TO QUALITY CORRECTIONS

1. Deliver the Accountability We Demand of Others

One of the realities of journalism is that our work causes us to highlight the mistakes of others. We expose failures, malfeasance and hidden dangers. We demand that someone be held accountable for these mistakes. We bring officials and business leaders and others to public account.

But when failures occur within our ranks, we are often suddenly not so committed to transparency and public accountability. Like Fox News, we insist on our rightness even when our failure is self-evident. This fundamental hypocrisy—of not meeting the same standard we demand of others—has a corrosive effect on our relationship with the public. It prevents the kind of connection that leads to a trusted relationship.

An essential guiding principle, a golden rule that should inform and direct newsrooms in how they handle mistakes and deliver transparency, is that news organizations must meet the same level of accountability and transparency they demand of the people and institutions they cover.

Thanks to social media, journalists are sharing more about their work, their reporting processes and themselves. They are being pushed to connect more closely with the public. These initiatives are put at risk, however, when the worst happens and individuals and organizations move from serving the public with information to closing off and circling the wagons.

To be more trusted and uphold the Contract of Correction, we must be more accountable and transparent. This is never more true and urgent than when the worst happens: plagiarism, major errors, fabrication, ethical lapses. This is when it's most important that we offer details, answer questions and otherwise provide the accountability and transparency journalists push for from public officials, business leaders and others. Delivering that kind of accountability requires that we embrace failure and vulnerability and take steps to publicly express them in meaningful ways.

2. Make Mistakes Easy to Report

News media are being transformed from a monologue—we report, you listen—to a two-way exchange. The press is still developing its listening skills. We tend to be responsive when trusted sources bring us new information or when we put out a targeted call for feedback and opinions. But it's harder to be all ears when the message is about our failures.

Some major media organizations lack clear contact information for people who want to report a mistake or request a correction. And when a request is submitted, it's often greeted by silence. People are left to their own devices to locate a correction or guess as to why one is not forthcoming.

There is little service mentality when it comes to encouraging error reports from the public and responding to these requests. This helps explain why Maier's 2007 study found such an alarmingly low correction rate: News media don't encourage people to report errors. Yet the vast majority of corrections are the result of members of the public speaking up and telling us about our errors. The press must provide a reasonable level of service and accessibility for those who wish to report an error or request a correction. That means a page on a website that lists ways to report an error and perhaps provides a button on content that invites people to do that easily. These buttons are already in place at publications such as *The Huffington Post* and *Toronto Star*.

The Washington Post and *Chicago Tribune* both have online error report forms that allow readers to offer information for a correction. *The New York Times* has a dedicated online corrections page that lists an email address and a toll-free phone number. These are good initiatives, but they vary from one outlet to the next. A good standard to meet would be to offer a dedicated online corrections page that is linked from the home page and that lists recent corrections, along with contact information to report an error. Even better, offer a straightforward form for readers to fill out—this ensures the person fielding the requests has all the necessary information.

Print publications should also offer consistent placement of corrections that includes the necessary contact information. Broadcast programs can also easily share contact information and encourage people to offer feedback *and* report errors.

3. Create a Corrections Workflow

Make time to ask, "What did we get wrong?" In 2009, *Washington Post* ombudsman Andy Alexander wrote a column to detail the "abysmal performance" of the paper's corrections process:[15]

> As of the beginning of last week, The Post had a backlog of hundreds of correction requests, a few dating to 2004. In many cases, readers never heard whether The Post had rejected their request, or why. For them, it was like sending a correction request into a black hole.
>
> The newspaper's process for handling correction requests has not worked properly. In some instances, reporters were never even notified that readers had requested corrections to their stories.[16]

This is what a broken corrections process looks like. Another common affliction is for an organization to write up a policy and process, then drop it in a drawer or hard drive, never to be opened or enacted. Or, they don't take the time to discuss and plan for when things go wrong. We know we will make mistakes. A successful news organization plans for errors.

Journalists by and large understand the importance of corrections, but they don't feel they have the time to think about them or react to error reports. Often, they lack guidance for how to handle correction requests or are simply not notified when something they reported has been questioned.

A corrections workflow will have clear roles and responsibilities for those involved, and it closes the loop by ensuring the requester of a correction is given an answer and can see any resulting fix. It's in everyone's best interest to have a clear process that integrates an efficient workflow for corrections. This helps provide the level of service and response the public deserves, and it helps correct errors quickly.

4. Corrections Must Be Clear and Sincere

When writing a correction, two goals should always be top of mind: clarity and sincerity. Clarity is essential to ensure people can understand both the mistake and the correct information. A correction must inform the reader. Too often a correction is confusing or vague because the goal in drafting it was to mitigate damage and blame. Sincerity is key to ensuring a correction repairs, rather than compounds, any damage. An effective correction is written with the head *and* the heart. Certainly, a simple factual error that doesn't induce harm requires less empathy than a correction to a mistake that falsely accused someone of a crime. Corrections often fail to adapt their tone and language to meet the severity and impact of an error.

There is also a related, important point: You will only feel better about a mistake if you offer a clear and full-hearted correction. Trying to hide, minimize or otherwise turn away from a mistake will result in unresolved feelings and shame. Your conscience will not be clear. Catholics can tell you that they feel better about their sins after they've gone to confession. The same principle applies to corrections, except a public act of journalism requires a public confession.

5. Corrections Must Be Spread and Promoted

The act of confession is a core part of correction, but a correction is about promotion as much as it is about admission. Professional journalists have a responsibility to promote corrections in order to ensure their efficacy. A correction that no one sees or reads is a failed offering; it exists to help spread the correct information to anyone who might have encountered the incorrect information.

This is even more urgent due to how easily and rapidly mistaken information spreads today over social networks and other means.[17] This, of course, requires a redoubling of prevention efforts. It also requires that journalists apply resources to making corrections as viral as any initial error. A basic approach is to match the distribution of a correction to the same channels used to promote the inaccurate content. Spreading corrections, promoting them, helps us turn our failures into powerful engines of trust and connection.

This was one way CNN stood out with the correction of its embarrassing U.S. Supreme Court error. The mistaken information was spread to multiple channels, such as email, Twitter, television. Soon after realizing its error, the network engaged these same channels to spread a correction. This matched the correct information to the error. It helped fight back against the misinformation spread by CNN itself. It also demonstrated that CNN cared about correcting its error and was willing to dedicate resources to helping fix it. This builds trust.

Another surefire way to help corrections spread is to make them worth sharing. "Correction: An earlier version of this article claimed that journalists at Bloomberg *Businessweek* could be disciplined for sipping a spritzer at work," read a 2012 correction from *The Economist*. "This is not true. Sorry. We must have been drunk on the job."[18]

When all else fails, a correction executed with humor and sincerity goes a long way.

NOTES

1. "CNN Correction: Supreme Court Ruling," *CNN Pressroom,* June 28, 2012, http://cnnpress room.blogs.cnn.com/2012/06/28/cnn-correction/.
2. Andrew Beaujon, "CNN Issues Correction, Fox Issues Statement on Supreme Court Reporting Mistakes," *Poynter.org,* June 28, 2012, http://www.poynter.org/latest-news/mediawire/179245/cnn-issues-correction-fox-issue-statement-on-supreme-court-reporting-mistakes/.

3. Jeff Sonderman, "ABC News Apologizes for Speculation That Theater Shooter James Holmes Linked to Tea Party," *Poynter.org,* July 20, 2012, http://www.poynter.org/latest-news/mediawire/181843/abc-news-speculates-theater-shooter-jim-holmes-linked-to-tea-party/.

4. Matthew Mosk, Brian Ross, Pierre Thomas, Richard Esposito and Megan Chuchmach, "Aurora Suspect James Holmes' Mother: 'You Have the Right Person,'" *ABC The Blotter,* July 20, 2012, http://abcnews.go.com/Blotter/aurora-dark-knight-shooting-suspect-identified-james-holmes/story?id=16818889#.UWI_9RlAuyZ.

5. Benjamin Harris, quoted in Walter Lippmann, *Liberty and the News* (New York: Harcourt, Brace and Howe, 1920), 1.

6. Stephen J. A. Ward, *The Invention of Journalism Ethics* (Montreal: McGill-Queen's University Press, 2004), 109.

7. Scott R. Maier, "Setting the Record Straight: When the Press Errs, Do Corrections Follow?" *Journalism Practice,* 1, no. 1 (2007): 33-43.

8. Allan M. Siegal, in *Kill Duck Before Serving: Red Faces at the New York Times: A Collection of the Newspaper's Most Interesting, Embarrassing and Off-Beat Corrections,* eds. Linda Amster and Dylan Loeb McClain (New York: St. Martin's Griffin, 2002), xiv.

9. Andrew Beaujon, "*This American Life* Retracts Mike Daisey Story about Apple Factory in China," *Poynter.org,* March 16, 2012, http://www.poynter.org/latest-news/mediawire/166825/this-american-life-retracts-mike-daisey-story-it-says-was-partially-fabricated/.

10. "Examining Our Credibility: Perspectives of the Public and the Press: The Findings in Brief," *American Society of News Editors,* Aug. 10, 1999, http://files.asne.org/kiosk/reports/99reports/1999examiningourcredibility/p7-10_Accuracy.html.

11. Brené Brown, "Want To Be Happy? Stop Trying To Be Perfect," CNN, http://www.cnn.com/2010/LIVING/11/01/give.up.perfection/index.html.

12. Brené Brown, "The Power of Vulnerability," *TED Talks,* filmed June 2010, posted December 2010, http://www.ted.com/talks/brene_brown_on_vulnerability.html.

13. Search results for David McCumber, New Canaan News website, http://www.newcanaannewsonline.com/?controllerName=search&action=search&channel=news&search=1&inlineLink=1&query=%22David+McCumber%22.

14. Search results for Hearst Connecticut Media Group, New Canaan News website, http://www.newcanaannewsonline.com/?controllerName=search&action=search&channel=news&search=1&inlineLink=1&query=%22Hearst+Connecticut+Media+Group%22.

15. Andy Alexander, "Ombudsman—The Post's Corrections Process Needs Correcting," *The Washington Post,* March 22, 2009, http://www.washingtonpost.com/wp-dyn/content/article/2009/03/20/AR2009032002272.html.

16. Ibid.

17. Craig Silverman, "Visualized: Incorrect Information Travels Farther, Faster on Twitter Than Corrections," *Poynter.org,* March 7, 2012, http://www.poynter.org/latest-news/regret-the-error/165654/visualized-incorrect-information-travels-farther-faster-on-twitter-than-corrections/.

18. "The boredom of boozeless business," The Economist, Aug. 11, 2012, http://www.economist.com/node/21560265.

Caitlin Johnston

Craig Silverman suggests that while inaccuracies are bad for journalism, corrections are good because they allow a news organization to establish a bond with the audience by admitting mistakes. In the case that follows, two newsrooms made the same mistake but dealt with the correction in different ways.

Breaking news doesn't always announce itself weeks in advance, but in June 2012, newsrooms across the country were preparing for the day when the Supreme Court of the United States handed down its decision about the President Obama's Affordable Care Act. Journalists had spent the last couple of years covering what would become one of Obama's signature initiatives. And all of that work was at stake as the Supreme Court ruled on whether a key component of the law—the individual mandate requiring citizens to have health insurance—was constitutional.

Reporters staked out the press room at the Supreme Court to be the first to have the decision in their hands. Images of journalists in suits and heels (the experienced ones wore tennis shoes) sprinting from the Supreme Court went viral. But snagging the 59-page majority decision was only part of the battle. They had to interpret it, too. Reporters furiously read over pages and pages of legal opinion trying to answer the questions of the day.

AP, Bloomberg and Reuters correctly informed their audiences that the mandate survived. CNN and Fox News initially got it wrong. Both news organizations tripped over the same language. The court had ruled that the individual mandate was not constitutional under the government's right to regulate commerce, but subsequently, the ruling stated that the law was permissible under the federal government's right to tax.

The mistake was apparent within minutes, but these two news channels went about correcting it very differently. The corrections were similar in length, with Fox News' at 106 words and CNN's at 82, but different in tone.

Fox News:

> We gave our viewers the news as it happened. When Justice Roberts said, and we read, that the mandate was not valid under the Commerce clause, we reported it. Bill Hemmer even added, be patient as we work through this. Then when we heard and read, that the mandate could be upheld under the government's power to tax, we reported that as well—all within two minutes.

> By contrast, one other cable network was unable to get their Supreme Court reporter to the camera and said as much. Another said it was a big setback for the President. Fox reported the facts, as they came in.[1]

CNN:

> In his opinion, Chief Justice Roberts initially said that the individual mandate was not a valid exercise of Congressional power under the Commerce Clause. CNN reported that fact, but then wrongly reported that therefore the court struck down the mandate as unconstitutional. However, that was not the whole of the Court's ruling. CNN regrets that it didn't wait to report out the full and complete opinion regarding the mandate. We made a correction within a few minutes and apologize for the error.[2]

Both news channels explained that the error stemmed from Chief Justice Roberts' initial statement that the individual mandate was not a valid exercise of congressional power under the Commerce Clause. But while CNN took the proactive role of admitting its error, saying it "wrongly reported that therefore the court struck down the mandate as unconstitutional," Fox News took a more defensive approach: "We gave our viewers the news as it happened." Both added that they reported the accurate decision only a couple of minutes after they first got it wrong.

But the cable outlets took different stances on where the blame lay for the mistake. Fox News ended by saying, "Fox reported the facts, as they came in." CNN owned up to the error: "CNN regrets that it didn't wait to report out the full and complete opinion regarding the mandate."

The cable channels had discovered and corrected the error. But they each faced a choice of how to disseminate the correction. CNN took to its broadcast, websites, mobile devices, Twitter and email. Fox News noted the mistake on air and posted the statement on its website.

A week later, nearly one-third of Americans (30 percent) surveyed were unclear how the Supreme Court ruled on the Affordable Care Act, according to the Pew Research Center for the People & the Press. Another 15 percent thought the law was overturned.[3]

QUESTIONS

- Both CNN and Fox news made the same mistake. But their approach to correcting it was different. What was each network trying to communicate to its audience? What conclusions can you draw about each news organization's definition of accuracy? What other evidence can you find that support or undermine your conclusions about CNN and Fox?

- What are the key elements that should be included in a correction? Write your own correction of the errors made by CNN and Fox including those elements.

- When issuing a correction, there is a certain danger in restating the error. Describe that danger. What can journalists do to avoid making matters worse when writing a correction?

- Where should corrections appear? What challenges do news organizations face when trying to reach citizens who consumed faulty information? What is the difference between making a mistake on your own platform compared with making a mistake on Facebook or Twitter?

CASE NOTES

1. Alex Alvarez, "Fox Media Releases Statement After Initially Reporting Individual Mandate Was 'Gone,'" *Mediaite,* June 28, 2012, http://www.mediaite.com/tv/fox-news-releases-statement-after-initially-reporting-individual-mandate-was-gone/.

2. "CNN Correction: Supreme Court Ruling," *CNN Press Room,* June 28, 2012, http://cnnpressroom.blogs.cnn.com/2012/06/28/cnn-correction/.

3. "Division, Uncertainty over Court's Health Care Ruling," *Pew Research Center for the People & the Press,* July 2, 2012, http://www.people-press.org/2012/07/02/division-uncertainty-over-courts-health-care-ruling/.

PART 3

The Community as a Goal

Kelly McBride and Tom Rosenstiel

When we gathered the authors for this book, we did so with the notion that what we created would be more significant than the mere sum of its parts. We knew that no one person, or even a small group of people, would be able to articulate a set of ideals that would guide journalism in the future. We knew we needed a community. So we tapped people who, in turn, were plugged into other communities. And when we asked these writers to test out their ideas, we did it in front of a broader group. In short, we layered community on community.

The benefit revealed itself to us midway through the morning of a symposium with the authors, when contributor Mónica Guzmán (whose chapter appears in this section) was discussing the relationship between community and journalism. Guzmán said:

> Forever, the product of journalism has been the article, the photo, the essay, the content. The digital ecosystem today is asking us why can't the product of journalism be the community? Why can't that be the space where we do our work? If the mission of journalism is to inform the public for the civic good, but citizens are showing us they can inform themselves with the right tools and the right guidance, then the community should be as much a product of what we do, as much an end, as anything else. *The differentiator for other industries is they think of the community as a means to an end. But for journalism, the community should be an end.*

One sign this moment was significant was that people on Twitter, the extended community to our gathering, immediately called attention to it. We had more than a thousand tweets that day. This was the single most tweeted moment. The community told us we were onto something.

On one level, community is an ideal that's impossible to achieve. It's not fixed in one space, and there is no one community. In fact, every newsroom serves many different communities, and many industries and groups are after the same community. But journalism is different. Sure, we all want *likes* and *shares* and *comments*; they help measure reach and impact. More than that, physical signs of engagement let journalists know that they are succeeding in becoming part of the community. They indicate that we are integrated into the community.

The signs of a successful, fully realized community are going to be different for every organization. They are also likely to change with time and topics. It matters more that newsrooms and journalists start by imagining what successful community would look like—around the topic of public schools or public transportation—then start working toward those goals. To do that, we need to look at the barriers that might prevent us from becoming whole communities, as well as identify the pathways that will get us there.

This notion of community as the end not the means of journalism defines the third broad ethical principle and is the focus of this final section of the book. Four authors tackle aspects of this concept here. Steven Waldman describes his experience with the creation of Beliefnet, one of journalism's first great experiments with community, and makes a business argument for investing in the tools and skills necessary to foster healthy community. danah boyd draws on her background as a Microsoft researcher, and, along with Kelly McBride, explores the rising tendency for journalists to use fear to sell their work and, as a result, cause harm to communities. Eric Deggans delves into the colliding values of different communities interested in telling the story of Trayvon Martin's death at the hands of a neighborhood watchman. Finally, Guzmán explains how she put together the puzzle pieces of her own experience as a journalist to arrive at the revolutionary conclusion that community is an end product for journalism, not the means to an end.

This section is just the beginning of what will be a difficult journey. Professional journalism must grasp this deeper, more complex idea of community and the ever expanding range of tools that make it possible. That will require a new mind-set, new work processes and a new rapport.

We said at the outset of this book that journalism must survive, if democracy is to survive. If journalism can accomplish this transformation into a service that creates and supports the community, rather than one that creates news products, this could be our best investment in survival.

The (Still) Evolving Relationship between *News* and *Community*

Steven Waldman

I n 1999, when we were building the first version of Beliefnet.com, a multi-faith religion and spirituality website, we hit upon a crazy idea: What if instead of having the readers post comments in a separate "message boards" area, they could comment right next to an article? We called them "mini boards" because they were slender message boards that ran vertically alongside an article.

We were travelling in mostly uncharted territory. The Internet had stimulated online community almost since its inception, news groups and bulletin boards being among the first popular uses of the new technology. Those tended to be separate, stand-alone forums, however. With this new experiment, we were inviting readers to engage with a piece of content, using that article to stimulate conversation and prompt readers to describe their own experiences in ways that could provide a richer experience for those who came to that page.

This grew out of my experience with newspapers and magazines, which had letters to the editor sections inviting reader comment on articles. These sections were popular yet absurdly restrictive; the number of people who ever got their letters published was tiny. We toyed with calling mini-boards "instant letters to the editor" but decided that would be meaningless to our younger readers.

Bringing the community into the editorial area raised all sorts of questions. Would we be able to get writers to contribute to Beliefnet if they knew they might see criticisms—or rude insults—right alongside their pieces? What if members posted false information? Would we be responsible for correcting it? What if the comments were nasty, rude or stupid? Wouldn't that somehow undermine the quality of the overall experience?

In some ways, this is ancient history. Commenting on articles is now ubiquitous. The rise of massive social media platforms—MySpace, Facebook, Twitter, Instagram and many others—offer far more complex and varied avenues for personal expression and human interaction. Indeed, even the term *community* seems quaint and old-fashioned, implying a group of users off in a segregated pen, even though the users (aka, readers, listeners, Tweeters, the crowd) are so deeply a part of and so influential in any media operation now.

Yet journalists are still dealing with some of the same questions about the relationship between community and journalists. What should be the role of the readers versus the professionals? Or stated more positively, how can the professionals harness the incredible value of the readers to improve the quality of journalism?

Beliefnet maintained a mix of traditional content—original reporting, bloggers, multimedia—and community features, including interactive prayer circles, dialogue groups, online memorials and many others. We often created editorial features out of the message board posts, in what is now referred to as user-generated content.

Beliefnet grew to the largest spirituality site on the Internet (12 million daily newsletter subscribers, 4 million unique visitors to the site per month) and was eventually bought by News Corp (which eventually resold it, but that's another story). We always believed it was the mix of traditional content, community and new hybrid formats that drove its success.

NEW ROLES FOR THE CROWD

When newspaper advertising started to collapse and newsrooms to shrink, distinct camps developed about the role of the "crowd" in the new world. Some digital evangelists viewed old-style journalists as virtually obsolete. Most of what the reporters did could be picked up by a swirling community of citizen reporters, fact-checkers and commentators, they said. Conversely, traditional editors caricatured the new media practitioners: The crowd resembled less the noble citizens at a virtual New England town hall than the pitchfork-wielding rabble in Frankenstein. The "pajama clad bloggers" were slightly better than the mob but not in the same league as real journalists, traditionalists said.

The lines have softened, the camps dispersed a bit. Traditional editors have long since integrated social media into their old media operations—adding comments to their articles, promoting their material on Facebook and Twitter, and inviting citizen reporting in certain circumstances (especially around weather-related disasters). New media advocates have come to realize that full-time professional reporters can do certain things better than an inchoate swarm of volunteers. It also has become clear that the crowd-based media operations have not, at least so far, been able to pay the salaries of full-time reporters. Eliminating the false choice between professional journalism and community-driven content is important because in the future mastering the proper relationship between media and the community will be essential to inventing news institutions and strategies that will be valuable, effective and sustainable.

Too many media managers still view social media primarily as a distribution system for content. It is that, but *community* (to use the old term) or *social media* (to use the new) serve various functions in a digital news world. The potential value of the community to building better media is significant. But to tap that value, we must better understand the potential roles of community, not just in terms of platforms—Twitter versus Instagram versus message boards—but in terms of functions. Here are the most significant ways community and news can interact.

Readers as distributors. At this point, most news organizations understand the significance of Twitter and Facebook as a way for readers to pass along content. In 2012, 19 percent of Americans got news via social networks, and 34 percent of those between the ages of 18 and 25 did, according to the Pew Research Center.[1] In the old model, the readers were the circulation endpoints; now they are midpoints. To paraphrase what public health officials used to say about sexually transmitted diseases, when a news organization reaches a reader, it is potentially reaching everyone in that person's network.

For all the distressing news about news economics, the cost-savings implicit in this new world order are significant: Legacy news organizations and startups can find their audiences at a fraction of the cost of old news or magazine models, which often involved ridiculously expensive and inefficient techniques like direct marketing.

It has also become clear that these reader/distributors may have different views about what's important. Readers do not merely pass along what legacy media folks think is important; they make their own editorial judgments. What's more, they continually insert into the information stream images or news that may not have made it to traditional media, as when the Reddit community generated public awareness about a YouTube video showing a bus monitor being bullied in Greece, N.Y.[2] In many cases, the phrase "gone viral" really means escaping the initial media ecosystem in which a story or video was born and passing into a much larger network of readers or viewers.

Ironically, while the Internet often smashes the traditional broadcasting model and its "one to many" approach, some news organizations have used social media distribution networks in a cramped way, as just another means to transmit a single piece of information from "one" (the newsroom) to many, without much interactivity going the other way.

There are other pitfalls: Organizations that see the benefits of social media-driven distribution can also become intoxicated by it, warping editorial decisions to push stories with great social media appeal. Just as a local TV newscast may become overly reliant on the crime and sex stories that can drive ratings, Twitter-obsessives can over-depend on stories that move the social media needle. There may be no more of a correlation between "importance" and social media pickup than there is between ratings and journalistic merit. I'm not suggesting we snobbishly ignore the crowd, but we should recognize that editors still must maintain a sense of balance between reader appetites and editorial judgment.

Readers as contributors. At first, news organizations were reluctant to accept reporting from regular folks. Then they began to accept photos, especially in times of disaster. Now they use information from readers in a great variety of ways. We have seen the "Twitter revolution" which awakened Western press not only to the role of new media in stirring world events but also in providing news. CNN uses "iReporters." The Public Insight Network, a nonprofit system run by American Public Media, enlists, organizes and prods citizen experts in a variety of areas. Ushahidi is a software tool that allows residents to report on crimes, fires, disasters or any other hyperlocal news event. We're now seeing parents upload box scores for high school games and photo galleries consisting entirely of user-created art; parents tweet from PTA meetings—just two of many examples of readers becoming content contributors.

I believe we're still at the early stages of tapping into the power of readers as content providers. Editors realize at this point that these tools can be valuable and an enormous force multiplier for news organizations. They have begun to understand what types of citizen contributions work best for particular stories: photography and on-the-ground reports during weather disasters, expressions of opinion during political campaigns, descriptions of personal experiences when reporting a medical story. We can hope that they will also realize that a little bit of curation has its rewards. An Instagram module capturing a raw flow of photos about a storm is fascinating; a gallery using the 10 best of those photos, with explanation and context, is even better.

Readers as sources. This is where news organizations really blew it. When craigslist came along and created cheap classifieds—a marketplace for users to share information with each other— newspapers stuck their heads in the sand. Or they decided (accurately) that it made more short-term economic sense to protect their paid classified revenue engines. But they ended up losing their classified business without having enough of a stake in what replaced it.

Many managers didn't realize that one of the most important roles a news organization can play is being a community *platform*—a way for users to exchange information with each other. This need not involve human intervention from editors or reporters. There's no reason that news organizations couldn't have been the ones to invent Yahoo Questions, craigslist, Foursquare, Match.com or any of the other new tools or businesses that thrived by connecting users with each other. These efforts have tended to focus on commercial transactions. The next wave will likely be the creation of tools that enable citizens to connect with each other to improve their own neighborhoods. Perhaps news organizations will play a bigger role in this second revolution. The term *media,* after all, comes from the Latin word *medius,* meaning in the middle of. Being a matchmaker between user and information is not only valuable, it's perfectly compatible with journalistic mores.

Readers offering support. Perhaps I developed a warped perspective working at Beliefnet, but online communities can provide people with tremendous support and inspiration. We had a "prayer circle" that went on for years in which parents whose children had died comforted other parents who had just suffered the same incomparably horrible fate. While the ability to post anonymously has led to an explosion of trolls who post mean, nasty comments to distract and incite, it also allows for extraordinary tenderness and honesty. People will open up about traumas or anxieties online in ways they won't in person, especially when it relates to sensitive topics like spirituality, grief, suicide or abuse.

But such communities cannot be cultivated merely through automated services that vote good posts up or down. Even seemingly sure-fire, safe rules of the road will be violated by creative people with agendas. At Beliefnet, we saw the birth of a novel new form of expression: the attack prayer. Prayer circles were mostly used to offer support, but we would occasionally see members innovate further, as in, "Lord, oh God, please provide wisdom and guidance to Jack, my deadbeat husband, who has been cheating on me with that whore, Darleene. Amen."

So there's no substitute for having skilled community managers. They are often recruited or identified from within the online community with special leadership skills. Editors—trained as we are to be cynics—may have trouble accepting that these sorts of communities grow from a mix of self-aggrandizement motives (who doesn't like to be an authority in a group?) *and* genuine compassion. Many people become online community leaders because they want to help; it's a way for them to contribute. Editors aren't used to acting as social workers or counselors, but it's worth the effort. It will help create a community that will be profoundly useful to their members and therefore help strengthen the ties between the readers and the news organization.

Readers expressing themselves. Sometimes a reader is really just looking for a means of one-way, personal expression. She doesn't want a conversation; she wants a soapbox. In one sense, this type of community is quite familiar. For years, a newspaper's letters to the editor section invited community members to express their views. But that's a little like saying a donkey and a jet fighter are similar because they both carry people. First, and most obviously, on the Internet there are no space constraints to personal expression. It's hard to overstate the importance of that basic fact: The ability to express oneself on a large platform has gone from being an unusual achievement—sometimes determined by eloquence, sometimes by luck—to an easy and ubiquitous one.

Second, the comments sections within a news organization's website or Facebook page do not discriminate by quality, ideological proclivity or mental health status. They can be conduits for eloquent expression or for vile ravings of some of society's most sociopathic and everything in between. News organizations have responded in a variety of ways, some shutting down the comments areas, some allowing for a Wild West attitude (figuring that everyone is now used to the raucous nature of message boards). Both approaches are unfortunate. To shut down comments because of fear of what might be said misses out on one of the great democratizing elements of the new media. It blinds news organizations to a source of story ideas, information and analysis. On the other hand, those that allow for unfiltered community drive away many readers from the discussion. Virtual loony bins are sometimes fun to watch, but most of us would just as soon not hang out there.

The truth is, allowing for readers to express themselves takes real work on the part of the news organization. And that requires an authentic belief in and commitment to the value of the audience as a content-producing community. Web tools enabling readers to flag or vote on different posts assist in the policing of communities, but they cannot substitute for human management. An example: On Beliefnet, some people would use scriptural references to attack other people, even in message boards that were ostensibly created to provide support around issues such as divorce or the death of a child. We found that if we merely banned users, they would come back again under different names. So we created the "doctrine and dissent" boards—basically free-for-all areas for the angriest members to argue. Whenever one of those flame wars broke out in a peaceful area, instead of deleting the thread we moved it to an area specifically geared toward argumentation. That way the most opinionated folks felt respected but we were able to protect the safety of the more contemplative areas. That solution wouldn't have been invented if we hadn't had a team of very skilled community managers. They had real salaries—but, wow, were they worth it.

Geographically bounded communities. The Internet has been especially effective at creating non-geographically bounded communities. Political sites draw ideological fellow travelers from far and wide. Ethnic sites connected scattered minorities into a place where they feel in the majority. Indeed, some believe that geographic communities are almost passé, replaced by the communities of the like-minded. As a business matter, these national or international communities of the like-minded make economic sense. A national collection of almost any interest or niche groups can run into the millions of people, already larger than the potential market of most local areas. Technological innovation has focused on the creation of platforms that connect people from around the world. Think of how Twitter or Facebook would have done if they had been limited only to the people in a particular city.

But as traditional local news organizations struggle, especially in the provision of accountability reporting, innovators must now create tools that will help strengthen geographically bounded communities. Because the economics of local are challenging, investors shy away from locally oriented media or technology businesses unless they are geared toward the creation of a national platform or focused on commercial transactions (i.e., Groupon or Foursquare). The struggles of both traditional newspapers and digital operations like Patch have convinced investors that investing in locally oriented content is risky.

The key is that local news organizations have to see themselves not only as providers of information but also as facilitators of community. In some cases, this may involve no traditional journalism at all. For instance, a newspaper could take a city's health data and create mobile apps enabling citizens to avoid restaurants with bad inspection records. This involves no storytelling but rather redefines the media organization's role as a facilitator of information exchange. Beyond that, news organizations can take the lead in promoting or even developing technologies that can actually strengthen neighborhoods or provide better services to residents. Groupon helps connect local consumers with local businesses, but so far there are not enough effective tools to help residents get their potholes fixed, to ensure that housebound seniors get their lawn mowed, or to advise parents on which teachers are best for their kids.

THE ECONOMICS OF COMMUNITY

There's a reason that venture capitalists these days will fund social media platforms but not news content companies. The cost-per-pageview of a community is much less than the cost of content creation. Yet if you look at the staffing of most newsrooms, you'll probably find that this logic is not yet reflected. Much more money is spent on reporting than community.

To be sure, community is no panacea. These areas have at times been hard to monetize. Traditional message board areas used to fetch ad rates at some fraction of the content areas, and no one has figured out how to monetize Twitter followers other than driving them to click back to a website. As noted earlier, making communities productive and healthy does not happen just by slapping up some message boards, spitting out a Twitter feed and calling it a day. It takes time and care.

But the value is clear. In economic terms, a news organization can lower distribution costs, improve retention and generate more pageviews per dollar of expense. Just as important, in intellectual terms, the audience is no longer merely a consuming group. People expect to participate, and media managers must make it easier for readers to interact with each other, the news organization and other institutions in the community. News organizations will become, in effect, community service organizations of a new kind and the process will become truly valuable.

NOTES

1. "In Changing News Landscape, Even Television Is Vulnerable: Trends in News Consumption: 1991-2012," *Pew Research Center for the People and the Press*, September 27, 2012, http://www.people-press.org/2012/09/27/section-2-online-and-digital-news-2/.
2. "Kids Call Bus Monitor 'Fat' until She Cries and They Still Don't Stop," *Reddit*, June 19, 2012, http://www.reddit.com/r/videos/comments/vb5gj/kids_call_bus_monitor_fat_until_she_cries_and/.

Caitlin Johnston

In Chapter 11, Steven Waldman describes how the editors at Beliefnet balanced content generated by professionals and content generated by the audience. Below are two examples from other news organizations.

In May 2011, a devastating tornado tore through Joplin, Mo., killing about 160 people and destroying one-third of the city.[1] Large areas were without electricity and phone service, making it difficult to reach family members and friends. The *Joplin Globe* created a tornado survivor page the same night the tornado whipped through the city.

Scott Meeker, the *Globe*'s enterprise editor and Facebook administrator, said the staff made the decision when they noticed the *Globe*'s main Facebook page was getting inundated with families desperately trying to get information on loved ones. People from far away—Texas, Utah and Illinois—inquired about friends and family they hadn't heard from. An auto mechanic in Florida searched for his missing 5-year-old niece. A 61-year-old grandfather from New York wanted to know where to send a sympathy card for parents who lost their young son: "I am so heartsick about him it feels like he could have been my own child." They posted names and photos, addresses and the last places the missing were seen. They searched for uncles and dads, mothers and daughters. And they shared posts of joy when those they loved were found.

For Meeker, the decision to create the Facebook page was an easy one, in the same vein of public service as any other journalism the newspaper creates. However, others argue that having too many sites dedicated to finding people after disasters—other citizens had the same idea, and the American Red Cross has a "Safe and Well" searchable registry on its site—can cause confusion and make it harder to know where to go.

But while the Red Cross is the expert in family reunification, Meeker was happy that a news staff of about 15 people was able to use social media to better connect with its readers during a time when information was of the utmost importance. "I've been the admin on our Facebook page for a little over a year," Meeker said in an interview with The Poynter Institute. "It didn't really hit me until now the power that social media can have in times of crisis."

For Andy Carvin, his audience—in this case, his Twitter followers—function as a sort of newsroom, helping with research, translation and information services.[2] Carvin, an avid Twitter user who works at NPR, made a name for himself in 2010 when he started extensively tweeting about the revolution in Tunisia and the resulting uprisings across the Middle East. Carvin had spent time in Tunisia and was able to use his contacts there while cultivating others in order to inform his following of 30,000 at the time.

Carvin calls his Twitter account an "open-source newsroom that anyone can come and participate in."[3] In 2011, Carvin and his Twitter newsroom debunked claims that Israeli weapons were being used in Libya. On the day Egyptian President Hosni Mubarak resigned, Carvin tweeted more than 1,400 times. He tweeted 1,200 times on a separate weekend during the Libyan revolution. He has been described as a "DJ of the revolutions," a hub for those on the ground.[4]

While some have equated Carvin's use of Twitter to a wire service, Carvin explains that it's more similar to the community of a newsroom, where people work together as researchers, producers and editors:

> So when I'm trying to capture what's going on in Syria, or Libya, or Egypt, my Twitter followers come out of the woodwork and they translate for me, they do research for me, they track shipping lanes and flights going in and out of airports. It's incredible the skills that people bring to the table. They may not be experts in the entire Arab spring, or a specific country, but they have either one area of expertise or local knowledge that allows them to contribute to the greater part of my newsgathering.

While his followers dig up information and help with translation and verification, Carvin must still work as the traditional journalism gatekeeper. He must constantly monitor the feeds, coordinate the conversation, and decide what parts of that conversation are important enough to focus on.

QUESTIONS

• When professional journalists invite the public to participate in the gathering and telling of news, what responsibilities do they take on? How should they moderate the participation? What techniques should they employ to ensure accuracy? Write a set of short guidelines for each of the examples above, outlining responsibilities for a journalist new to the role.

• Virtual communities across the Internet are organized around an issue or event. Find an example of one such community that is gathering and sharing news. What is the value of the news created by the community you have identified? How would that news be different if it were generated by professionals?

• News organizations employ a variety of systems for gathering user-generated content. Some encourage comments; others ask for photos or other submissions. Some create their own custom spaces within their websites. Others use independent spaces like Facebook and Twitter. Identify three different places where news organizations are gathering user-generated content. Describe how the content is gathered and the strengths and weaknesses of each approach. How does each approach build community?

• Some news stories lend themselves to community participation. Identify three such topics and craft a plan that would encourage citizen engagement.

Identify the platform, what you would expect citizens to contribute, and how you would verify, organize and curate those contributions so that they would be most helpful to others.

CASE NOTES

1. Adam Hochberg, "Joplin *Globe*'s Facebook Page Locates, Reunites Missing People in Tornado Aftermath," *Poynter.org*, May 24, 2011, http://www.poynter.org/latest-news/making-sense-of -news/133446/joplin-globes-facebook-page-locates-reunites-missing-people-in-tornado -aftermath/.
2. Jeff Sonderman, "Andy Carvin Explains How Twitter Is His 'Open-Source Newsroom,'" *Poynter.org*, January 3, 2012, http://www.poynter.org/latest-news/mediawire/157874/andy -carvin-explains-how-twitter-is-his-open-source-newsroom/.
3. Ibid.
4. Jeff Sonderman, "How Andy Carvin Keeps His Sanity While Live-Tweeting World News," *Poynter. org*, September 7, 2011, http://www.poynter.org/latest-news/media-lab/social-media/145279/ how-andy-carvin-keeps-his-sanity-while-live-tweeting-world-news/.

The Destabilizing Force of Fear

danah boyd and Kelly McBride

Fear is perhaps the most immediately powerful emotion. While lust, anger and love move people to do great things, make sacrifices and change the world, fear inspires in all animals—humans included—an immediate, rapid, sometimes involuntary response. Fear makes you jump or yell or fight. Fear motivates mobs, which go on to commit violence. Fear makes rational behavior unlikely. Fear overwhelms compassion.

Increasingly, certain aspects of the Internet run on fear. Thanks to technology, people have more access to more information at their fingertips than ever before in human history. This creates a new challenge for those who are trying to produce and disseminate information in the attention economy. Organizations that rely on people's attention—including news media—must go to great lengths to seize focus by any means possible.

Of course, the attention economy has always been a companion to the world of media. It's why the commercials are louder and sometimes more clever, certainly more obnoxious on TV and radio, than the programming. It's why billboards and cereal boxes are designed to draw your eye. But the technology explosion that has shepherded us into the 21st century has magnified the value of attracting an individual's attention such that it can pose a challenge to journalism's core values of truth, transparency and community. Or to put it another way, everyone has a limited span of attention available to consume information. And fear sells.

Indeed, journalism has a tradition of fear. TV news and radio programs use auditory cues, linguistic patterns and segment cliffhangers to entice people to stay attentive. Teasers for the upcoming newshour often hook viewers with stories of scary events that "could happen to you." Media organizations regularly employ fear because it works. Fear generates attention and helps draw an audience.

Fear sells particularly well in a social media environment. How many times have you seen a friend click (and thus share) an ad on Facebook like the warning about three things that happen before you have a heart attack? How tempting is it to click a link to a site that promises that you can see who's viewing your profile, even though you know it's a phishing scheme meant to trick you into revealing your password? The more likely it is you'll pass the information by, the greater the payoff when the creator taps into your anxieties and grabs your attention.

As our society grows increasingly networked, and as our attention is increasingly trained on a device—be it a laptop, tablet or phone—we face a critical crossroad. We are presented with an increasing volume of information, while our capacity for attention remains the same. Thus our attention is increasingly commodified, and countless actors go to great lengths to be the ones that catch our eye. What are the costs? What are the implications?

Democracy depends on a citizenry, if not fully informed, at least episodically engaged and willing to render judgments on public policy. Ideally, that notion works best when the media play the role of directing the public's attention to issues and concerns of public significance. As news organizations compete for audience, however, and as data and demographics tie specific audiences to specific stories or topics, the product of a journalist's effort can increasingly be valued in commercial terms. Thus, journalists and newsrooms are not just pursuing information in order to inform the public. They are increasingly tempted to select narratives that will entice desirable demographics to sell to advertisers. To do so, they are playing into the attention economy. Given these very real pressures, how should we understand the ethics of using fear to capture attention?

THE CULTURE OF FEAR

Fear trickles down in a society. While it's easy to look at historic examples of xenophobia and recognize the real consequences, it's harder to see the damage it's causing as it unfolds right in front of you. An individual act of fear-mongering causes little damage, but the additive effects of repeated episodes are huge.

Consider contemporary parenting culture. Every day, we wake up to news reports about the dangers that youth face when they go online. Parents, surveyed by researchers, are patently afraid of online sexual predators. When parents explain their decisions to place restrictions on their kids' freedoms, they point to the risk of abduction and sexual victimization. It is rare for these parents to know anyone who has ever been kidnapped or sexually assaulted by any stranger, let alone one met through the Internet. Instead, they point to television news shows like *Dateline's* "To Catch a Predator" series as proof of the pervasiveness of lurking pedophiles.

Yet the data on sex crimes against children show that, more often than not, family members and friends of family members are the aggressors in sexual assaults of children. People hold onto the image of innocent children who are duped by lurking abusers because we refuse to accept the possibility that dad or grandpa, coach or mom's boyfriend, could be a predator. This is not to suggest that those with disturbing sexual desires don't use the Internet to engage in illegal or problematic behavior. They do. But the story that is told is rarely the full story. In the extremely rare cases where the Internet was involved in sexual assaults, researchers have found that teenagers who have previously been abused sometimes invited the attention of strangers in an effort to feel loved by someone in their mid-20s or early 30s.[1] These teenagers are being violated, but the model of their abuse is far from the public image of an online sexual predator.

The story of sexual predation captures people's attention. Every parent out there is worried that terrible things might happen to their child. News media play on this fear by amping up any and all stories that suggest that an evil man lurking in the corner has abducted an innocent child. The price of the simplistic narrative is that is makes us ignore the more complex issues.

For example, in February 2006, two girlfriends, ages 13 and 15, disappeared in the middle of the night from the same condominium complex in Los Angeles. The girls left behind their wallets and prescription medication and had not packed anything of sentimental value. Quite reasonably, police and family immediately assumed they had been abducted. As law enforcement investigated, the news media told stories about the dangers of MySpace, the perils of the Internet and the prevalence of sexual predators.

As the story unfolded and the girls were found, it became clear that the teens had not been kidnapped. Instead, they had run away together because they were lovers and their parents had barred them from seeing one another or even communicating with one another online. Instead of correcting earlier stories that implicitly drew a connection between the disappearance and the dangers of technology, most news media outlets covering the story went silent. As a result, many parents and teens in Southern California continued to see this story as evidence of sexual predators on the Internet even though the real story was about the costs of parental homophobia.

When we accept the stranger-danger story of children on the Internet, as the media did in this instance, we fail to tell other stories: Most child sexual abuse victims are harmed by someone close to them, and teens sometimes engage in risky behaviors online. Often these kids are acting out partially as a result of previous trauma and abuse. Rather than educating the public to recognize these behaviors as warning signs, journalists often demonize the technology and ramp up the narrative about the risks all teens face. They do so at the expense of accuracy. But more devastatingly, they do so at the expense of youth who seriously need attention, support and help.

THE COST OF FEAR

By most measures, today's youth are safer than ever before in history. Yet parents perceive the exact opposite, then act on those perceptions by restricting independence and curbing opportunities that allow children to grow and engage in public life. As a result, we've seen an increasingly fractured youth culture where teens have few opportunities to socialize unsupervised or take risks.[2]

In *The Culture of Fear*, sociologist Barry Glassner provides numerous examples of how fear has stymied people's willingness to engage publicly or take risks that lead to personal growth. For example, elderly populations often grow fearful of the possibility that they will be victims of violent crime because of how news media cover violent crime. This leads some senior citizens to not leave their homes and isolate themselves out of fear of potential abuse. Some have died of starvation because they were too afraid to purchase groceries.

For every headline meant to capitalize on fear, an opportunity is lost. The premise of fear is easy, whether it's a story about bedbugs, dirty restaurants or contaminants in your food. Again, this is not a new device to journalism. You can look no further than local television sweeps week or the grocery store tabloids to see examples that predate the Internet. But layer on the massive explosion in information, as well as the new platforms through which information is delivered—phone, social media, tablet—and you intensify the competition for people's attention. This gives rise to an attention economy where competing interests are vying for a limited resource. Appealing to fear may seem like an easy solution. Fear is not predicated on risk assessment but on the perception of risk, and that perception is shaped through exposure to a narrative through media, friends and social messages.

In the days that followed Sept. 11, Americans scrambled to understand what was going on and to get their heads around the potential threat they faced as a community. This wasn't the first time Americans endured national confusion and chaos. Read accounts of the Cuban missile crisis and you'll hear a similar set of fears, born out of uncertainty. The government can and does use those fears to justify particular policies and to get public buy-in. The media both serve the government's mission by producing these stories and capitalize on the opportunity to sell stories that are part of widespread cultural anxieties. For the last decade, the U.S. government has tapped into this fear to mold the behavior of its citizens. More than a full decade after the 9/11 attacks, the United States is still on orange alert.

In an information-rich world, it stands to reason that forces would rise up to counter corruption and push back against institutional oppression reliant on fear. Indeed, even in the months following 9/11, when it was clear that the United States would invade Afghanistan, we saw survivors rise up to state "Not in our Name." But in many communities where the media-driven narrative was disconnected from the physical realities of those attacks, the fear sold by the media had much more traction and provided much greater fuel to justify a reaction.

Healthy fears are those that encourage survival. Burn yourself on an open flame, and you'll be more wary next time. In a journalistic context, healthy fears would translate into those that are true to the context of the events—for instance, that sexually predatory behavior is more likely to come from family or friends than strangers. Healthy fears would also relate to problems that rise to appropriate significance—for instance, the implications of climate change or the consequences of the rising costs of entitlement programs on future fiscal policy. The more outrageous the perceived threat, the more willing people are to go to extremes to avoid it, even if such trade-offs do significant cultural damage. But who is responsible for fueling the flames of fear? When is doing so acceptable?

BEGGING FOR ATTENTION

Plenty of journalists—indeed probably most in the profession—don't set out to scare people with their work, but they are traveling upstream in the information flow. The fear element is often teased out of the most respectable work in order to help information travel far and wide via social media. It emerges in the headline that adorns an otherwise tempered article, and it emerges in how a particular segment is juxtaposed with another.

Part of journalism is presenting information in a way that will capture people's attention, and some publications have looser standards than others about what means can be used to do so. In an era of fragmented media, even the most traditional media organizations must now leverage the Internet to broadcast stories and attract attention. To increase the likelihood of their success, they often make it easy for viewers to spread stories via email, Facebook or Twitter, where those who originate the stories lose control over how they are presented. What circulates is often the content that has the least geopolitical consequence and is most likely to scare universally. Fearful messages spread especially far, particularly stories that play into broad cultural anxieties. When journalists are rewarded for viewership, there's a perverse motivation to play into people's attraction to freak shows and horror, regardless of the broader social consequences.

Journalists and news media are responding to existing incentives. They're incentivized to generate audiences that they can then sell to advertisers. They're incentivized to capture attention by any means possible. The underlying incentive to inform and educate is still there, but it's muddied by the corporate incentives to increase audience. Left unchecked and incentivized to increase viewership at whatever costs, news media will continue to capitalize on fear and increase the culture of fear in the process.

Consider the 2012 story surrounding the "Innocence of Muslims." This atrociously produced, low-budget film had few redeeming qualities. In a badly acted narrative, the film suggested that the prophet Muhammad was a pedophile, a womanizer and an egomaniac. The movie was created by a California man, Nakoula Basseley Nakoula, and clips were uploaded to YouTube in the summer of 2012. An Egyptian man living in Virginia then added Arabic subtitles and posted the clips to his own website. Media in the Middle East found the film clips on YouTube and broadcast them as evidence of America's Islamophobia.[3]

While trying to track down information on the film, some journalists decided to call Pastor Terry Jones of the Dove World Outreach Center in Gainesville, Fla., who could be depended on to say something controversial. Jones had gained notoriety in 2010 when he promised to burn a Koran on the anniversary of the Sept. 11 attacks. After much attention and international pressure, he backed down. He actually did burn a Koran in March 2011, which sparked protests in the Middle East. Asked about the "Innocence of Muslims," Jones seized the opportunity to say that, yes, he supported the film and would be showing it in his church. Within hours, dozens of reporters were outside Jones' church in Gainesville representing the nation's media outlets.

Jones had nothing to do with the creation of the "Innocence of Muslims" video. In fact, until reporters called it to his attention, he wasn't even aware of it. Suddenly, his statement that he "supported" the video made it seem like there was a network of Islam haters working to incite riots in the Middle East. Within hours, the chairman of the joint chiefs of staff was asking Jones to withdraw his support for the film, furthering the impression that Jones was part of a network.[4]

Meanwhile, in the Middle East, discussion of the footage took on an equally hateful narrative as commentators used the film to make broad claims about American attitudes toward Muslims, which were then used to justify anti-American sentiment. Networked conversations online fueled those messages, which were in turn reinforced by people having broad anytime access to the disturbing video. The news media helped create a spark that turned into a bonfire.

Fear's influence over information can be subtle, as well as overt. In the case of the "Innocence of Muslims" video, journalists invited Jones to insert himself into the story. When he did, the resulting impression was greater than the sum of its parts. Journalists didn't simply report on a story; they helped create it. And in doing so, they leveraged an opportunity to capitalize on existing fears and phobias.

SERVING CITIZENS, FUELING CITIZENS

Historically, journalists have focused on creating media that citizens consumed. While word-of-mouth and water cooler conversations always served as vehicles for their reporting to circulate, news media did not actively rely on the audience to play an active role in distribution and circulation. In an era of social media where news organizations traffic in *likes* and depend on readers to forward along anything they find interesting, that is no longer the case. Newspapers like *The New York Times* prominently display the most emailed articles while news aggregators like Yahoo! News and Google News depend heavily on user interactions to determine what is most popular or most interesting.

Newsrooms control their own websites—and editors are passionate architects of what goes above and below the digital fold—but when millions of people find news through what's posted on Facebook or what appears at the top of an aggregator, editors quickly lose control of their stories.

In February 2012, *The New York Times* published an extensively detailed and rich feature article about the ways in which Target used customer data, in which reporters raised serious questions about privacy in a world of data analysis. The article was posted under a relatively neutral headline "How Companies Learn Your Secrets."[5] A few hours after the *Times* published this well-researched article, *Forbes* posted an article that provided a synopsis of *The New York Times* story, complete with a link to the original *Times* story in the second paragraph. Their story, "How Target Figured Out a Teen Girl Was Pregnant before Her Father Did," played on consumer fears.[6] Needless to say, this latter story spread like wildfire on social media as people actively shared the link. While it's not clear how many people clicked through to read the full *New York Times* exposé, it was quite obvious that *Forbes* capitalized on a fear-provoking aspect of *The New York Times*' investigative work.

Just as news media consider what might capture their potential audience's attention, so too do everyday people participating on social media. They craft status updates and publish tweets meant to entice their friends to pay attention, either to them or to the content that they're suggesting. When the media give them an inflammatory message to spread, they take that language and roll with it. Even when the media is more neutral in its tone, people often pick up the most fearful component of the story and use that as link bait.

Social media has made information overload a de facto part of everyday life, and it can be difficult to manage the onslaught of personalities, brands and messages vying for people's attention. Some have adopted a Zen-like approach, letting the flood of information flow over them and grabbing onto the occasional message just to check in.[7] Others obsessively try to prioritize what to consume. But either way, there's always the question of what will stand out, what will capture someone's attention. It's no longer the message that's at the top of the hour or above the fold. It's often the message that's repeated the most or framed in a way that's too juicy to ignore. Journalists aren't the only ones struggling to find their voice in an information-saturated world. This is now everyone's challenge and everyone's dilemma.

COMBATING FEAR IN AN ATTENTION ECONOMY

There is no magic bullet to solve the problem of fear-selling in media, but it starts with awareness. It's clear that journalists are for the most part fully cognizant of the pressures of the attention economy. Have journalists articulated how those pressures undermine their core commitment to truth? Do we understand the costs that fear has to society? Have we considered the role that journalists play in setting societal norms?

As we fully embrace a networked society, we need to consider what guiding principles should influence decisions about the spread of information. This book has articulated three core principles—Truth, Transparency and Community—as guideposts by which to navigate. These principles become increasingly essential as we navigate the costs and consequences of an attention economy, and they also raise serious questions about how we move forward to achieve these higher goals.

Is it possible to break down the workflow in newsrooms and identify where the influence of fear is inserted into the news product and then ask if those small decisions are undermining those big principles? When a reporter focuses on a sensational anomaly, what obligation does she have to place that information in a broader context? When a Web producer writes a catchy headline in order to grab people's attention, how much distortion is tolerated? What are the ethical responsibilities of an editor or publisher, who has both a fiduciary responsibility to attract audience and advertisers, as well as a commitment to journalism? How can we assess the influence that journalists have on the public's use of fear-mongering? Can we articulate best practices for packaging pictures and words for social media distribution? Who is responsible for making journalists accountable in a networked age?

Just as societies are dependent on information to enable citizens to participate in democracy, societies can be undermined and fragmented through fear. There is nothing neutral about the practice of reporting, and it behooves journalists to draw from a practice widespread among anthropologists and reflexively account for how their work affects the communities they serve.

Beyond thinking about a commitment to accuracy in reporting, journalistic principles should include accounting for accuracy in interpretation. In a mediated world where information flow isn't just par for the course, but something that is highly visible, it becomes imperative for news agencies to examine how their acts of journalism are influencing the public's understanding of the world.

As our society gets increasingly networked, we need to hold onto the importance of serving the citizenry in ways that support democracy rather than undermine it. Journalists are not simply in the business of reporting the news; they are in the business of making sure that the public is meaningfully informed. Key to that is a commitment to prevent fear from taking over.

NOTES

1. Janis Wolak, David Finkelhor, Kimberly J. Mitchell, and Michele L. Ybarra, "Online 'Predators' and Their Victims: Myths, Realities, and Implications for Prevention and Treatment," *American Psychologist,* 63, no. 2, 111–128 DOI: 10.1037/0003–066X.63.2.111, http://www.apa.org/pubs/journals/releases/amp-632111.pdf.

2. Gill Valentine, *Public Space and the Culture of Childhood* (Burlington, VT: Ashgate, 2004).

3. "The Worldwide Protests Against Anti-Islam Film *Innocence of Muslims:* By the Numbers," *The Week,* September 17, 2012, http://theweek.com/article/index/233439/the-worldwide-protests-against-anti-islam-film-innocence-of-muslims-by-the-numbers.

4. "General Asks Gainesville Pastor to Withdraw Support of Anti-Islam Film," *Tampa Bay Online,* September 12, 2012, http://www2.tbo.com/lifestyles/life/2012/sep/12/3/gainesville-pastor-terry-jones-indirectly-tied-to-ar-495749/.

5. Charles Duhigg, "How Companies Learn Your Secrets," *New York Times Magazine,* February 16, 2012, http://www.nytimes.com/2012/02/19/magazine/shopping-habits.html?_r=1&.

6. Kashmir Hill, "How Target Figured Out a Teen Girl Was Pregnant before Her Father Did," *Forbes,* February 16, 2012, http://www.forbes.com/sites/kashmirhill/2012/02/16/how-target-figured-out-a-teen-girl-was-pregnant-before-her-father-did/.

7. danah boyd, "Streams of Content, Limited Attention: The Flow of Information through Social Media," *Web2.0 Expo,* November 17, 2009, http://www.danah.org/papers/talks/Web2Expo.html.

Caitlin Johnston

In their essay, danah boyd and Kelly McBride suggest that journalists reflexively use fear as a means of generating interest in their work. In the example that follows, critics argued that journalists were tapping into fear after a traumatic event. Supporters argued the newsroom was making public information accessible to an interested citizenry.

In December 2012, *The Journal News,* which serves the suburban communities north of New York City, published an interactive map showing the names and addresses of every registered handgun permit owner in two nearby counties.[1] The paper filed a Freedom of Information Act request in the wake of the Sandy Hook Elementary shooting in Newtown, Conn., in which 20 children and six adults were killed. In the wake of the shooting, debate on gun control raged throughout the country. Politicians spoke of gun reform. Gun owners advocated for their rights. The subject dominated the news.

FIGURE 12-1   **This map shows pistol permits registered with the Westchester County Clerk's Office as of December 2012.**

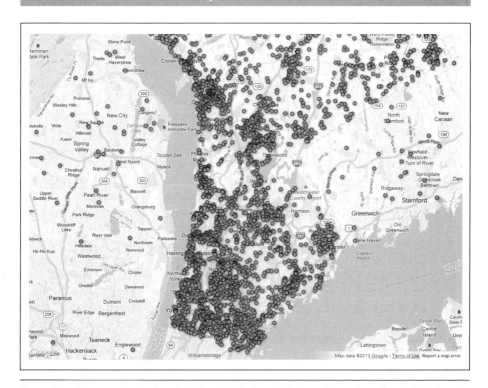

Source: "Map: Where are the Gun Permits in Your Neighborhood" *The Journal News,* December 22, 2012, http://www.lohud.com/interactive/article/20121223/NEWS01/121221011.

The *Journal News* headline—"The gun owner next door: What you don't know about the weapons in your neighborhood"—urged readers to click on the story and explore the map.[2] The story itself started with a chilling anecdote: "In May, Richard V. Wilson approached a female neighbor on the street and shot her in the back of the head, a crime that stunned their quiet Katonah neighborhood. What was equally shocking for some was the revelation that the mentally disturbed 77-year-old man had amassed a cache of weapons — including two unregistered handguns and a large amount of ammunition — without any neighbors knowing."

The story went on to quote law enforcement pointing out how very little the public knows about the privately owned weapons and a neighbor who said she would not have purchased her house had she known someone nearby owned so many weapons.

The database did not include shotguns, rifles or assault weapons. Nor did the inclusion of a name and address mean that person currently owned a handgun[3]—only that he or she had a permit to do so. The article garnered about 2,000 mostly critical comments before it was taken down about a month later.[4] Some said the map endangered former police officers, domestic violence victims and local residents *without* guns, whose homes might be considered safer to burglarize. Others compared it to publishing the names and addresses of pedophiles, except the people listed on the gun map were not violating any laws by holding these pistol permits.

"People obtain permits for personal safety reasons," Andrew Arulanandam, director of public affairs for the National Rifle Association, told *USA Today* "It is incredibly ignorant and irresponsible for the newspaper to publish a map of which houses have firearms in them. There is no public service component (to the database) no matter how you look at it."[5] In response, bloggers published addresses for the newspaper's publisher and editor, the story's reporter and Gannett's CEO. Dozens of other publications, including the Drudge Report, Yahoo, ABC News and Fox News, discussed the ethics of publishing the database.

The newspaper defended its decision, stating the information was a matter of public record. A couple days after the story went live, the paper published an article explaining the controversy and responding to critics. "We knew publication of the database would be controversial, but we felt sharing as much information as we could about gun ownership in our area was important in the aftermath of the Newtown shootings," said CynDee Royle, editor and vice president/news. "People are concerned about who owns guns and how many of them there are in their neighborhoods."[6] The newspaper's office was flooded with threats and calls from angry readers. In response the paper hired armed guards to protect its employees.

A few weeks later, the state responded by enacting a law that allowed registered handgun owners to request their name be kept out of the public record by claiming an exemption based on a long list of privacy reasons.[7] While the law did not require the paper to take down the story, *The Journal*

News removed the data from its website days after the law was passed. Still, the paper argued that the story and map contributed to the national conversation on gun control. "One of our core missions as a newspaper is to empower our readers with as much information as possible on the critical issues they face, and guns have certainly become a top issue since the massacre in nearby Newtown, Conn.," said Janet Hasson, president and publisher of The Journal News Media Group.[8]

Timeliness alone isn't reason enough to publish the information, nor is privacy a strong enough argument against it, argued The Poynter Institute's Al Tompkins.[9] After all, journalists infringe on privacy frequently when publishing drunk-driving records, arrest records, professional licenses and other private information. The justification comes after weighing the journalistic purpose of the information against the potential harm.

QUESTIONS

- When looking at the interactive map of pistol permit holders, different people might experience different fears. What are those fears? Some might argue that because *The Journal News* tapped fears on both sides of the gun control debate, its choices were a model of neutrality and independence. How would you respond to that?

- Editors at *The Journal News* said their journalistic purpose was to give their audience information. Are there other higher journalistic purposes for publishing this database? What are those purposes, and what type of reporting or execution would be required to achieve those higher purposes?

- What alternatives did the staff at the *The Journal News* have besides publishing all the information in the database the way they did? How could they have published the information differently without invading personal privacy?

- In the digital age, data is one of the growth areas of journalism. What essential notions should guide the creation of journalism from data? What is the difference between data and news?

- Various government agencies generate lots of public databases. Identify one database that is public but not easily accessible. How might a professional journalism organization make that information more accessible? Can you articulate a journalistic reason to do that?

CASE NOTES

1. "Map: Where Are the Gun Permits in Your Neighborhood?" *lohud.com*, December 22, 2012, http://www.lohud.com/interactive/article/20121223/NEWS01/121221011?gcheck=1.

2. "The Gun Owner Next Door: What You Don't Know about the Weapons in Your Neighborhood," *lohud.com*, December 23, 2012, http://www.lohud.com/apps/pbcs.dll/article?AID=201231223 0056&nclick_check=1.

3. "Many Rockland Handgun Permits Have Outdated, Inaccurate Data," *lohud.com*, January 26, 2013, http://www.lohud.com/article/20130127/NEWS03/301270041/Many-Rockland-handgun-permits-outdated-inaccurate-data?odyssey=tab|topnews|text|Frontpage.

4. Andrew Beaujon, "Journal News Removes Gun Map," *Poynter.org*, January 18, 2013, http://www.poynter.org/latest-news/mediawire/201195/journal-news-removes-gun-map/.

5. Randi Weiner, "N.Y. Newspaper's Gun-Owner Database Draws Criticism," *USAToday*, December 26, 2012, http://www.usatoday.com/story/news/nation/2012/12/26/gun-database-draws-criticism/1791507/.

6. Julie Moos, "Newspaper Publishes Names, Addresses of Gun Owners," *Poynter.org*, December 26, 2012, January 7, 2013 (updated), http://www.poynter.org/latest-news/mediawire/199148/newspaper-publishes-names-addresses-of-gun-owners/.

7. Andrew Beaujon, "N.Y.'s Tough New Gun Law Also Prohibits Disclosure of Gun Owners' Names," *Poynter.org*, January 15, 2013, January 16, 2013 (updated), http://www.poynter.org/latest-newsmediawire/200714/n-y-s-tough-new-gun-law-also-prohibits-disclosure-of-gun-owners-names/.

8. Jim Fitzgerald, "NY Newspaper Removes Handgun Permit Holder Data," *Associated Press*, January 18, 2013, http://news.yahoo.com/ny-newspaper-removes-handgun-permit-holder-data-002910027.html.

9. Al Tompkins, "Where the Journal News Went Wrong in Publishing Names, Addresses of Gun Owners," *Poynter.org*, December 27, 2012, January 7, 2013 (updated), http://www.poynter.org/latest-news/als-morning-meeting/199218/where-the-journal-news-went-wrong-in-publishing-names-addresses-of-gun-owners/.

13

How Untold Stories Can Reflect Diversity

Eric Deggans

I f anyone asks why ethnic, cultural and gender diversity is important in journalism, advocates have a ready answer: Greater diversity equals greater accuracy and fairness. This belief is based, in part, on bitter experience. From turn-of-the-century lynchings[1] in the American South to the women's suffrage movement and the civil rights protests in the 1950s and 1960s,[2] U.S. history is filled with stories journalists got wrong because they excluded the perspectives of anyone who wasn't a white male. Coverage was so distorted during the civil rights era[3] that some newspapers—including the *Tallahassee Democrat* in Florida, the *Lexington Herald-Leader* in Kentucky and the *Hattiesburg American* in Mississippi—all apologized for their misguided work decades after the initial mistakes were made.[4]

Beyond hurt feelings or appearances, a diverse newsroom better reflects the population, which should enable fairer, more accurate and incisive reporting.[5] But what if that idea isn't entirely true? As journalism continues to adapt to a new digital reality, journalists will encounter a number of blockbuster news stories with race and cultural differences at their core. The result: Reporters can stumble over a host of pitfalls as their work is affected by limited perspectives.

The shape of modern media has only multiplied these problems. With a range of politically partisan, specifically targeted cable news channels, social media platforms and websites adding to the noise, ethical journalists face even more complicated questions. What separates an opinion journalist from a news reporter and a straight-up pundit? And what are the ethical requirements for each of these figures, especially in covering a race-based controversy? In the age of Fox News, MSNBC, the *Huffington Post* and Breitbart.com, is there such a thing as a completely honest broker in today's news media?

But increasing diversity in newsrooms and giving journalists of color more leeway to cover stories centered on race is only a partial solution to a more complicated problem. Put simply, we often don't know how to talk about race and difference outside of a crisis. Such subjects are covered so infrequently— sometimes with multipart series making a great splash every couple of years or so—that the only time media turn as a collective toward such issues is in the shadow of a larger event. Discussions about racial implications are hung onto journalism like ornaments on a Christmas tree, often distracting and obscuring the core issues in the process.

After a concert in 2012, a group of African-American youths attacked two non-black reporters from *The Virginian-Pilot* newspaper. Their employer initially failed to report on the crime to its readers.[6] Later, after an editorial columnist at the paper wrote about the assault,[7] Fox News Channel anchor Bill O'Reilly[8] and The Drudge Report website implied journalism was stifled for political correctness. But even the reporters who were attacked now say there was no indication from the attackers that race was a factor in the assault. They blame O'Reilly and Drudge for distorting the issue from more basic questions about how the newspaper should report on staffers who are victims of a crime.[9]

After anchor Ann Curry was pushed from her job at NBC's *Today* show, *Seattle Times* digital associate opinions editor Sharon Pian Chan wrote a short piece lamenting the loss of an important role model for Asian American journalists.[10] But many of her readers responded with anger, convinced she was saying Curry lost her job because she was Asian-American. Chan's conclusion: She had mistakenly assumed her readers had a more sophisticated understanding of the race issues at hand and failed to give them enough context to understand her message. "My . . . reaction was, 'Wow, dialogue on race is far less evolved in our society than I expected it would be,'" said Chan, a former president of the Asian American Journalists Association, during a phone interview. "People were shocked that we would A: notice (Curry's) race, and B: say that her race was important to us."

Of course, real success in covering race comes when perspectives are tempered by a clear strategy for preserving the traditional journalism values of fairness and accuracy. One of the biggest stories to test these concepts—from the power of including diverse perspectives in media coverage to the danger of letting opinions cloud facts in an explosive, internationally known news event—centered on the fate of an unarmed 17-year-old male shot dead while walking back from a convenience store in a small central Florida town.

Many of the complex dimensions of diversity can be found in one of the biggest stories of the digital age so far to involve race—the killing of Trayvon Martin. Let's examine the story, as it evolved.

PART 1: THE EARLY DAYS

What stands out about Trayvon Martin is how easily his name might not have become a household word. Martin, 17, was shot dead by George Zimmerman on Feb. 26, 2012, while walking to a home he was visiting in a subdivision of Sanford, Fla. Later, after his case became a worldwide cause, people learned the youth was unarmed, holding a bag of Skittles and a container of iced tea, after a trip to a nearby convenience store.[11]

Zimmerman, who was a volunteer neighborhood watch captain, killed the youth with a gun he was legally licensed to carry after they got in a fight. The state's Stand Your Ground law provided possible justification for using lethal force if Zimmerman felt his life was in jeopardy.

One of the first reports on the shooting, an 86-word piece printed in the *Orlando Sentinel* on February 27, noted simply that "two men were arguing before shots were fired."[12] The next day, the newspaper published another, 152-word story naming Martin, citing his age and noting his Facebook page listed Miami as his hometown, quoting a local TV station's report that there had been a fistfight before the shooting. But the newspaper didn't name Zimmerman, it wrote, "because he has not been charged."[13] By March 2, the *Miami Herald* had published a report noting erroneously that Martin was shot dead at a convenience store, quoting the teen's uncle. It did name Zimmerman but understated the 28-year-old's age by three years.

None of these stories, however, had the detail that would turn Martin's case into an international media tsunami: Martin was black, and the shooter who killed him was not. Race was the engine that eventually turned Trayvon Martin's death into the first story to briefly eclipse the presidential race in coverage during 2012;[14] sparking "million hoodie" marches across the country (the teen was wearing a hooded jacket when he was killed) and eventually costing Sanford police chief Bill Lee his job.[15]

With the race difference, police reticence to arrest Zimmerman took on a new light, raising fears of a southern town's good ol' boy network in action. Journalists had an angle that could elevate the unfortunate shooting of a young boy into a story with implications about racial profiling, small town justice and the struggle for a working-class, black family to get fair treatment from a mostly white police force and criminal justice system.

"It's clear this kind of thing just doesn't happen to white people . . . so race played some role in it," said Trymaine Lee,[16] a Pulitzer Prize–winning reporter who covered the case for *The Huffington Post's* Black Voices site.[17] Lee spoke with me in late 2012, just before leaving the *Huffington Post* to join MSNBC .com as a senior writer. "Obviously, Trayvon wasn't doing anything illegal at the time," added Lee, who jumped onto the Martin case early, after Martin's father hosted a press conference on the steps of the Sanford Police Department. Lee wrote one of the first extensive national stories about the family's concerns that police wouldn't prosecute Zimmerman. "But to paint (Zimmerman) as a homicidal devil incarnate is also a little . . . (much)," he told me.

Notions of racial implications behind the killing didn't emerge until more than a week after the teen's death, when CBS News, the *Huffington Post* and Reuters were among the first national news outlets to publish stories on that angle. The family's attorney, Benjamin Crump, said in Reuters' March 7 story that race was "the 600-pound elephant in the room. Why is this kid suspicious in the first place? I think a stereotype must have been placed on the kid."[18] Lee wrote a March 8 story for the *Huffington Post* noting "an unarmed African-American teenager was shot and killed in a gated community in Florida late last month by a white neighborhood watch captain, according to police. But the watch captain, George Zimmerman . . . still walks free."[19]

Why did it take so long for the story to surface? The nearest newspaper, the *Orlando Sentinel*, had closed its local Sanford bureau,[20] and police early on insisted they had no cause to arrest Zimmerman.[21] More bluntly, it seemed nobody was all that interested in a neighborhood watch captain killing a black teen in a subdivision, until Martin's parents began to speak up. This is a sore subject for some diversity advocates, who say media outlets may cover crime victims differently based on their race. In missing persons cases, for instance, critics have assailed the habit of extensively covering white females who have gone missing as breaking news, while missing people of color are covered only in stories about how little media attention they get.

The Trayvon Martin shooting, barely covered as a breaking news event, seemed to follow the pattern of attracting more coverage for the racial implications of its aftermath than the news of the killing itself. And a problem surfaced early in these first accounts. Although the initial police report on Martin's killing listed shooter George Zimmerman as white,[22] he self-identified as Hispanic on both his driver's license and voting records.[23] Because Zimmerman was already in hiding and didn't have anyone speaking publicly for him, that fact didn't surface until March 15, when his father, Robert Zimmerman, delivered a letter to the *Orlando Sentinel,* noting "George is a Spanish-speaking minority with many black family members and friends."[24] (George Zimmerman's mother is from Peru, and his father is a non-Hispanic white man.)

Others—notably, Pulitzer Prize–winning African-American columnist Leonard Pitts Jr.— noted that Zimmerman still could have racially profiled a young black teenager regardless of his own cultural background.[25] Still, the wrinkle with Zimmerman's ethnic heritage—*The New York Times* and ABC News even called him a "white Hispanic"[26] in some stories, straining to encompass the situation's racial dimensions in a single, crude identifier— highlighted some early, race-centered issues exposed by this story.

PART 2: EARLY PROBLEMS, CLASHING VALUES

Because people want race issues to be simple, often news stories centered on race are crafted simply. They feature shocking tales complete with heroes, villains and injustice, often with people of color presented as the noble victims. But the drive to fit real-life circumstances into these molds can be the enemy of accurate journalism. In the Trayvon Martin case, journalists quickly found themselves balancing conflicts between several different journalism values. There are three values that collided in the Martin case: the call for social justice, the notion that diversity adds context and the drive for exclusive scoops.

The social justice imperative. Journalists often seek to pursue social justice in their work, living up to fourth estate ideals of speaking up for those who lack power in society, opposing unfair treatment in government systems and holding big institutions accountable. In the Martin case, early reports suggested a white man might have gunned down a black teenager and received no prosecution or punishment, allowing journalists to feel free to even the score by bringing attention to the situation, amplifying the family's calls for more information and the prosecution of Zimmerman.

Here, the Martin family emerged as the noble victims, pressing big institutions such as the Sanford police department, local prosecutors and even Florida's statewide law enforcement agencies to pay attention to their concerns.

Better, fuller context through diversity. In the early days of the case, as public pressure grew for Zimmerman's arrest and prosecution, journalists of color added insights and urgency to the case by sharing their own experiences. *Washington Post* columnist Jonathan Capehart[27] wrote "one of the burdens of being a black male is carrying the heavy weight of other people's suspicions,"[28] recounting the instruction he got as a teen on how to deal with police to stay safe. Jesse Washington, who covers race and ethnicity for the Associated Press, wrote about explaining the "black male code" to his 12-year-old son, instructing him on how to "go above and beyond" to show strangers he isn't a threat.[29]

Referencing Ralph Ellison's classic novel *The Invisible Man*, the *Miami Herald*'s Pitts wrote, "That's one of the great frustrations of African-American life, those times when you are standing right there, minding your business, tending your house, coming home from the store, and other people are looking right at you, yet do not see you."[30] Some media figures of color obviously felt a personal stake in the Martin case that those unaffected by race prejudice or racial profiling may not have felt. And that led to some compelling pieces.

But was it fair for noncolumnists and journalists who don't express opinions to assume the case centered on racial profiling, when the man at the center of the case, shooter George Zimmerman, wasn't telling his side of the story publicly yet?

The push for scoops. Forget political bias; most journalism outlets are biased toward being first to break news, dominating the story everyone is talking about, and influencing the direction of the story by continuing to reveal information no one else has.

As interest in the story began to explode, news outlets crossed a number of lines in trying to find new information, from CNN using audio analysis of a 911 call[31] to mistakenly conclude Zimmerman used a racial slur, to ABC examining blurry video of Zimmerman's arrival at police headquarters in Sanford the night of the shooting to mistakenly theorize he might not have been injured in a fight with Martin as he claimed.[32]

Audiences concerned about the racial implications of the Martin story were seeking as much information as possible to understand what happened. But when reporting morphed from uncovering new facts to speculating on unverified claims, journalists wound up muddying the waters for news consumers, harming their own credibility in the process.

These three values, already in conflict as interest in the case began to heat up, collided with each other in earnest when the story took another turn: The 911 tapes from the shooting were made public.

PART 3: THE NATIONAL EXPLOSION

Media coverage of the Trayvon Martin case can easily be divided into two parts: Before the 911 tapes were heard by the world, and after. Police in Sanford had resisted releasing audio from 911 calls—including Zimmerman's call while following Martin and calls from neighbors during their fight and the shooting—saying the case was still under investigation. But they were made public March 16, supercharging national interest in a case, which was already percolating on CNN and ABC News, in local newspapers and in pockets of social media.[33]

Indeed, the *Huffington Post's* Lee, who tweeted steadily about developments in the case, said social media kept outrage over Martin's death alive, as people could sign petitions and participate in discussions about the case with a mouse click. The most visible petition, posted on Change.org and eventually embraced by Martin's parents, racked up 1 million signatures in less than two weeks to become the fastest-growing petition in the site's history.[34] "The more eyes this case got in front of, the more people got angry—in one way or another," Lee added. "It was amplified in a way I'd never seen . . . with petitions, people being active in a way they never felt motivated to do before, but it was so simple and easy. I don't think Trayvon would have been (such a phenomenon) without social media."

Audio of the 911 tapes turned that simmering heat into a raging fire. The most controversial moments indicated Zimmerman continued to follow Martin even after a police dispatcher told him "we don't need you to do that" and proved he knew Martin's race, despite a statement from police chief Bill Lee indicating he had not.[35] In calls from neighbors, high-pitched screams were abruptly cut short after a gunshot.

The tapes produced an explosion of media coverage on network TV news shows, cable news channels, national newspapers and websites. After their release, MSNBC anchor Al Sharpton[36] became officially involved as spokesperson for the Martin family, leading a March 22 rally in Sanford[37] to protest Zimmerman's freedom on the same day he interviewed the family for his TV show, less than a week after the 911 audio was released.

While media ethicists fretted, MSNBC president Phil Griffin insisted hosts such as Sharpton were not bound by the traditional codes of journalism.[38] Less than 18 months after MSNBC hosts Keith Olbermann[39] and Joe Scarborough had been suspended[40] from their jobs for donating to political candidates without approval, Sharpton was interviewing a family he also represented as an advocate—on the same news outlet.

In some of its coverage of the case, NBC News aired clips of Zimmerman's 911 call in which he seemed to be volunteering information on Martin's race. After complaints from media critics and conservative media outlets, the network admitted it clipped out audio of the dispatcher asking for the teen's race,[41] and it fired several staffers connected to the misleading, mistaken edits.[42] The firings didn't prevent Zimmerman from filing suit against NBC,[43] accusing the network of distorting facts and employing "the oldest form of yellow journalism"[44] to make him look racist. NBC denied the allegations and promised to fight the lawsuit in court.

The involvement of Sharpton and President Obama's March 23 statement that "if I had a son, he'd look like Trayvon,"[45] seemed to galvanize conservative media outlets, fracturing coverage further along political lines. Conservative-friendly websites such as the Daily Caller,[46] Twitchy.com[47] and Breitbart.com[48] published photos and stories questioning whether Martin was the innocent teen presented by his family and supporters. Some conservative news outlets seem to resent the power they believe nonwhite activists and advocacy groups have to define race-based controversies in the public space; thus, insisting that Martin may have been oversold as an innocent victim seemed to fit squarely with their mission.

Using photos and messages taken from the dead youth's social media accounts, the sites suggested Martin was a rougher figure, even as reports in the *Orlando Sentinel* and *Miami Herald* revealed the youth had been suspended from school for possession of a plastic baggie with marijuana residue.[49] On Fox News Channel, where its biggest stars lean conservative, some worried the shooting would be used to pursue stricter gun control laws.[50] Conservative media watchdogs Newsbusters.org wondered why media outlets used photos of Zimmerman's mug shot from a 2005 arrest next to images of Martin, who looked younger than 17.[51]

At MSNBC, liberal-oriented anchors such as Melissa Harris-Perry wore hooded jackets and denounced Zimmerman's continued freedom.[52] According to the Project for Excellence in Journalism, MSNBC devoted 49 percent of its news time to the story between March 19 and March 28, compared to 40 percent on CNN and 15 percent on Fox News.[53]

But even as this news story accelerated into the stratosphere, there were lessons about covering race to be learned from the trip.

LESSONS LEARNED

The most maddening part of the Trayvon Martin shooting is a question that may never be fully answered: Was this killing motivated at all by race?

Absent direct evidence, the struggle for answers often pushed journalists into a fight over the images of both victim and killer. If Zimmerman could be shown to have racial bias in his past, perhaps he acted on those biases when he saw a 17-year-old black kid he didn't recognize in his housing development. If Martin could be shown as a "thug"—which increasingly seems a nicer way of saying "violent, criminally inclined person of color"—then perhaps he was the one who began the confrontation that ended in his death. Decoding those two notions led reporters to excavate social media accounts maintained by both people, with the content of each examined to prove different points in the same way.

The *Miami Herald* drew international notice for its report on an old MySpace page maintained by Zimmerman in which he complains about

Mexicans, calling them "soft ass wanna be thugs messin with peoples cars when they aint around."[54] Later, he wrote of "Workin 96 hours to get a decent pay check, gettin knifes pulled on you by every mexican you run into!" The page, which Zimmerman's legal counsel admitted was genuine but abandoned years ago,[55] also featured pictures of Zimmerman with black friends, boasting of avoiding serious charges over a domestic dispute and a 2005 arrest after pushing a law enforcement officer arresting his friend for underage drinking.[56]

In Martin's case, media outlets reported on messages and pictures from the dead teen's social media accounts, which could have made him look oversexed, violent or unstable—the stereotypical picture of a criminally minded, thuggish young black man. The Daily Caller website featured a large picture of Martin with gold caps on his teeth taken from his Twitter account, where they say Martin tweeted under the name NO_LIMIT_NIGGA, using all the profanity and bravado about sex you would expect from a 17-year-old boy.[57] But if a white teen had kept a Facebook page with pictures of himself in a hoodie and gangster gear, talking pridefully with friends, would the same assumptions be made about possible criminality? Or would it just be chalked up to youthful exuberance?

This highlights one of the biggest problems in covering race for journalists: the temptation to "prove" the person at the center of a controversial story involving prejudice or stereotyping is racist. While a person's past history is important, finding unassailable evidence of racism is tough because it is often impossible to judge someone's thinking on race by outside factors. Worse, such notions also assume that only bigots can act on unfair prejudices.

It is entirely possible that a person who doesn't usually prejudge people of color might do so in a special circumstance—say, encountering that type of person at night on the street in a neighborhood where burglaries have been a problem. Early in Zimmerman's 911 call, he told the police dispatcher the area had a problem with break-ins.[58]

Still, if trying to read minds is one of the biggest pitfalls of race coverage, the next biggest problem is equally troublesome: We only talk about race issues on a national level in a crisis. I've written about this issue in The Poynter Institute's *Tampa Bay Times*[59] and in my own book, 2012's *Race-Baiter*,[60] ancillary discussions often spring up around race-based controversies because this is the only time the world is really paying attention.

A local TV news director once told me about the "myth of life" pitfall that journalists can fall into while discerning what is newsworthy. He noted that too many journalists assume that news is defined as an event that violates the myths of how we think life works: White suburbanites rarely are shot to death, or black teens from poor neighborhoods often don't get into Ivy League colleges. Such attitudes can keep journalists from seeing news in what happens every day, even when what happens daily is so horrific it would make the front pages of newspapers in most every other city instantly. And social media can make the dynamic worse, as more comments and Twitter posts focus on similar issues.

Given the "myth of life" issues with mainstream press, it's no wonder so many commentators addressing the Martin case tried to talk about racial profiling, the stereotyping of young black males, the history of law enforcement's role in enabling profiling and more. It's a dynamic that only gets worse as online and social media speed up the news cycle. With so few nuggets of news connected to the real questions the audience wants answered, a default for some media outlets can involve talking about ancillary issues, which distract and complicate.

Journalists are uniquely positioned to lead communities out of this trap, focusing on factual reporting and consciously working to sidestep misleading, myth-of-life–based attitudes. Years ago, a news event might unfold over a longer period of time where the focus would first fall on fact-gathering and reporting the story, with follow-up pieces devoted to the implications of the news and connected issues. These days, that process runs together. In the Martin/Zimmerman case—when news consumers needed as many facts about the case as journalists could provide—they instead got commentary, fact-based reporting and prognostication all wrapped up in one often-toxic ball.

Other problems with covering issues of race often fall into four categories:

Reflex: News media cover issues a certain way because they've always done it that way. Trusting police reports too much or failing to see the news in a teenager's violent death could be a result.

Fear: We fear being criticized for unfairly injecting race into a story, particularly if it isn't the central issue. One of the thorniest questions involves referencing race when it may not be the central issue in a story or may not be an issue at all.

Lack of history: We don't understand the community we're covering and its specific issues. Black residents in Sanford had specific gripes about how police treated them that many national media outlets didn't discuss.

Avoidance: When a newsroom is diverse, sometimes staffers of color are expected to provide the bulk of coverage on issues relating to race. That's not fair to the staffers or to the community, which deserves news outlets where every journalist is attentive to such stories and issues.

In the Martin case and others like it, the toughest task journalists may face is ignoring the perceptions and judgments of the outside world to focus on telling the most accurate, incisive stories possible.

Beyond its troubling facts, the story of Trayvon Martin's death also stands out for the way it straddles so many growing trends; from frictions sparked by the increasing diversity of the nation's under-18 youth (expected to be majority nonwhite by the year 2015) to the disappearance of traditional journalists from the biggest jobs in cable TV news and the growing influence of social media on the news cycle.[61]

In the midst of growing uncertainty and chaos, one comforting fact remains true. The organizations that excelled at covering this story provided the most accurate facts, told the public much that they didn't know, kept their commentaries fair, and resisted the temptation to turn their coverage into vehicles for self-promotion.

This story also taught many important lessons about covering race in media: Talking about race isn't necessarily racist. Examining people of color and their unique view of diversity isn't necessarily racist. Even biracial people such as Zimmerman often self-identify as members of a minority group. Acknowledging that isn't racist, either. For people of color, incidents like losing jobs, career setbacks, even traffic stops by the police can be an ambiguous experience. In other words, even when a situation doesn't seem to be focused on race, sometimes you wonder.

One of the consequences of media diversity for white news consumers is that they will see more columns, commentary and stories created from these perspectives, which can feel so different from their own. As the expanding world of digital media brings new voices into journalism's mix, traditional news values can be an invaluable guide for news outlets providing coverage to meet this cultural moment. The challenge to traditional journalists is to embrace new voices, bringing new perspective, ideas and values to news coverage, while keeping the accuracy, ethical conduct and fairness required by top-notch reporting. All while holding an audience in the most competitive media environment in modern history.

If the Trayvon Martin case teaches us anything about media, it's that the digital world's ability to spread information and galvanize opinion means little without ethical, accurate, fair-minded journalism to help everyone make sense of it all.

NOTES

1. Richard M. Perloff, "The Press and Lynchings of African Americans," *Journal of Black Studies* (January 2000), 315–330, http://academic.csuohio.edu/perloffr/lynching/.

2. Mary C. Curtis, "The Civil Rights Struggle and the Press," *Nieman Reports*, Summer 2007, http://www.nieman.harvard.edu/reports/article/100233/The-Civil-Rights-Struggle-and-the-Press.aspx.

3. "Journalism and Black America: Then and Now," *Nieman Reports*, Fall 2003, http://www.nieman.harvard.edu/reports/issue/100025/Fall-2003.aspx.

4. Patrick Dorsey and Bob Gabordi, "Fifty Years in Coming: Our Apology," *Tallahassee.com*, May 21, 2006, http://www.tallahassee.com/legacy/special/boycott/apology.html.

5. "Newsroom Census," American Society for News Editors, http://asne.org/content.asp?admin=Y&contentid=121.

6. Denis Finley, "Memo on Coverage of Assault on Pilot Reporters," *HamptonRoads.com*, May 2, 2012, http://hamptonroads.com/2012/05/memo-coverage-assault-pilot-reporters.

7. Michelle Washington, "A Beating at Church and Brambleton," *The Virginian-Pilot*, May 1, 2012, http://hamptonroads.com/2012/05/beating-church-and-brambleton.

8. Bill O'Reilly, "Bill O'Reilly: The Bias Crime Coverup in Virginia Grows," *O'Reilly Factor*, May 07, 2012, http://www.foxnews.com/on-air/oreilly/2012/05/08/bill-oreilly-bias-crime-cover-virginia-grows#ixzz2K8ffQtTn.

9. Denis Finley, "Column | Pilot Stands By Handling of Attack on Staff Members," *The Virginian-Pilot*, May 3, 2012, http://hamptonroads.com/2012/05/column-pilot-stands-handling-attack-staff-members.

10. Sharon Pian Chan, "Ann Curry's Departure from 'Today' Stings," *The Seattle Times*, June 29, 2012, http://seattletimes.com/html/edcetera/2018559635_ann-curry-today-nbc.html.

11. Julia Dahl, "Trayvon Martin Shooting: A Timeline of Events," *CBSNews.com*, April 11, 2012, http://www.cbsnews.com/8301-504083_162-57412417-504083/trayvon-martin-shooting-a-timeline-of-events/.

12. Susan Jacobson, "Boy, 17, Shot to Death in Sanford during 'Altercation,' Police Say," *Orlando Sentinel*, February 29, 2012, http://articles.orlandosentinel.com/2012-02-29/news/os-fatal-shooting-sanford-townhomes-20120226_1_gated-community-death-sunday-night-shothttp://articles.orlandosentinel.com/2012-02-29/news/os-fatal-shooting-sanford-townhomes-20120226_1_gated-community-death-sunday-night-shot.

13. Ibid.

14. "Trayvon Martin Killing Is Public's Top News Story," *Pew Research Center for the People and the Press*, March 27, 2012, http://www.people-press.org/2012/03/27/trayvon-martin-killing-publics-top-news-story/.

15. Meredith Rutland, "Sanford Police Chief Bill Lee Fired in Wake of Trayvon Martin Case," *The Miami Herald*, June 20, 2012, http://www.miamiherald.com/2012/06/20/2860209/sanford-police-chief-bill-lee.html#storylink=cpy.

16. "Trymaine Lee," The Huffington Post, http://www.huffingtonpost.com/trymaine-lee/.

17. "Black Voices," The Huffington Post, http://www.huffingtonpost.com/news/trayvon-martin-case.

18. Barbara Liston, "Family of Florida Boy Killed by Neighborhood Watch Seeks Arrest," *Reuters*, March 7, 2012. http://www.reuters.com/article/2012/03/08/us-crime-florida-neighborhood watch-idUSBRE82709M20120308.

19. Trymaine Lee, "Trayvon Martin's Family Calls for Arrest of Man Who Police Say Confessed to Shooting (UPDATE)," *The Huffington Post*, March 8, 2012, http://www.huffingtonpost.com/2012/03/08/family-of-trayvon-martin-_n_1332756.html.

20. Kelly McBride, "Trayvon Martin Story Reveals New Tools of Media Power, Justice," *Poynter.org*, March 23, 2012, http://www.poynter.org/latest-news/making-sense-of-news/167660/trayvon-martin-story-a-study-in-the-new-tools-of-media-power-justice/.

21. Rene Stutzman, "Sanford Police Took One Position on Trayvon Shooting in Public, Another in Paperwork to Prosecutors," *Orlando Sentinel*, July 7, 2012, http://articles.orlandosentinel.com/2012-07-07/news/os-george-zimmerman-sanford-police-lied-20120707_1_special-prosecutor-angela-corey-chief-bill-lee-arrest-warrant.

22. "Trayvon Martin Shooting Death—Initial Police Reports and '911' Call Transcript," *Chicago Tribune*, March 27, 2012, http://blogs.chicagotribune.com/news_columnists_ezorn/2012/03/trayvon-martin-shooting-death-initial-police-reports.html.

23. Mike VanOuse, "Mediapulation," *jconline.com*, March 29, 2012, http://php.jconline.com/blogs/mikev/mediapulation/.

24. Rene Stutzman, "George Zimmerman's Father: My Son Is Not Racist, Did Not Confront Trayvon Martin," *Orlando Sentinel*, March 15, 2012, http://articles.orlandosentinel.com/2012-03-15/news/os-trayvon-martin-shooting-zimmerman-letter-20120315_1_robert-zimmerman-letter-unarmed-black-teenager/2.

25. Leonard Pitts, "Trayvon Martin: What If George Zimmerman Had Been Black?" *The Baltimore Sun*, May 6, 2012, http://articles.baltimoresun.com/2012-05-06/news/bs-ed-pitts-zimmerman-20120506_1_trayvon-martin-george-zimmerman-zimmerman-supporters.

26. Erik Wemple, "Why Did *New York Times* Call George Zimmerman 'White Hispanic'?" *The Washington Post*, March 28, 2012, http://www.washingtonpost.com/blogs/erik-wemple/post/why-did-new-york-times-call-george-zimmerman-white-hispanic/2012/03/28/gIQAW 6fngS_blog.html.

27. "Jonathan Capehart, Opinion Writer," The Washington Post.com, http://www.washington post.com/jonathan-capehart/2011/02/24/AB1tR7I_page.html.

28. Jonathan Capehart, "Under 'Suspicion': The Killing of Trayvon Martin," *The Washington Post*, March 18, 2012, http://www.washingtonpost.com/blogs/post-partisan/post/under-suspicion-the-killing-of-trayvon-martin/2011/03/04/gIQAz4F4KS_blog.html.

29. Jesse Washington, "Trayvon Martin, My Son, and the Black Male Code," *The Huffington Post*, March 24, 2012, http://www.huffingtonpost.com/2012/03/24/trayvon-martin-my-son-and_1_n_1377003.html.

30. Leanord Pitts, "Tragic Teen Shooting Raises Old Fears, Questions," *The Miami Herald*, March 17, 2012, http://www.miamiherald.com/2012/03/17/2698133/tragic-teen-shooting-raises-old.html#storylink=cpy.

31. Jonathon M. Seidl, "CNN Enhances Zimmerman 911 Call Again—And Reporter Now Doubts Racial Slur Used," *The Blaze,* April 5, 2012, http://www.theblaze.com/stories/2012/04/05/cnn-enhances-zimmerman-911-call-again-and-reporter-now-doubts-racial-slur-used/.

32. Matt Gutman, "Trayvon Martin Video Shows No Blood or Bruises on George Zimmerman," *abcNews,* March 28, 2012, http://abcnews.go.com/US/trayvon-martin-case-exclusive-surveillance-video-george-zimmerman/story?id=16022897#.UU81KTm3l7M.

33. Trymaine Lee, "Trayvon Martin Case: 911 Audio Released of Teen Shot by Neighborhood Watch Captain (AUDIO)" *The Huffington Post*, March 16, 2012, http://www.huffingtonpost.com/2012/03/16/trayvon-martin-911-audio-_n_1354909.html.

34. Tracy Martin and Sybrina Fulton, "Prosecute the Killer of Our Son, 17-Year-Old Trayvon Martin," *Change.org*, April 2012, http://www.change.org/petitions/prosecute-the-killer-of-our-son-17-year-old-trayvon-martin?utm_source=share_petition&utm_medium=url_share&utm_campaign=url_share_before_sign.

35. "George Zimmerman 911 Call Reporting Trayvon Martin," *Orlando Sentinel*, March 27, 2012, http://www.orlandosentinel.com/videogallery/68871920/News/George-Zimmerman-911-call-reporting-Trayvon-Martin.

36. "Rev. Al Sharpton," MSNBC, http://www.nbcnews.com/id/45901721/ns/msnbc-meet_the_faces_of_msnbc/.

37. "Al Sharpton at Trayvon Martin Rally: 'We Are Tired of Going to Jail for Nothing and Others Going Home for Something' (video)" *The Huffington Post*, March 23, 2012, http://www.huffingtonpost.com/2012/03/23/al-sharpton-trayvon-martin-rally_n_1374975.html.

38. David Bauder, "Should Al Sharpton Be Trayvon Martin Activist and MSNBC Host?" *Associated Press*, March 27, 2012, http://www.csmonitor.com/USA/Latest-News-Wires/2012/0327/Should-Al-Sharpton-be-Trayvon-Martin-activist-and-MSNBC-host.

39. "Keith Olbermann Suspended over Political Donations," *MSNBC.com*, November 2, 2010, http://www.nbcnews.com/id/40028929/ns/politics-decision_2010/t/keith-olbermann-sus-pended-over-political-donations/#.URKieSJ218F.

40. "Joe Scarborough Suspended over Political Donations," *MSNBC.com*, November 19, 2010, http://www.nbcnews.com/id/40277217/ns/politics-decision_2010/t/joe-scarborough-suspended-over-political-donations/#.UQLzvY5Cfao.

41. David Boroff, "Trayvon Martin Shooting: NBC News Apologizes for Airing Edited Version of 911 Call Placed by George Zimmerman," *NY Daily News*, April 2, 2012, http://www.nydaily

news.com/news/national/trayvon-martin-shooting-nbc-apologizes-airing-edited-version-911-call-george-zimmerman-article-1.1055599#ixzz2K95qI7ty.

42. Andrew Beaujon, "Second Reporter Loses Job over NBC George Zimmerman 911 Call Edit," *Poynter.org*, May 4, 2012, http://www.poynter.org/latest-news/mediawire/172798/second-reporter-loses-job-over-nbc-george-zimmerman-911-call-edit/.

43. Julie Moos, "George Zimmerman Sues NBC over Editing of 911 Call about Trayvon Martin," *Poynter.org*, December 6, 2012, http://www.poynter.org/latest-news/mediawire/197363/george-zimmerman-sues-nbc-over-editing-of-911-tape-after-trayvon-martin-shooting/.

44. Michael Martinez, "George Zimmerman Sues NBC Universal over Edited 911 Call," *CNN*, December 7, 2012, http://www.cnn.com/2012/12/06/us/florida-zimmerman-nbc-lawsuit/index.html.

45. "Obama: If I Had a Son He'd Look Like Trayvon Martin," *CBSNews*, March 23, 2012, http://www.youtube.com/watch?v=Yt_g5JPdP8Y.

46. David Martosko, "Second Trayvon Martin Twitter Feed Identified," *The Daily Center*, March 29, 2012, http://dailycaller.com/2012/03/29/second-trayvon-martin-twitter-feed-identified/.

47. "Why TeamDueProcess Is Important for Justice; Correction and Update: Twitchy Issues Apology for Fake Trayvon Martin Photo," *Twitchy Media*, March 25, 2012, http://twitchy.com/2012/03/25/why-teamdueprocess-is-important-for-justice/.

48. Ben Shapiro, "House Dems Offer 'Trayvon Amendment' to Punish States for 'Stand Your Ground'" *Breitbart.com*, May 8, 2012, http://www.breitbart.com/Big-Government/2012/05/08/Trayvon-Martin-Amendment-Stand-Your-Ground.

49. Frances Robles, "Reports of Suspensions Paint More Complicated Picture of Trayvon Martin," *The Miami Herald*, March 26, 2012, http://articles.sun-sentinel.com/2012-03-26/news/sfl-reports-of-suspensions-paint-more-complicated-picture-of-trayvon-martin-20120326_1_suspensions-jewelry-report.

50. John Lott, "Trayvon Martin, George Zimmerman and the Media's Misleading Rhetoric on Guns," *FoxNews.com*, April 03, 2012, http://www.foxnews.com/opinion/2012/04/03/trayvon-martin-george-zimmerman-and-medias-misleading-rhetoric-on-guns/#ixzz2K98YFUOS.

51. Alicia Shepard, "The Iconic Photos of Trayvon Martin & George Zimmerman & Why You May Not See the Others," *Poynter.org*, March 30, 2012, http://www.poynter.org/latest-news/top-stories/168391/the-iconic-photos-of-trayvon-martin-george-zimmerman-why-you-may-not-see-the-others/.

52. Thomas Roberts and Melissa Harris-Perry, "Sound Off: Trayvon Martin Case, a Case of Hate?" *MSNBC*, March 23, 2012, http://video.msnbc.msn.com/msnbc/46836089#46836089.

53. "Themes of Trayvon Shooting Differ by Media," *Journalism.org*, March 30, 2012, http://www.journalism.org/taxonomy/term/59?page=1.

54. Frances Robles, "George Zimmerman's Crude Myspace Page from 2005 Uncovered," *The Miami Herald*, May 1, 2012, http://www.miamiherald.com/2012/05/01/2778234/myspace-page-is-latest-salvo-in.html#storylink=cpy.

55. "Revealed: George Zimmerman's MySpace Page from 2005 Includes Slurs Against Mexicans—But Shows He Has Many Black Friends" *Daily Mail Reporter*, May 2, 2012, http://www.dailymail.co.uk/news/article-2138238/Travon-Martin-case-George-Zimmermans-unseen-2005-MySpace-page-includes-slurs-Mexicans.html#ixzz2K9BMQnEd.

56. Gene Demby, "George Zimmerman's MySpace Disparages Mexicans, Mentions 2005 Criminal Charges," *The Huffington Post*, May 2, 2012, http://www.huffingtonpost.com/2012/05/02/zimmerman-myspace-page_n_1471818.html.

57. David Martosko "The Daily Caller Obtains Trayvon Martin's Tweets," *The Daily Caller*, March 26, 2012, http://dailycaller.com/2012/03/26/the-daily-caller-obtains-trayvon-martins-tweets/.

58. Isabelle Zehnder, "George Zimmerman's 911 Call Transcribed," *The Examiner,* March 24, 2012, http://www.examiner.com/article/george-zimmerman-s-911-call-transcribed.

59. *Tampa Bay Times:* Media Blogs, http://www.tampabay.com/blogs/media/.

60. "Race-Baiter," *Ericdeggans.com* http://ericdeggans.com/?page_id=80.

61. Ronald Brownstein, "The Next America," *National Journal,* April 1, 2011, http://www.nationaljournal.com/magazine/u-s-transforming-into-majority-minority-nation-faster-than-expected-20110331.

Caitlin Johnston

In Eric Deggans' analysis of media coverage of the Trayvon Martin shooting, he suggests that newsrooms must confront their competing values in order to provide the public with accurate information on stories that are still developing.

When the Trayvon Martin story exploded as a national conversation in early 2012, it did so because a handful of national columnists and bloggers took interest. Martin, 17, was shot dead by George Zimmerman on February 26, 2012, in a gated community in Sanford, Fla., where he was staying with his father. Martin had just come from a 7-Eleven convenience store,[1] and was carrying a bag of Skittles candy and a can of Arizona Watermelon Fruit Juice Cocktail. The teen was wearing a black sweatshirt with its hood up: The hoodie would become an iconic image of protest in the months following his death.

The next day, February 27, the *Orlando Sentinel* published a news brief on the shooting, which didn't name either Martin or Zimmerman. Two days later, the local paper wrote a longer story naming Martin but getting some of the facts of the shooting wrong. On March 8, Martin's family held a press conference on the steps of the police department, demanding that Zimmerman be charged.

At that point, national media began publishing stories about the case. Many of them, such as CBS News, *The Huffington Post* and Reuters, directly stated what smaller news briefs had left out: Martin was black, and his shooter was not. Furthermore, much of this early coverage was in the form of editorials and columns from analysts and pundits. What started as a cops brief about a shooting—a fairly run-of-the-mill story for many newspapers—morphed into a highly volatile debate about racial profiling, other forms of racism, and Florida's controversial Stand Your Ground law.

Trymaine Lee, then writing for *The Huffington Post,* argued it was a journalist's task to get people to care about these issues and to bring the story to light. "As a young black man this story can't help but settle in a certain place inside of you," Lee told Poynter.[2] Two other writers, both columnists, are credited along with Lee for shifting this story from a local brief to a national headline. They were also black males: Charles Blow of *The New York Times* and Ta-Nehisi Coates of *The Atlantic.* In addition to that, Al Sharpton, an anchor for MSNBC, became a personal advocate for Martin's family. At the same time, he continued to report on the story for the MSNBC audience.

Meanwhile, the grio, an African-American website owned by NBC, published more than 250 stories in the first two months after the shooting. Many of those ended up on MSNBC and NBC.

QUESTIONS

- The story gained a national audience largely through columnists and commentators who work from a point of view. Look up some of the early columns written by Trymaine Lee or Charles Blow. What is their point of view? How did it impact the way they tell the story?

- Al Sharpton became an advocate for Trayvon Martin's family while remaining an anchor on MSNBC and reporting updates on the story. How does that enhance or detract from his credibility with different audiences?

- Newsrooms are criticized for their failure to have diverse viewpoints. Yet in this chapter, Deggans criticizes newsrooms for allowing people with a point of view to frame the Trayvon Martin story at the expense of accuracy. How can newsrooms do both? In this case, how could a newsroom encourage columnists and opinion writers to tell the story, and ensure that the story frames are appropriate for the facts?

CASE NOTES

1. Kyle Hightower and Tamara Lush, "Cache of Evidence Provides Little Clarity in Trayvon Martin Case," *The Associated Press*, May 19, 2012, http://www.denverpost.com/nationworld/ci_20657491/cache-evidence-provides-little-clarity-trayvon-martin-case.
2. Tracie Powell, "How Pulitzer-Winning Writer Moved Trayvon Martin Story from Margins to Mainstream," *Poynter.org*, April 9, 2012, http://www.poynter.org/latest-news/making-sense-of-news/169323/how-pulitzer-winning-writer-moved-trayvon-martin-story-from-margins-to-mainstream/.

Community as an End

Mónica Guzmán

On the morning of November 29, 2009, a man named Maurice Clemmons entered a coffee shop in Parkland, Washington, shot to death four police officers who were getting ready to begin their shifts, and, with the help of a driver, got away.[1] Over the next two days, police searched for the suspect and people searched for answers. Where was Clemmons? Who would harbor a cop killer? Were citizens safe? Reporters in nearby Seattle filled their websites with stories and updates.

But something else happened, too. Instead of clicking from one newsroom's account to another, a large chunk of news readers in this tech-savvy city went to the one place where all the information was coming together—Twitter. Anyone who followed the manhunt thoroughly could tell you that Twitter, not any one news site, was the best first source for up-to-the-minute information.

This wasn't just because a hashtag, #washooting, made it easy to track tweets about the manhunt or because so many journalists—including the executive editor of *The Seattle Times*—smartly tweeted their updates before they published them on their news sites. It was also because anyone could participate. Not just editors in the newsroom or reporters in the city, but workers who saw patrol cars zoom by, neighbors who noticed something suspicious, newsies who'd caught an interesting report, and nervous residents who just wanted to know they weren't alone.

The staff at *The Seattle Times* would go on to win a Pulitzer Prize for its breaking news coverage of the shooting.[2] That coverage included updates and links its staff shared on #washooting. Reporters, photographers and editors all made posting to the hashtag a priority, and as the largest news organization in the region, *The Times* did much to strengthen the conversation there.

But on #washooting, the public's story was the public's to tell. All the region's journalists, meeting on that neutral ground, could guide, collaborate and even lead in a raw but real and ultimately more powerful search for understanding. The #washooting news stream was just one early example of what digital connection has made possible. And the lessons it offers journalists are nuanced.

People are gathering in inclusive, open spaces to do what a new generation of online tools lets them do—inform themselves. But a self-informing public needs more from its journalists than information. It needs guidance. Direction. Support. Someone to show the way, then make the most of what everyone gathers. That Pulitzer Prize could have gone to every journalist and every citizen who worked, in whatever small way, to bring important information together.

In a world where everyone can participate in newsgathering, cultivating self-informing communities is itself an act of journalism. To accomplish it, we need to know not only the language of these spaces but also smart ways to join, respect, and inspire the voices within.

A STRONGER USE OF SOCIAL MEDIA

Journalists are already familiar with the set of tools and spaces most often associated with cultivating and joining online community: social media. But journalism is not about tools. It's about people. Working well with social media is not the same as working well with community.

Many news organizations have mastered ways to use social media to distribute their content. Most have Facebook pages and Twitter accounts—many with tens of thousands of followers—where they post updates in real time. After years of not knowing what to do about journalists on their staffs who had taken to the social media channels themselves, news media today mostly encourage reporters to talk about their work there, with relatively little supervision. It's been a smart move for Web traffic, which comes increasingly from social channels. Facebook and Twitter have not overtaken news websites as primary pathways to news, but their influence has exploded and will likely continue to grow. A 2012 report from the Pew Center's Project for Excellence in Journalism found that just 9 percent of digital news consumers follow links from these sites very often, compared to 32 percent who follow links from search engine results.[3] But five months after it installed a Facebook news reader app, *The Guardian* saw more than 30 percent of its traffic one month come from Facebook, beating search engine referrals for the first time in its history.[4]

Then there's branding. Social media make it easier than ever for journalists to build their own brands. Reporters, in particular, use these channels to speak in their own voices to (and with) their own audiences, quickly establishing connections that can make their bylines more visible and marketable. They become their own distribution channels, so readers can follow people like Steven Levy of *Wired* without ever buying *Wired* or using its website. Thanks to social media's ability to distribute personality, journalists are becoming as aware of the state of their "personal brands" as they are the comings and goings of their beats.[5]

Social media's power to promote both content and brand has made these tools an obsession not just for journalists, but for every communications industry. More and more, journalists are finding themselves sitting next to marketing and public relations professionals at conferences that round up the latest ways to use social media to grow. In one sense, we all want the same things: retweets, Facebook *likes, shares,* and, every now and then, some piece of content that goes magically, wonderfully viral. We want them for different reasons, but we want them all the same. It is now so easy for journalists to participate in the promotion of our work that we are feeling a stronger and stronger obligation to be not just its creators, but its marketers. That impacts not just how our content spreads but also how it looks.

BuzzFeed is a great example. The blockbuster site doesn't pretend to be the most serious of news sources, but two minutes of clicking shows how far content creators have gone to shape what they produce so it soars on social. Headlines like "35 Things You Will Never See Again in Your Life" promise brevity and amusement in exchange for your attention, while its images, bold and prominent, beg to be shared. The content is packaged to be spread.

It can be fun to market our work and make it addictive. Journalists are brands, most news sites are businesses, and traffic, of course, matters. But journalists can't just be promoters of content or sellers of a product. We are here not just to satisfy, but to serve. Like the search for the Washington state shooter, other incidents have also shown the growing value of social media as a news-gathering force.

INFORMING THE SELF-INFORMED

On July 20, 2012, 24-year-old James Holmes walked into a movie theater in Aurora, Colo., and opened fire, shooting and killing 12 people and injuring 58 others. As reporters scrambled to get the news,[6] another young Colorado man saw a Facebook post from 9 News in Denver about a shooting at a movie theater and went to the popular social site, Reddit.[7]

That night and the following day, 18-year-old Morgan Jones gathered information from news organizations, Aurora police and fire department feeds, and victims who were posting their experiences online to create the most exhaustive timeline of events anywhere.[8] As his timeline grew, other Reddit users joined in, making his posts compelling magnets for what could have otherwise remained disparate bits of information. One user linked the final tweet from a confirmed victim. Another shared what he was hearing on the news. Many, many more offered something equally important, though often overlooked—gratitude and encouragement. "Belgium calling in. Thanks for doing this," wrote one user. "British guy in Japan here," began another. "Thank you for the amazing coverage of this tragic event."

Jones was playing a video game before the Facebook post led him to spark a self-informing community. He didn't have to do it. But like many in the digital age, something drove him to tap the wealth of data available to inform himself and—*so* important—share his findings online, so others could do the same. The hunger for information is a powerful thing. Thanks to what digital communication makes possible, it alone can drive people not only to gather news, but also to rally others in the effort.

This is the higher calling for journalism: to grow communities that can self-inform. All of us share a need to understand our world. When our audience shows us that they are capable and willing to inform themselves, they are no longer just an audience, and we no longer serve them by treating them as such. It's not about how we beat Morgan Jones but how we join him, encourage him and inspire more like him. In a self-informing world, journalists must go beyond championing information to champion the civic act of staying informed.

That means that to best serve a self-informing public, journalists must provide good information *and* encourage the public's instinct to self-inform. Those dual purposes may appear to conflict. They don't. Or at least, they shouldn't. To understand how these purposes actually complement each other, we must learn to see all sources of information as a self-informing public sees them—as voices to hear and consider, not competitors to ignore or bystanders to dismiss.

JOURNALISM AS COLLABORATION

This is a time of extreme participation in journalism. And that's exciting. The rise of the #washooting hashtag is a simple example of what this perspective makes possible. Soon after the shooting, *The Seattle Times* used the hashtag #washooting to mark its tweets about the developing story. As residents began to see the hashtag on Twitter, other local news media had a choice. They could mark their tweets with #washooting and post their content to a stream started by a competitor. Or, they could create their own hashtag and compete with the conversation as they already compete with their content.

Social media managers at Seattle's largest news outlets had already learned during their coverage of flooding the previous winter that in today's digital landscape, collaboration works. Professional newsrooms immediately adopted the hashtag, and it was thanks to that small gesture that #washooting became such a comprehensive information hub.

Segmenting the audience would have made sense in a shrewdly competitive analog media world, but it makes no sense in the digital one. Separate conversations would have scattered the participatory audience and denied it an opportunity to build momentum and grow. It also would have scattered the information, weakening, rather than strengthening, the public's ability to self-inform.

Critics will say it's one thing to join a conversation with fellow journalists and another to welcome to that conversation the people formerly known as the audience. At the heart of quality journalism is verification: How do you know which contributions from the crowd are true and which are not? There's good sense in the question. Journalists make mistakes but are held to account for them, or should be. Nonjournalists suffer fewer consequences. It's smart to approach with added skepticism any source whose informational discipline is at best untested and at worst nonexistent.

Hurricane Sandy's destructive trek up the East Coast was just one example of a news event during which the experiences of millions could be fodder for news, but journalists had to remember not to believe everything they read on social media.

On September 16, 2010, tornado warnings led the news in a stormy New York City. A young man named Dave Carlson found a photo of a tornado over the Statue of Liberty and posted it on Twitter, where *Time Magazine* writer Steven James Snyder saw it and posted it to the magazine's website as a shocking image from a tumultuous day. But the photo, as then–*Huffington Post* traffic and trends editor Craig Kanalley pointed out, was from 1976, not 2010. Carlson had posted it to "mess with friends," as he tweeted to Kanalley, and he was stunned to see that a journalist assumed he was reporting the news.

Public voices might never speak as carefully as journalists do. But that's no reason to avoid publicly shared information, dismiss it or feel you're working against it. It's a reason to dive in and help steer. The photos residents shared of Hurricane Sandy's destruction led everyone to a richer, more personalized understanding of a disruptive storm. Journalists can play a role in helping organize and verify information shared by the public to arrive at that understanding more quickly and credibly.[9] A self-informing public is better served with support than suspicion.

COMMUNITY OVER COMPETITION

Welcoming new voices is just the beginning. To empower those voices, journalists need to connect with them, and, more importantly, help them connect to each other—all in a way that honors their independence in a self-informing world.

Enter NPR's Andy Carvin. At a time when most journalists create content first and community second, if at all, Carvin has shown that we can accomplish the goals of the former by doing almost exclusively the latter—even from thousands of miles away. Carvin was not a reporter when the revolutions of the Arab Spring began to rumble in 2011 and he began to tweet and retweet the network of contacts he'd developed through travels in the region.[10] He was NPR's social media strategist, tasked with helping its journalists understand and wield social media.

Fueled by his interest in what was happening, and under little pressure to prepare his own content about the upheaval, Carvin spent time curating the information being shared on Twitter by people on the ground—highlighting it, distributing it, even tapping those same people to help verify it. Some voices he already knew. The ones he didn't, he scrutinized, engaging them if they seemed genuine and helpful. Before long, his Twitter feed, @acarvin, could be counted on to feature a growing number of authentic, credible voices few others could find. It became its own indispensable, real-time news source for anyone following the revolution.

In the process, Carvin linked not just information, but people—and not for his benefit, exclusively, but for theirs. Carvin calls it *situational awareness*—the big-picture understanding he gleaned from following his collection of on-the-ground voices speaking in real time on Twitter. One man planted in the middle of Cairo's Tahrir Square could not hope to get that comprehensive view on his own. By curating the Twitter collection thoughtfully and openly, Carvin gathered the most important on-the-ground reports, turned the random chatter into collected wisdom and gave that wisdom right back to the people who needed it most—people thousands of miles away, living history. He informed more people in more ways than many journalists thought possible. All without writing a single traditional news story.

If you've been following the step-by-step integration of social media in journalism, this might not be the first time you've heard of Carvin. His work during the Arab Spring has become one of the most celebrated examples of what journalists can do to inform a curious, connected public from within the spaces where that public gathers. Where most journalists conduct their news-gathering in private, Carvin's tweets made his explorations public, inviting both established contacts and new observers to contribute.

While we celebrate Carvin for creating a rich network, it's important to understand that because it lived in a neutral, public space, it was never really *his* network, never *his* sources, never *his* information—and that's why it worked. Carvin encouraged and empowered the voices he gathered, but he did not pretend to control them. And though NPR paid his salary, it built no walls around his work. This is the difference between using community and engaging it. Everyone—including the people formerly known as the competition—could both learn from and contribute to the gathered wisdom. And when the revolution led to a new government and new struggles, the community endured.

This is what the openness of social technology makes possible: Rather than develop sources to serve himself, Carvin developed community to serve anyone. He let the benefits of his work divide and multiply in the service of a self-informing public.

INSPIRING CONVERSATION

The role of the journalist in the age of the self-informing public is to embrace public voices, partner with them and connect them—and then take what the public has shared, increase its value and give it back.

On Sept. 11, *The New York Times* asked its readers the question that most news media asked readers that day: Where were you on Sept. 11, 2001? Instead of collecting the answers in a comment thread or on a Facebook page, the *Times* built an elegant, easy-to-use map. It invited readers to plot where they were on 9/11, identify how they felt about the event 10 years later—scared, angry, hopeful and so on—and recall their experiences.[11]

The result was a moment in time, told in thousands of memories that meant more together than they would have meant apart. Besides plotting their own memories, people could discover the memories of people who were near them that day and take some new context or comfort in that discovery. Every recollection, for being part of this organized collection, became more valuable. As a result, every contributor could see how his or her memory fit into a larger story.

It helps, of course, to have the capacity to build spaces customized with tools to best fill each information need, but we don't need technical wizardry to bind the contributions of the public into something more. Good rules, good moderation and plain old dedication can be enough. It begins with an acknowledgment that working with communities, and not just with content, is part of the job.

In 2008, a columnist at the *Chicago Tribune* invited the public to join her in a candid conversation about race. It was a bold move. The topic can get so toxic, many news websites had gotten into the habit of closing comments on stories in which race played a role.[12] But Dawn Turner Trice made it work. When people responded to her initial questions about race, she turned their answers into different sections on "Exploring Race," a forum she created around the topic. People were invited not just to read and respond to content she created, but to submit their own stories and questions, guided by prompts tailored for the topic.[13] "I want this to be a safe place where people of all races can explore their views and biases, openly and honestly," reads a note at the top of the site. Thanks to her thoughtful, committed moderation—she watched over the comments to encourage the right tone—it was.

A self-informing public has an instinct to delve into issues that interest them most. To serve that public, journalists can cultivate new and existing spaces where that instinct, when it strikes, can do the most good. That work can do much to stabilize understanding over time, even as the frenzied conversations around news events overwhelm us. To accomplish the mission of journalism at a time when journalism has burst from containment, we must go beyond the old task of inspiring the public to be diligent news consumers and adopt a new call to activate them, wherever we can, as responsible self-informers. The key is collaboration. People can and will come together on their own to seek understanding. How can journalists help them do it better?

So back to BuzzFeed. The site, like many others, is good at making content that people will share. It's part of its DNA. What if more journalists made it part of their DNA to engage a public of informers and partner with that public to circulate good information?

BuzzFeed is a big site with a lot of resources, but news organizations don't need to be big to serve a self-informing public well. Just one person can make the difference. If you know who is most interested in the news you gather, and how to reach those people, you can cultivate relationships that lead to better understanding.

Since 2006, the West Seattle Blog has served the residents of the 90,000-resident West Seattle neighborhood as a combination news source, bulletin board, and forum. Its founder and editor, Tracy Record, was anonymous at first. Without a face or name, she spoke with a voice that so authentically channeled the concerns and interests of her neighborhood that she became a crisp, clear conduit for information in the neighborhood's interest. Before long, the simple blog grew to become the neighborhood's most popular information hub.

Before it became commonplace among digital journalists to acknowledge readers as more than an *audience,* Record was renouncing the term. To her, every reader of West Seattle Blog is at least a potential contributor.[14] She leaves the door open to them day and night. This way of seeing her public informs everything she does in their service. Record's readers have long been her partners. And she doesn't shy away from engaging with her community directly. She responds to comments and questions on the site's posts and forums. She gets into conversations with residents on Twitter and Facebook. And though she authors many of the site's posts, most include credits to one or another resident or group of residents for the information she passes on. Plus, many posts remain open, inviting the public to fill in whatever blanks are left.

News in the age of the self-informing public is a process, not a product, and it is shared. When Record is not writing, her partners still are talking, moving their understanding forward in a space informed by her example. The community awards and commendations received by the West Seattle Blog signify what many in the neighborhood already know: West Seattle is stronger because of the West Seattle Blog.

Record does not report *to* her partners. She reports *with* them. That makes her, the reporter, like them, the people. And it encourages them, the people, to be more like her, the reporter. Journalists have for years now wondered who can and can't be described by that term. In an age when anyone can commit acts of journalism, asking who is a journalist has become the wrong question. It's not who we are but what we do that matters, and whether we do it right by the public we serve, the self-informing public of which we're only a part.

We're all in this together. Ethical practice in digital journalism begins and ends there.

NOTES

1. "A Path to Murder: The Story of Maurice Clemmons," *The Seattle Times*, December 6, 2009, http://seattletimes.com/html/localnews/2010436039_clemmonsprofile06m.html.

2. "The 2010 Pulitzer Prize Winners: Breaking News Reporting," The Pulitzer Prizes, 2010, http://www.pulitzer.org/citation/2010-Breaking-News-Reporting.

3. Amy Mitchell, Tom Rosenstiel, and Leah Christian, "What Facebook and Twitter Mean for News," *The State of the News Media 2012: An Annual Report on American Journalism, 2012,* http://stateofthemedia.org/2012/mobile-devices-and-news-consumption-some-good-signs-for-journalism/what-facebook-and-twitter-mean-for-news/.

4. Tanya Cordrey, "Tanya Cordrey's Speech at the Guardian Changing Media Summit," *The Guardian*, March 21, 2012, http://www.guardian.co.uk/gnm-press-office/changing-media-summit-tanya-cordrey.

5. Sarah Fidelibus, "Branded Journalists Battle Newsroom Regulations," *Poynter.org*, March 2, 2012, http://www.poynter.org/how-tos/digital-strategies/163019/branded-journalists-battle-newsroom-regulations/.

6. Julie Moos, "How News Spread of the 'Dark Knight Rises' Shooting at Colorado Movie Theater," Poynter.org, July 20, 2012. http://www.poynter.org/latest-news/mediawire/181793/how-news-spread-of-the-dark-knight-rises-shooting-aurora-james-holmes/.

7. Andrew Beaujon, "Reddit Covers the Colorado Movie Theater Shooting," *Poynter.org*, July 20, 2012, http://www.poynter.org/latest-news/mediawire/181840/reddit-covers-the-aurora-movie-theater-shooting-dark-knight-rises/.

8. Alan Stamm, "If I Were an 18-Year-Old Aspiring Journalist, I'd Want to Be Like Morgan Jones," *Poynter.org*, July 21, 2012, http://www.poynter.org/latest-news/media-lab/182082/if-i-were-an-18-year-old-aspiring-journalist-id-want-to-be-like-morgan-jones/.

9. Craig Silverman, "How Journalists Can Avoid Getting Fooled by Fake Hurricane Sandy Photos," *Poynter.org*, October 29, 2012, http://www.poynter.org/latest-news/regret-the-error/193470/how-journalists-can-avoid-getting-fooled-by-fake-hurricane-sandy-photos/.

10. Steve Myers, "NPR's Andy Carvin on Interplay between Social Media, Offline Organizing in Egypt, Tunisia," *Poynter.org*, January 28, 2011, http://www.poynter.org/latest-news/top-stories/116799/live-chat-today-what-role-is-social-media-playing-in-the-egypt-tunisia-uprisings-for-journalists-and-protesters/.

11. "Where Were You on Sept. 11, 2001?" *The New York Times*, September 8, 2011, http://www.nytimes.com/interactive/2011/09/08/us/sept-11-reckoning/where-were-you-september-11-map.html.

12. Patrick Thornton, "Racism, Attacks Lead News Sites to Disable Story Comments," *Poynter.org*, July 23, 2009, http://www.poynter.org/latest-news/top-stories/97416/racism-attacks-lead-news-sites-to-disable-story-comments/.

13. Mallary Jean Tenore, "Exploring Race, Asking Tough Questions," *Poynter.org*, May 5, 2008, http://www.poynter.org/how-tos/newsgathering-storytelling/diversity-at-work/88684/exploring-race-asking-tough-questions/.

14. Anna Tarkov, "How Hyperlocal Sites Handle 'Micro-News' in Their Communities," *Poynter.org*, July 19, 2012, http://www.poynter.org/latest-news/top-stories/180926/how-hyperlocal-sites-handle-micro-news.

Caitlin Johnston

Mónica Guzmán describes a new facet of journalism that guides and supports citizens as they "self-inform." When a man killed four police officers in 2009, The Seattle Times *and other northwest newsrooms modeled that process.*

In November of 2009, Maurice Clemmons walked into a Parkland, Wash., coffee shop and opened fire on a group of police officers working on their laptops, killing four of them. He jumped into a getaway vehicle driven by a friend. For the next 48 hours, the Seattle-Tacoma area watched the manhunt for Clemmons unfold. Police stopped cars and searched houses. Clemmons, who had been shot by one of the officers, received help from friends and family as he moved from location to location.

As the shooting occurred on the Sunday morning after Thanksgiving, only one reporter and one editor were in *The Seattle Times*' newsroom at the time. Within a few hours, though, a full newsroom was covering the story with reporters on the scene, working from their desks, and gathering and organizing information on the Internet. The Twitter hashtag #washooting became the primary way to track news about the shooting across the community. The hashtag also worked as a way to aggregate output from multiple media outlets, guaranteeing that readers had access to the most up-to-date information, no matter who produced it. The newspaper invited citizens to contribute everything from sightings of police cars to photos to statements of concern.

The role of the readers in producing such outstanding journalism was not lost on the staff of *The Seattle Times*. "First of all, I want to say this belongs to all of you. We want the whole community to share in this prize," editor David Boardman said during an event at the Greater Seattle Chamber of Commerce after *The Times* was awarded the Pulitzer Prize for breaking news coverage of the shooting.[1] "*The Seattle Times* jumped into digital news with both feet," local TV anchor Lori Matsukawa said at the event, "noting that many bloggers and dot-commers were 'shocked' that *The Seattle Times* could become so 'digitally nimble' in such a short time."

The newspaper used social media tools such as Google Wave (a now defunct aggregation service designed to merge platforms such as social networking, instant messaging and email) and Dippity, a free program for interactive timelines on any topic. These tools made it easier to integrate user-generated content with material produced by the staff.

One challenge of using content submitted by readers is that average citizens don't usually hold themselves to the same standards of integrity and accuracy maintained by a professional news organization. They may not even be aware of the professional standards of veracity. While this risk has led some news organizations to exclude material submitted by individuals outside their staffs, *The Seattle Times* did not see this as a reason to avoid outside content. Instead, the staff worked to verify as much of the information as it could.

Managing editor Suki Dardarian "said they checked tips and rumors constantly," according to a Washington News Council article about the event. "When a new report came in, people in the newsroom would ask: 'How do you know that? Are you sure of that? We've always had those conversations, but to have them every 15 to 20 seconds was new.'"[2] While *The Times'* staff included a substantial amount of information submitted by readers, it did so after moderating what was of value to its audience and fleshed out the narrative already created by the news organization. Ultimately, *The Seattle Times* found the proper balance between its role as a traditional gatekeeper and a facilitator of the information community.

QUESTIONS

• *The Seattle Times* not only informed readers but entered a conversation with them about the shooting and its effects. What are the best opportunities for journalists to engage with their audience? How can journalists best inspire their audience to want to engage?

• In addition to aggregating reporting, photos and social media from its own staff and its competitors, *The Times* included information its readers submitted. Describe the tension between the information gathered by professionals in your news organization and information collected by citizens. When should a news organization promote a reader's photos, reporting or information ahead of its own content?

• What sort of vetting, if any, should a news organization do before using user-generated content? Does this change when covering a breaking news story?

• For many of *The Seattle Times'* journalists, coverage of the 2009 shooting was a most intense introduction to Twitter. How much freedom should news organizations give their reporters on Twitter? What type of oversight should editors provide? Does this change when covering a breaking news story?

• Guzmán proposes that community is not simply a means for journalism, but an end in itself. How does *The Seattle Times* experience—in putting community over competition, for example—illustrate that concept? Pick a story covered in the last year that treated community as an end and explain how that process unfolded.

CASE NOTES

1. John Hamer, "Anatomy of *The Seattle Times'* Pulitzer Prize," *Washington News Council*, June 23, 2010, http://wanewscouncil.org/2010/06/23/anatomy-of-the-seattle-times%E2%80%99-pulitzer -prize/.

2. Ibid.

The Future of Journalism Ethics

Kelly McBride and Tom Rosenstiel

The news has never belonged to journalists. It has always belonged to the public. News is the social flow, the stream of information, the spark of discovery, the spotlighting of problems, the working through of solutions, the gathering to celebrate, the full range of generating knowledge that creates community.

To the extent that we have a history of news, we can trace it to the *agora*, the market where people gathered to shop in ancient Athens. We can track it to the coffee houses that sat alongside the ports of Europe. Eventually, people were paid to capture and communicate the conversation that occurred in those places, to retell the stories from foreign lands revealed by the people who disembarked from the ships, to publish the manifests of the cargo and the passengers who had arrived. It was printed in partisan papers, later in a commercial penny press. News was carried eventually over telegraph lines, then over radio, and soon enough on television. Over time, the communicators of that news formed routines, styles and ethics to make their work more credible—so the public, the audience, the community, found it more useful.

The digital age has taken us back to the agora. The conversation that the news has always inspired is now public for anyone to see and participate in if she wants. It is as if what once happened around the breakfast table in one home, as someone would read parts of a story to the family and others would react and comment, is now occurring in front of everyone. What does that mean for the practice of journalism? Where, in other words, does this shift leave the ideas advanced by years of professionalization about how to make news more reliable?

That's what this book has been about. *The New Ethics of Journalism: Principles for the 21st Century* is predicated on the idea that the digital age has made journalism's principles more important—not less. These ethical dilemmas are now the province of anyone who wants to produce news—even only momentarily in special circumstances—and of everyone who consumes it. Ethics is no longer just the concern of professionals.

Gone are the days when consumers could trust news simply because it was produced by a caste of people. Now, we must determine whether news is reliable by looking for evidence of its credibility. Does what I am reading, watching or hearing have an internal integrity? As consumers, we may have a general and intuitive sense of whether we see integrity in what we are consuming. But in a user-controlled media world, our senses must be honed, our thinking disciplined, our consumption informed and our journalism transparent. That is what the chapters contained in this volume, and the case studies that accompany them, are about—how to produce news so that the public knows it can be trusted. That begins with the three broad concepts that form the structure of this book: truth, transparency and community.

The idea that news should be as accurate as possible is the first principle. While on its face that may be no surprise, it is not without argument. We know, for instance, that our judgment about what accuracy and truth mean vary with the nature of the story. We know that coverage of a breaking-news event in which facts are fluid, such as a hurricane making landfall, may be less certain than coverage of a news event that is planned, such as the president's inaugural address. We can sense that an analysis of why something occurred involves judgment and interpretation and is by its nature softer. Yet news media must strive for accuracy as a principle of journalism, however elusive the goal may be, for a practical reason: The public good requires it. Truth is the foundation on which news is built.

Transparency allows the public to determine for themselves whether they should believe the truth as it's presented. Transparency is the currency that shows whether news is produced in good faith and in ways that make it trustworthy. What is the evidence for what is asserted? Why were certain choices made about how to gather the news? Who are the sources in this story? How close to the events were they? Is their account firsthand, secondhand, or something even more remote? And what should consumers know about the news producers? Is there a partisan agenda attached? Do they strive for neutrality and disinterest? Are they citizen witnesses? Is this news produced by a commercial interest or a partisan or political one, or is it driven by some other motive?

We can rely on one law of human nature here that's proved true in every age. The less willing a news producer is to being open about these things, the more our alarms should go off. Transparency, in other words, is not only evidence of good motive. It is also the antiseptic against shoddy work. Transparency is the public's to demand. The more we expect it from our news, the more we will receive.

Here, technology offers the promise of a rich new journalism. The depth and links and interactivity of the digital environment are all evolving forms of new proof, new footnotes, new sidebars, a new archive. A close attachment to transparency should make it clear that the process and product built into 20th-century journalism—news provided by a press that strove to be independent and professional as evidence of its reliability—remain. Indeed, the demand for transparency is a quest for the same value—to know where news is coming from so that it can be judged for its trustworthiness.

That leads to the third and final broad concept: The news serves the community for which it was produced. Nothing could come closer to the idea of journalism in the public interest. Nothing aims more squarely at the existential question: What is journalism's value? What is it for? The future of journalism is secure, we believe, as long as it creates value for the community.

This notion, in the end, is at the center of the debates over journalism past and future. We find traces of it in the earliest legal battles over journalism in the American colonies, which formed our notions of truthfulness in news; we find traces in the writings of Walter Lippmann and John Dewey, which asked whether journalism could ever come close to serving the public; and we find traces in the arguments of this digital age over whether journalism's professional ethics retain their value or ever had any. Can the news serve the community or not? Will it fail the public? Is the public up to understanding the news they help create, discover and spread?

Whether one falls closer to the skeptical side of the spectrum (doubting whether the news can ever be delivered well enough) or the more optimistic side (confident that more news will get us closer to the truth no matter how it is delivered), we share one thin line of common ground. All those who produce news should aim high and strive hard to live up to their public responsibility. And the public, over time, will engage with this growing debate over what happens and what it means. It will be messy and chaotic as we all move closer to knowing what happened and what to make of it, closer to the truth.

ABOUT THE EDITORS

Kelly McBride is a writer, teacher and consultant. She has worked on faculty at The Poynter Institute since 2002. Before that she was a reporter for 15 years, working at *The Spokesman-Review* (Spokane, Wash.), the Cleveland *Plain Dealer* and *The Blade* (Toledo, Ohio). She teaches ethics at Poynter, specifically addressing the transformation of journalism from a profession for a few to the calling of many. She served for 18 months as the lead writer for the ESPN–Poynter Review Project, an ombudsman service for the sports network. She has taught journalists in their newsrooms and in professional workshops across the United States, in South Africa and in Denmark. She writes and lectures widely on ethics and the transformation of journalism. Born and raised in Toledo, Ohio, she graduated from the University of Missouri-Columbia School of Journalism and Gonzaga University. On Twitter she is @kellymcb.

Tom Rosenstiel is an author, journalist, researcher and media critic. The executive director of the American Press Institute, he also founded and directed the Pew Project for Excellence and was co-founder and vice chair of the Committee of Concerned Journalists. He spent a decade as media writer for the *Los Angeles Times* and also was chief congressional correspondent for *Newsweek,* media critic for MSNBC, business editor at the *Peninsula Times Tribune* and a reporter for columnist Jack Anderson. He began his career at the Woodside Country Almanac in his hometown in California. A graduate of Oberlin College and Columbia University, he has written and lectured around the world long enough to collect lifetime achievement awards among others. His six previous books include *The Elements of Journalism: What News People Should Know and the Public Should Expect* (2001, 2006) and *Blur: How to Know What's True in the Age of Information Overload* (2010), both with Bill Kovach.

ABOUT THE CONTRIBUTORS

danah boyd is a senior researcher at Microsoft Research, a research assistant professor in media, culture and communication at New York University, and a fellow at Harvard's Berkman Center for Internet and Society. She was selected as a Young Global Leader of the World Economic Forum in 2011 and was

listed by *Technology Review* as one of its 2010 Young Innovators under 35. Her research examines the intersection of technology, society and youth culture and regularly appears in new media. *Fortune Magazine* dubbed her "the smartest academic in tech." Currently, she is focused on privacy, youth meanness and cruelty, big data and human trafficking. She co-authored *Hanging Out, Messing Around, and Geeking Out: Kids Living and Learning with New Media.* Her monograph titled *It's Complicated: The Social Lives of Networked Teens* is scheduled to come out in February 2014. She blogs regularly at Apophenia (http://www.zephoria.org/thoughts) and is @zephoria on Twitter.

Roy Peter Clark has taught writing at The Poynter Institute since 1979. Over three decades he has served the institute as dean, vice president, senior scholar and member of the Board of Trustees. Clark has written or edited 15 books on writing and journalism, the most popular and influential being *Writing Tools: 50 Essential Strategies for Every Writer.* Podcasts of the book have been downloaded more than a million times. *The New York Times Book Review* praised Clark's latest book, *The Glamour of Grammar,* as "a manual for the 21st century." Born in New York City, Clark attended Catholic schools through his graduation from Providence College in 1970. He earned a Ph.D. in English from Stony Brook University. He began his teaching career in Montgomery, Ala., where he became interested in journalism, and he was hired by the *St. Petersburg Times* as one of America's first writing coaches in 1977. He is the founding director of the National Writers Workshops. His work has been highlighted on NPR, *Today,* and *The Oprah Winfrey Show.* Selected as a distinguished service member of the American Society of News Editors, he was inducted into the Features Hall of Fame.

Eric Deggans serves as TV/media critic for the *Tampa Bay Times.* He also provides commentaries on television and pop culture for NPR and writes on sports media issues for the National Sports Journalism Center at Indiana University. He is the author of *Race-Baiter: How the Media Wields Dangerous Words to Divide a Nation,* a look at how prejudice, racism and sexism fuel some elements of modern media, published in October 2012. His work has also appeared in *The Washington Post, Chicago Sun-Times, Chicago Tribune, The Miami Herald, Ebony* magazine, Rolling Stone Online and CNN.com. Named in 2009 as one of *Ebony's* "Power 150"—a list that also included Oprah Winfrey and PBS host Gwen Ifill—he has lectured at Columbia University, Loyola University, The Paley Center for Media, The Poynter Institute for Media Studies, the University of Tampa, Indiana University and many other schools. In addition, he worked as a professional drummer in the 1980s, touring and performing with Motown recording artists The Voyage Band. He continues to perform with area bands and recording artists as a drummer, bassist and vocalist.

Ann Friedman is an editor and writer based in Los Angeles. She writes a politics column for *New York* magazine's website and a weekly advice column for the *Columbia Journalism Review.* Her work has also appeared in *The New Republic, NewYorker.com, ELLE, Time Out Chicago, TheAtlantic.com, Bookforum, The Gentlewoman,* and more. She is a co-founder of a crowd-funded magazine called *Tomorrow,* which was nominated for an Utne Media Award for general excellence. She maintains a GIF blog, Real Talk From Your Editor, and she curates the work of women journalists at LadyJournos! She was previously the executive editor of *GOOD* magazine and the deputy editor of *The American Prospect.* In July 2012, the *Columbia Journalism Review* named her one of 20 "women to watch." She grew up in Iowa and attended the University of Missouri-Columbia School of Journalism. She now speaks on campuses and at conferences around the country about making journalism in the digital era. You can find her at www.annfriedman.com and @annfriedman on Twitter.

Dan Gillmor has spent his career in media—music, newspapers, online, books, investing and education. He teaches digital media entrepreneurship and is founding director of the Knight Center for Digital Media Entrepreneurship at Arizona State University's Walter Cronkite School of Journalism and Mass Communication. His latest book (a project that is much more than a book) is *Mediactive.* His goal with this project is to help turn passive media consumers into active users—as participants at every step of the process starting with what we read. He writes articles and commentary, including a regular online column for *The Guardian* newspaper, and somewhat more frequently at the Mediactive blog. His last book, *We the Media: Grassroots Journalism by the People, for the People* (2004 and 2006), has been translated into many foreign languages, most recently Korean and Arabic.

Mónica Guzmán is a columnist for *The Seattle Times* and Northwest tech news site GeekWire and a community strategist for startups and media. She emcees Ignite Seattle, a community-fueled speaker series, and dissects media tech trends on PBS *MediaShift's* Mediatwits podcast. From 2007 to 2010, she ran the award-winning Big Blog at the *Seattle Post-Intelligencer,* drawing a community of readers with nonstop online conversation and casual weekly meetups. After a year tracking Seattle news and culture at seattlepi.com, the online-only successor to the *Post-Intelligencer*, she helped Seattle startup Intersect launch an innovative storytelling platform. She serves on the boards of the Western Washington Chapter of the Society of Professional Journalists and the University of Washington iSchool's masters in science and information management program. In 2012, she began her tenure as a member of the National Advisory Board for The Poynter Institute for Media Studies and was selected as a member of the World Economic Forum's Global Shapers community. She has been named one of the Top 100 Women in Seattle Tech, one of Poynter's 35 social media influencers and one of the Society of Professional Journalists' *Quill* magazine's 20 journalists to follow on Twitter.

Adam Hochberg is a veteran journalist with more than two decades of experience with national news organizations. He currently teaches at the University of North Carolina School of Journalism and Mass Communication. He spent 15 years as a correspondent for NPR, mainly covering the southeast United States. He traveled with candidates in three presidential elections, played a major role in the network's coverage of the 2000 election recount in Florida, covered the Atlanta Olympics and reported from the scene of more than a dozen hurricanes. His work also has been featured on CBS Radio, ABC Radio and the *PBS Newshour*. In 2012, he served as editorial project manager for the State Integrity Investigation, a $1.5 million investigative reporting initiative sponsored by Public Radio International, the Center for Public Integrity and Global Integrity, which led to the passage of new ethics laws in six states. He also is a fellow at The Poynter Institute, where he writes about the effects of new technology on the values of traditional journalism. A Chicago native, Hochberg earned his master's degree in 1986 from the University of North Carolina at Chapel Hill. He graduated from Ohio University in 1985.

Tom Huang is Sunday and enterprise editor at *The Dallas Morning News* and reporting, writing and editing fellow at The Poynter Institute, where he oversees the school's writing program. He has worked at *The Dallas Morning News* since 1993, first as a feature writer, then as features editor, and now as the Sunday Page One editor. During his time as features editor, the newspaper's features coverage was named one of the nation's best by the Missouri Lifestyle Journalism Awards and by the American Association of Sunday and Feature Editors.

His reporting has taken him from Bosnia and Vietnam and the Athens Olympics to the aftermath of the Oklahoma City bombing and the 9/11 attacks in New York. At Poynter, he teaches sessions in ethics, diversity, writing and leadership, and he was co-editor of Poynter's *Best Newspaper Writing* book for 2008 and 2009. Before moving to Dallas, he worked at *The Virginian-Pilot* in Norfolk, Va. He is president of the Society for Features Journalism Foundation and serves on the governing board of the Asian American Journalists Association. He is a 1988 graduate of the Massachusetts Institute of Technology, with bachelor's and master's degrees in computer science and engineering.

Kenny Irby is senior faculty, director of community relations and diversity programs at The Poynter Institute. He is an integral figure in visual journalism education, having founded Poynter's photojournalism program in 1995, and is currently leading an academic enrichment and mentoring program called The Write Field for middle school male youth. He leads seminars and consults in areas of photojournalism, leadership, ethics and diversity. He has traveled to Nigeria, the Netherlands, Denmark, Canada, Jamaica, Singapore, South Africa and Russia, preaching excellence in photojournalism. In addition, he chaired the 2007 Pulitzer Prize photography categories and has lectured at the World Press Photos buddy training program and the International Center of Photography. He is a founding member of the National Press Photographers Association, The Best of Photojournalism (BOP) Committee, and is the recipient of numerous awards: 2007 Sprague Award (the NPPA's highest honor), the 2006 Society for News Design President's Award, and many others. He is a frequent lecturer, teacher and author on photographic reporting issues.

Gilad Lotan is the chief data scientist at betaworks, where he leads the data science team focused on building data products across the portfolio companies. Previously he was the vice president of research and development at SocialFlow. Before that, Gilad built social data visualizations at Microsoft's FUSE labs. His past work includes *Retweet Revolution,* visualizing the flow of information during the 2009 #IranElection riots, and a study investigating the relationship between mainstream media and social media channels during the Tunisian and Egyptian revolutions. He and his team provide insights and analysis for major brands and media outlets, more recently powering an Olympics data visualization for the *The New York Times.* His work has been presented at the MIT Center for Civic Media, Harvard's Berkman Center, TED, Personal Democracy Forum and SXSW. His company's work has been featured in *The New York Times, The Guardian, Fast Company* and the *Atlantic Wire.* You can find him at http://giladlotan.com, and as @gilgul on Twitter.

Steve Myers is managing editor of *The Lens*, a non-profit, in-depth news site based in New Orleans, La. As managing editor of The Poynter Institute's website, he wrote about emerging media practices such as citizen journalism, nonprofit news models, real-time reporting via social media, data-oriented news apps, iPhoneography and the fact-checking movement. He's spoken at South by Southwest Interactive twice: in 2012 about citizen journalism with the man who live-tweeted the raid on Osama bin Laden's compound and in 2013 about the fact-checking movement. He was a 2006 Ohio State University Kiplinger fellow and an Open Society Institute Katrina Media Fellow. His 10 years as a newspaper reporter included six years at the *Press-Register* in Mobile, Ala., where he focused on local government accountability, from jail management to hurricane preparation and response. In 2000, he and a friend started a website to cover the presidential primaries, logging 8,000 miles in three months. He has a bachelor's degree from the University of Notre Dame, where he majored in great books.

Clay Shirky is teacher, writer and consultant on the social and cultural effects of the Internet and mobile phones, particularly where they allow for amateur access to the public sphere and easy coordination for group action. He holds a joint appointment at New York University in the graduate Interactive Telecommunications Program in the Tisch School of the Arts and at the Arthur L. Carter Journalism Institute in the Faculty of Arts and Science. His courses address how communications networks shape culture and vice versa. He is the author of two recent books on social media: *Cognitive Surplus: Creativity and Generosity in a Connected Age* (2010) and *Here Comes Everybody: The Power of Organizing without Organizations* (2008). He has written extensively about the Internet since 1996, and he has given talks all over the world. He graduated from Yale University with a Bachelor of Arts degree in fine arts. He founded Hard Place Theater in New York City in 1990, where he created and directed several nonfiction theater pieces using only found materials such as government documents, transcripts and cultural records.

Craig Silverman is an award-winning journalist and the founder of Regret the Error, a blog that reports on media errors and corrections, as well as trends regarding accuracy and verification. The blog moved to The Poynter Institute

in December 2011, and he joined as adjunct faculty. He serves as director of content for Spundge and is national president of the Professional Writers Association of Canada. He is a former columnist for *Columbia Journalism Review, The Globe And Mail, Toronto Star* and BusinessJournalism.org. He previously worked as managing editor of PBS MediaShift and was part of the team that launched OpenFile.ca, a Canadian online news startup. His journalism and books have been recognized by the Mirror Awards, National Press Club, Canadian National Magazine Awards and the Canadian Online Publishing Awards.

Steven Waldman is senior media policy scholar at the Columbia University Graduate School of Journalism. He was senior adviser to the Federal Communications Commission and principal author of *Information Needs of Communities: The Changing Media Landscape in the Broadband Age.* He was the founder, editor in chief and CEO of Beliefnet.com, the largest multifaith spirituality website, which won the National Magazine Award for General Excellence Online. Previously, he had been national editor of *US News & World Report* and national correspondent for *Newsweek.* He is the author of *Founding Faith: Providence, Politics and the Birth of Religious Freedom in America.*

CASE STUDY AUTHOR

Caitlin Johnston is a journalist whose work has appeared in the *Tampa Bay Times, The Dallas Morning News* and the *Baltimore Sun.* While with the *Tampa Bay Times,* she spent 10 days on the road with a local band, detailing their journey to the Bonnaroo summer music festival. She covers regional news, including military life, human trafficking and county politics. Prior to her work in Florida, she was an editorial assistant for the *American Journalism Review,* where she wrote the Spring 2012 cover story on the effects of tablets on legacy news outlets. She is a 2011 graduate of Indiana University, where she studied journalism and political science. While at IU, she competed in the Hearst National Journalism Awards Championship, placing second. Other honors include Indiana Society of Professional Journalists Collegiate Journalist of the Year, the European Union Press Fellowship and awards in news and feature writing from the Columbia Scholastic Press Association. She earned her master's in journalism from the University of Maryland in 2012.

FOREWORD AUTHOR

Bob Steele is a Distinguished Professor of Journalism Ethics at DePauw University and the Director of The Janet Prindle Institute for Ethics. He spent nearly 20 years on the faculty of The Poynter Institute, and he still serves as the Nelson Poynter Scholar for Journalism Values. He has consulted on ethics standards and practices for dozens of news organizations and advised thousands of journalists and media leaders on real-time ethical challenges. He is the co-author of *Doing Ethics in Journalism: A Handbook with Case Studies.*
Steele earned his BA from DePauw in economics, his MS from Syracuse in television-radio and his PhD from the University of Iowa. He also received Honorary Doctorates from both DePauw and Emerson College. The Society of Professional Journalists honored him in 2010 as a Fellow of the Society, the highest honor SPJ bestows upon a journalist for extraordinary contributions to the profession. He served as an Army officer in Vietnam in 1971–72.

The Poynter Institute is a school dedicated to teaching and inspiring journalists and media leaders. Through its teaching, publications and website (poynter .org), the institute promotes excellence and integrity in the practice of craft and in the practical leadership of successful businesses.

Poynter stands for a journalism that informs citizens, enlightens public discourse and strengthens the ties between journalism and democracy. The school offers training at its Florida campus throughout the year in the areas of online and multimedia, leadership and management, reporting, writing, and editing, TV and radio, ethics and diversity, journalism education, and visual journalism. Poynter's custom programs address specific needs of news organizations, universities and associations in the United States and abroad.

Poynter's e-learning portal, News University (newsu.org), offers newsroom training to journalists, journalism students and educators through faculty-led, online seminars, Webinars and more than 250 self-directed courses. Most of these courses are free or low cost and are open to the public.

The institute was founded in 1975 by Nelson Poynter, chairman of what was then the *St. Petersburg Times* (now the *Tampa Bay Times*). Before his death, Mr. Poynter willed controlling stock in his companies to the school. As a financially independent, nonprofit organization, the Poynter Institute is beholden to no interest except its own mission: to help journalists seek and achieve excellence.

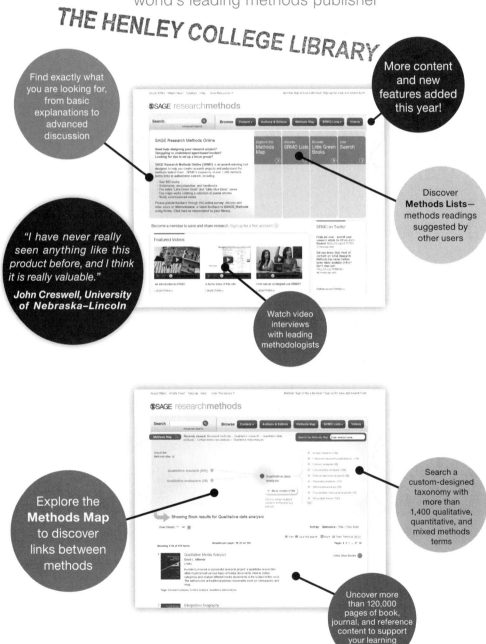

⑤SAGE research**methods**

The essential online tool for researchers from the world's leading methods publisher

THE HENLEY COLLEGE LIBRARY

Find exactly what you are looking for, from basic explanations to advanced discussion

More content and new features added this year!

Discover **Methods Lists**— methods readings suggested by other users

"I have never really seen anything like this product before, and I think it is really valuable."

John Creswell, University of Nebraska–Lincoln

Watch video interviews with leading methodologists

Explore the **Methods Map** to discover links between methods

Search a custom-designed taxonomy with more than 1,400 qualitative, quantitative, and mixed methods terms

Uncover more than 120,000 pages of book, journal, and reference content to support your learning

Find out more at
www.sageresearchmethods.com